Of Hominins, Hunter-Gatherers and Heroes

First published by Jacana Media (Pty) Ltd in 2019

10 Orange Street
Sunnyside
Auckland Park 2092
South Africa
+2711 628 3200
www.jacana.co.za

© David Bristow, 2019
Poem on page 173 permission courtesy of Chris Mann

All rights reserved.

ISBN 978-1-4314-2905-9

Also available as an ebook.

Cover design by publicide
Layout by Alexandra Turner
Editing by Megan Mance
Proofreading by Linda Da Nova and Josephine Bestic
Set in Minion Pro 10.8/15pt
Printed by ABC Press
Job no. 003578

See a complete list of Jacana titles at www.jacana.co.za

Of Hominins, Hunter-Gatherers and Heroes

*Searching for
20 Amazing Places in South Africa*

STORIES FROM THE VELD (II)

David Bristow

Amazing Places in South Africa

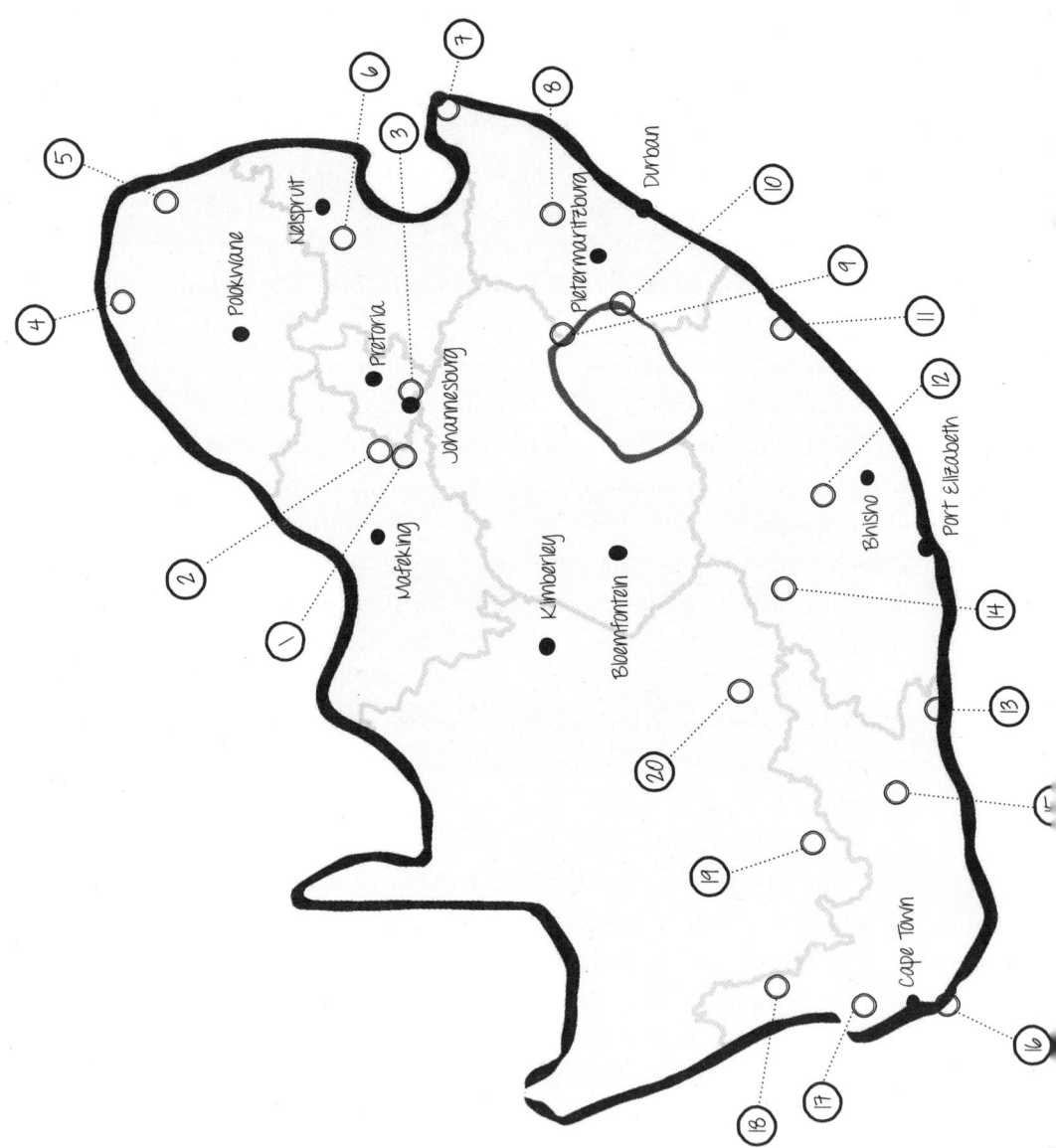

Contents

Introduction: Searching South Africa for Amazing Places 7

1. The Cradle of Humankind
   Pre-Human, Nearly Human and Almost Human: Searching for Our Forebears 11
2. National Heritage Monument, Maropeng
   Lost Wax, a Lost Statue and Freedom Lost and Found: Searching for Heroes of the Past 19
3. The Johannesburg Museum of Military History
   Civil War and Uncivil War: Searching for an Acre Full of Guns and Heroes 27
4. Mapungubwe
   Stone Citadels, Cities of Gold and Protective Spirits: Searching for Ancestral Treasures 35
5. Kruger National Park
   Big Game, Big Trees and a Ticking Conservation Time Bomb: Searching for a Game Reserve That Very Nearly Wasn't 43
6. Adam's Calendar
   Lost Worlds, Celestial Almanacs and Off-World Visitors: Searching for Truth Among Standing and Lying Stones 59
7. Kosi Bay
   Fish Traps, Turtle Eggs and Skokiaan: Searching for Amphibious Invaders Between the Tides 69
8. Isandlwana and Rorke's Drift
   Imperial Arrogance, Victorian Pride and African Spartans: Searching for Honour on a Field of Blood 77
9. Mont-aux-Sources and the Amphitheatre
   A Vulture-Eagle, a Tsunami in Stone and a Ladder to Heaven: Searching for the Country's Most Amazing Landscape 91

10. Kamberg, Game Pass Shelter
   The Story of !Xabo, Images of Power and a Secret App: Searching for the Meaning of Bushman Art 103
11. Lambazi Bay, Port Grosvenor
   A Lonely Bay, the Wondrously Wild Coast and a Terrible Saga of Castaways: Searching for the Fate of the Grosvenor 117
12. Hogsback
   A Place of Waterfalls, Gunsmoke and a Faerie Garden: Searching for a Rare Bird 137
13. The Garden Route
   A Post-Apocalyptic Gateway, a Man with a Theodolite Eye and a Very Small Flag: Searching for the Real Garden Route 147
14. Nieu Bethesda
   An Owl House, a Camel Yard and a Stream of Fossils: Searching for South Africa's Geo-Psychic Centre 165
15. Swartberg Pass and Die Hel
   A Bone-Jarring Passage, Hard People and Harder Wood: Searching Hard for a Forgotten Valley 175
16. Cape Point
   A Fearsome Wind, a Ghost Ship and a Bay of Plenty: Searching for a Paradise, Almost-Lost 187
17. West Coast Fossil Park
   Four-Tusked Elephants, Giant Giraffes and an African Bear: Searching for a Paradise Lost 201
18. The Heerenlogement
   A Cave, a Chisel and a Wagon Road: Searching for Fabled Kingdoms 209
19. Karoo Petroglyphs
   Bushman Songs, Broken Strings and Stories That Sing on the Wind: Searching for Sacred Rocks in the Karoo 223
20. Sutherland
   High Plains, Clear Skies and Starry, Starry Nights: Searching for Bright Objects and Dark Matter 233

Companion Reading List 243
About the author 248

Introduction

Searching South Africa for Amazing Places

THE OLD SOUTH AFRICAN TOURISM BUREAU claim that South Africa was "a world in one country" was appealing, but not altogether honest. For starters, we get very little snow here like you would in the Alps or the Antarctic. Also, there isn't any real desert, not in the league of a Namib or a Sahara. Then again, as far as I am concerned, we can be mightily grateful for that.

The main problem with snow is that it is miserably cold (I've been up enough ice-covered peaks to know this first hand). And deserts ... just to begin, there is that uncomfortable lack of water. It's so much nicer to pop in to places like Namibia or the Antarctic, then come home again to temperate, sunny South Africa, a real Goldilocks country where – at the very least in a climactic sense – things are "just right".

After more than three decades as a travel and nature writer who has seen much of the planet, I find that more and more I want to stay at home and explore my own little patch of paradise, otherwise known as South Africa, or Mzansi. Which is not to say I have not already done more than my fair share of exploring around here.

I was 14 when I hit the road big time, hitchhiking from Joburg to Cape St Francis. Things were never the same. I was hooked on travel and stuck a fold-out Mobil road map of South Africa to my bedroom wall. After every subsequent school holiday, I plotted my "roads done" with a blue marker. I wish I still had that map.

I know there are others who have travelled the place more than I: such as the late great veld scientist JPH Acocks, who reckoned he'd driven around a million miles while documenting the veld types of this country. But not many. Even fewer have been so fortunate as to get the opportunity to write about it.

This book is my list of must-see places in South Africa. It won't be everyone's list: for example it does not include the Augrabies Falls, Golden Gate, Hole in the Wall, Bourke's Luck Potholes or Blyde (Motlatse) River Canyon (which is not, in spite of marketing claims to the contrary, the third-largest canyon in the world; it's not even among the 10 biggest; in fact, it is not listed among the world's top 100).

It was never my intention to produce a book that featured only the pin-up models of our beautiful country. I created books like that early on in my writing career when I was young, had small children and needed the cash. Now that I write for the pleasure of it, I wanted to tell my own, hopefully deeper, stories.

That is why you will find unexpected places like the Heerenlogement, which most people will not have heard about previously. What it is, other than being a really interesting place, is a geographical and literary device to tell a story about the early exploration of the Cape by European adventurers.

And the Johannesburg war museum. This gave me a chance to tell the stories upon which I was raised by my saintly soldier father. Like so many of his generation, "the war" defined everything that came after shipping off to Egypt while still a teenager and helping Winston Churchill and Spike Milligan defeat both Mussolini and Hitler. But it is not so much a story about war as it is about heroes. We all need to know their stories, or I might be writing this in German.

Narrowing down my list to just 20 places was challenging, but it had to be done. Some admittedly very interesting places that did not make the final cut include De Hoop, Groot Marico, Rhodes Village,

Introduction

Riemvasmaak and Wonderwerk Cave. But I'm pretty sure you will enjoy the ones that did well enough. Visiting each of them, or at least the ones you have not already, would make for one heck of a road trip.

I have been accused of being an "olologist" – someone who is obsessed with places archaeological and palaeontological. I admit it's true, and I'm proud of it, and that is why you will find the Cradle of Humankind, Mapungubwe, Karoo petroglyphs, West Coast Fossil Park and Game Pass Shelter cave in this collection. In my humble opinion, they are so much more interesting than Augrabies or Golden Gate.

But I am also aware that a book simply about all the scientific sites in South Africa would have a rather narrow appeal … then again, maybe I'll keep that one for a later collection of veld stories. *Hominins, Hunter-Gatherers and Heroes* is the third in the series "Stories from the Veld", the other two being *Running Wild: The Story of Zulu, an African Stallion* and *The Game Ranger, the Knife, the Lion and the Sheep*.

I have also been accused of being a latter-day hippie, which is not altogether true, or false. For this project I found a tired, sad old 1988 Kombi and gave it as much TLC as I could, painted it jolly white and green, fitted a few modern conveniences and named it umKhombe (isiXhosa for rhino). Admittedly, it broke down a few times, but still it carried me for around 10 000 kilometres, some of them along some of the worst roads in the country, and it's still going strong.

The format of *Hominins* might not at first seem to, but it does follow a logical geographical route: the storytelling spiral starts in Gauteng and then unwinds clockwise through Limpopo, Mpumalanga, down KwaZulu-Natal, into the Eastern Cape, then round the Western Cape and ending in the Northern Cape.

It's never too late to have a happy childhood, so sit back and enjoy the journey with me.

David Bristow
Cape Town, September 2019

The Cradle of Humankind

Pre-Human, Nearly Human and Almost Human: Searching for our Forebears

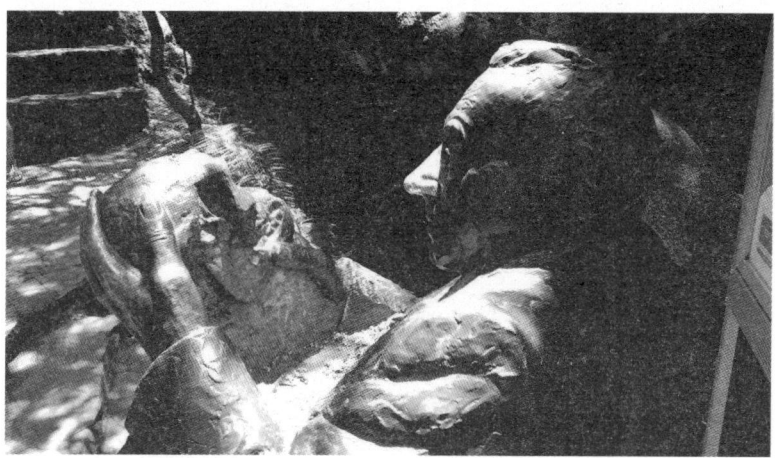

The Cradle of Humankind consists of a grouping of limestone caves, mainly in the Sterkfontein area of northwest Gauteng (also known as Maropeng), as well as satellite sites such as Makapansgat in Limpopo. It is the world's richest repository of hominin, or pre-human, fossils and accordingly has been declared a World Heritage Site.

"Mommy, Daddy, where do we come from?"

Apart from the obvious specific reply of Boksburg, or Bryanston, the broad answer is complicated, and ever increasingly so the more we find out about it. The main problem is that we know so little about our earliest ancestors.

Until not much more than a decade ago, all the fossil bones of all the pre-humans ever found would hardly fill the top of a coffee table: a bunch of partial skulls here, a jawbone there, a handful of teeth, some broken ribs and femurs, a cracked pelvis or two and not much more. Lucy (*Australopithecus afarensis*), the most famous pre-human fossil persona until recently, consists of just a partial skull, a few broken ribs, bits of humerus and ulna, half a pelvis, a femur and part of a tibia.

The fossilised remains of Turkana Boy (*Homo erectus*), the most complete hominin (pre-human) skeleton found outside of South Africa, are about double that. From the time Professor Raymond Dart discovered, in the scientific sense, the first correctly identified "ape-man" back in 1936, the search has been on for the so-called missing link among our human-like ape and ape-like human forebears.

Dart, Professor of Anatomy at Wits University, correctly identified the partial skull, and later the brain casing, of a pre-human creature that had been found among the rubble of the lime works at a place called Taung, not far from Kimberley. In those days, limestone, excavated from dolomite caves around the country, was used first as an agricultural additive to neutralise acidic soils, later for refining gold, and then to make cement, and even the first commercial antacid tablets. The Taung Child skull was being used by the mine manager as a paperweight.

Just 11 years later Dr Robert Broom, a struggling medical doctor and amateur dinosaur fossil collector who had found a job at the Transvaal Museum, was called out to a place called Sterkfontein, about half an hour west of Pretoria these days. This area is underlain by the largest dolomitic formation in South Africa and is perforated with caves. The area had been well gone over by miners, who hacked and blasted the limestone out from the hollow caverns.

And there, among the discarded piles of rubble near the main entrance to the cave, Broom found first one and then more parts of a skull of a creature that appeared to be an adult of the same species as the Taung Child. It was an extinct primate, very human-like but still clearly of the ape clan, that, after much debate, was given the name *Australopithecus africanus* – the southern ape from Africa.

Broom described the find of this extinct pre-human as being "nearly human", and thus began the race to find what was dubbed the missing link, that one relation between we *Homo sapiens* and the other living ape species. As more and more fossil findings have come to light in the intervening years, it has become evident that we do not sit on a single bough of the evolutionary tree, but on a many-branching limb, with monkeys at the first point of divergence.

There are currently 13 known members of the hominin family, including ourselves, with four links missing from the schematic. All four lie on the direct line to our own species so, while we have quite a few evolutionary aunts, uncles, cousins and second cousins, we still don't know who our own evolutionary parents were, or theirs.

The Star newspaper named Broom's find Mrs Ples, although recent re-examination of the teeth and upper jaw suggests it was that of a young male. Thereafter the focus of pre-human archaeology shifted to East Africa. The Leakey family, and then American fossil-finder supremo Donald Johanson, seemed to be the only people making any significant new finds. And so it remained throughout most of the rest of the 20th century.

Nevertheless, all this time the fossil hunters from the Bernard Price Institute at Wits were busy, at Sterkfontein, at Makapansgat, Blombos, Border, Wonderwerk caves and a few other fossil sites around the country. They were finding remarkable stuff, but the government of the time did not like what they were digging up, or saying about it, and anyway apartheid South Africa was a pariah state, so few people outside took much notice.

Palaeontology has been perhaps the most secretive branch of the extremely possessive scientific world, so not much gets shared between dig sites, countries and even among academic institutions. But the work here went on and over time the fossil remains of more hominin species were being uncovered: first the gracile *Australopithecus*, as well as a much brawnier *Paranthropus robustus* (it was nicknamed "the nutcracker" for its huge jaws), *Paranthropus boisei* and *Homo erectus, habilis* and *rudolfensis* in East Africa.

In the early 1990s the extremely reticent Wits fossil hunter Ronald Clarke came upon the traces of a skeleton in a lateral tunnel of the Sterkfontein cave system and, with his team, began excavating the site. Actually, some ankle bones had been collected there in 1980 and identified as belonging to an upright walking creature, but they got mixed up with a whole lot of other mammal bones from site Stw 573 (the Silberberg Grotto). Some years later Clarke identified a few more foot bones from bags collected at the same site and thought they just might all come from a single individual.

In 1997 two of Clarke's assistants returned to site Stw 573 with the hope that they might find matching tibia and fibula fragments among the rubble of the debris cone (what forms where sediment has fallen into a cavern through a sinkhole, of which there are many in this area). Within two days they had found them and more: matching leg bones protruding from the breccia (a rock type that forms when rubble inside a dolomite cave is cemented together by dissolved limestone) wall of the tunnel, which looked like they had been sheared off.

They had indeed, by dynamite. Sterkfontein, along with other similar caves, including Makapansgat, had been worked by limestone miners until they became unviable economically. Stalactites (from the Greek *stalakos*, dripping), stalagmites (from the Greek *stalagma*, to drop) and sparkling flowstones were almost pure limestone, so they were first to go.

You could knock them off with a sledgehammer. The denser limestone cave walls were blasted to smithereens. It was in the rubble pits from these workings that the earliest hominin fossils – the Taung Child, Mrs Ples, *Bos makapania*, a pygmy buffalo, and others – were discovered.

Back in tunnel Stw 573 at Sterkfontein, Clarke, Stephen Motsumi and Nkwane Molefe, working delicately with hammers and chisels, began to expose the leg bones and pelvis of a fossilised skeleton lying face-down in the breccia. Then the outside ends of upper-body bones, then shoulder bones and finally a skull still attached to the spine. It was an almost complete skeleton, the first ever found. Just the feet were missing, but Clarke already had most of the constituent bones.

In all it took 15 years of painstaking work to expose the full skeleton, but Clarke was being so furtive that not even his immediate boss, Dr Lee Berger, knew anthing much more than that he (Clarke) was working on "something special". Clarke called his find Little Foot and believed it belonged to an as-yet-unnamed hominin species, possibly in the genus of *Australopithecus*, but substantially different from the other *africanus* remains that dominated the Sterkfontein and related sites. What it was, exactly, and how old, would take another "little foot" to discover.

In 1990 an eager young American palaeontologist named Lee Berger had arrived at Wits. Not much new was going on there, other than going over and over the old bones from Sterkfontein and Makapansgat, trying to tease new data from them. His career was progressing on a predictable timeline: he married, had children and the world moved along with him. Then he received a grant from America and decided to use it to fund a team to return to the Cradle of Humankind landscape, hoping they'd find something, anything, new. For a long time they did not.

Then, on a warm spring day in 2008, he was out walking the most beaten tracks of the paleontological world, the Cradle of Humankind site, with a Kenyan colleague named Job Kibii. Lee's nine-year-old son Matthew and their dog Tau went along for the fun. They were still trying to find any caves or limestone sinkholes that had not yet been located and searched.

Out beyond the industry of Krugersdorp and the plots of Muldersdrift, the Witwatersberg and area around Sterkfontein is the best of what is left of the vigorous natural Highveld ecosystem. Red-oat grass would have been reaching knee height, delightful little brown-and-beige cisticolas would have been tinkling, wailing, wing-snapping and zitting in the air, because that is what they do.

Clumps of wild olive and white stinkwoods lined the ridges and protea bushes were just coming into bloom on the warm north-facing slopes of the Witwatersberg and shoulders of the Crocodile River valley and its tributaries, like the Bloubank. Long-tailed widowbirds would have just started to show their breeding colours, with their emerging banner-like tails dragging across the top of the dense grass cover.

"Dad, I've found a fossil," called young Matthew from where he was rummaging in the shade of a white stinkwood. At that moment, and with those words, the world of Lee Berger, Professor of Palaeoanthropology and National Geographic Explorer-in-Residence, as well as the world of hominin research, made a quantum leap. A block of breccia close to an old limestone quarry pit showed a jawbone and some small teeth protruding. When prepared back in the lab, the block revealed more bones from a juvenile of a hominin species Berger did not recognise.

In time that sinkhole, which he named Malapa ("home" in Sesotho) gave up not one, but two nearly full skeletons of a new species of pre-human, one mature female and the other a juvenile. It is quite possible it was a mother and child in search of water when they fell to their deaths and were covered with debris before predators could get at their remains.

Of this find Berger writes: "In the entire history of palaeoanthropology in Africa, never before had two (nearly complete) skeletons been found in close proximity." That would have been enough to make the career of anyone in his field. But still there was hard science to be done: what, who, were they?

The debate raged among the team of international experts assembled by Berger to study the old bones. Some bits were *Homo*-like, others *Australopith*-like. Some fancied *habilis*, others *robustus*. This had happened before when Phillip Tobias (Berger's mentor at Wits) and Louis Leakey had debated the provenance of what – eventually – came to be named *Homo habilis*.

It took the team a long time, using every available technology, to come to the conclusion that they had a new species: it was not anatomically advanced enough to be put in our own *Homo* class, so was ascribed to *Australopithecus*. With that Berger had the honour of naming the first new hominin species from southern Africa in several decades. He chose the Sesotho name for a spring, and so *A sediba* came to be. Various modern dating techniques put their age at around two million years old.

The prevailing thinking is that Little Foot is *A sediba*, but not everyone agrees about that, or its age. The most recent estimate is that Little Foot is around 3.4 million years old, but not everyone agrees about that either. What does become clear from all this is that our family tree is a lot older and a whole lot more convoluted than was previously thought. And that's not the end of it.

In fact *sediba* was only the beginning of this new fountain of discovery. Berger was fired up and decided to ask, and pay, some cavers he knew to explore the Cradle's cave systems. The full story is told in his book *Almost Human*, how he commissioned two skinny, out-of-work palaeontologists to scour the area for caves like no one had before. Rick Hunter and Steve Turner returned to an old cave system they had started to explore and, following its long, dark and winding tunnels deep underground, found a chamber full of bones at the very end of the Rising Star subterranean labyrinth that came to be called the Dinaledi Chamber.

Not just any bones, mind, but human-like ones. And not just a few human-like bones, but many, many more than had ever been seen before, never mind in one place, but in every other place ever discovered. In order to fully and scientifically excavate and research the site, he needed a special kind of person.

The story is excellently documented in a multimedia display inside the Tumulus, the focal point of the Maropeng Cradle of Humankind World Heritage Site. Berger advertised worldwide for females with master's degrees or higher qualifications. They would need to be able to work in confined areas, not be claustrophobic, be good team players, preferably have some climbing or caving experience and, most important, be skinny.

Berger's six successful candidates became known as the "underground astronauts" and they helped to unearth the greatest horde of hominin remains ever found – more than all the rest of the pre-human fossil bones ever found on Earth. Placed together, in sequence, the 1 700 or so bones and bone fragments, representing, it is thought, 15 individuals, would cover a banqueting table.

But they were not just any old, same-old same-old bones. Firstly, unlike just about all the bone fragments from the Cradle cave systems that were not encased in breccia, they had not been predated upon; they had not been carried there by water or otherwise fallen in. They were all in near mint condition. They lay on the floor like they had been put there.

At first it seemed like a wild idea, but as more evidence piled up the more it seemed like no other explanation fitted the evidence: they had been placed there deliberately. It was the first ever example found of some species (because we cannot really call them people) having a concept of an afterlife. To look up at the night sky and ask that fundamentally human question: What is it all about? Not wishing to place too spiritual an emphasis on the place, the scientists refer to the Dinaledi Chamber as a disposal site for the dead.

So who, or what, were they? Again, it took years and the largest team of scientists – 60 in all – ever to collaborate in the history of palaeontology, to come up with some answers. And it turned out that, if ever there was a missing link, this was it. The fossilised bones in the Dinaledi Chamber revealed a creature with half its characteristics decidedly human, and the other half unquestionably ape.

Those parts that interacted directly with the environment were human, fully *Homo* – hands, legs, feet – but the rest, including the brain, were *Australopithecus*. This was a species that sat on the evolutionary fence. In the end, based on deep analysis of bone morphology, and especially teeth structure, it was allowed to sit in the *Homo* classroom.

And once again Professor Berger got to select its species name (not something many people in his line of work get to do even once in a lifetime). He named it *naledi,* Sesotho for stars, both for the name of the cave system as well as for that curiously human characteristic of looking up at stars and thinking: What's out there, and what comes after this?

For decades the Sterkfontein Caves were an interesting day outing for countless Gauteng schoolchildren, an exciting exploration of an old cave system and some information about strange ape-men. It still is, but these days it is so much more.

The Cradle of Humankind is a monument to the most important and amazing archaeological site on the planet. Tours of the cave system at Sterkfontein are thoroughly professional, not something we enjoyed "back in the day" when the most scientific aspect was being asked to identify peculiar shapes like you might with clouds.

The Tumulus is arguably the finest exhibition space, and best-conceived scientific display in South Africa. To do it justice you need to take your time and really get involved with the various exhibits and information boards. The "four elements" water ride is a fun way to release brain tension after the heavy information bombardment.

Homo naledi is not the oldest fossil hominin yet found, but it might very well be the last hominin to have existed before we, humans, emerged on the African landscape. The species roamed the Highveld just 450 000 to 250 000 years ago, and could well have shared the area with other as yet unidentified archaic African humans, our lost parents.

This fact alone makes it is the most exciting palaeontological find ever. And to top this, Berger and his team have not finished searching the area for new finds; in fact, they've really only just begun.

National Heritage Monument, Maropeng

Lost Wax, a Lost Statue and Freedom Lost and Found: Searching for Heroes of the Past

From small beginnings at Newtown in downtown Johannesburg, this group of statues depicting struggle heroes down the centuries has grown substantially and moved three times.

THERE IS A GRASSROOTS group moving like a groundswell across the Highveld. It started with 20 or so well-known struggle stalwarts gathering in the Walter Sisulu Square in Kliptown, Soweto in 2012. That was the same place the watershed Freedom Charter was publicly and defiantly aired for the first time back in 1955.

Then they seemed to go underground, only to re-emerge some time later in Pretoria. By 2017 the number had swollen five-fold – an official statement said a hundred but some say they counted only 96, or 97, depending. They were marching – metaphorically speaking, since they were, and are, an assembly of bronze statues – down a green acre of the Groenkloof Nature Reserve, more popularly known as Fountains, a favourite picnic spot in the capital city.

Among them were not only political leaders and revolutionaries, but also lawyers, writers, preachers, cricket players, mystics, musicians, tribal warriors, even the emperor of an ancient dynasty. It was like a phalanx of the who's who in the struggle for liberation of all the downtrodden, the subjugated, the underdogs and the abused in the history of South Africa, some marching defiantly, steadfastly, some galloping, others admittedly strolling, and all heading to some undisclosed destination.

Then, for the second time, towards the end of the 2018, they disappeared. In March 2019, the bronze army, if you could call it that, was seen to be gathering out to the northeast, where the undulating Highveld begins rolling into the hills that mark the beginning of the Bushveld region.

For reasons that now seem predestined and appropriate, the bellicose crowd was re-assembling outside the information centre at Maropeng, in the heart of the Cradle of Humankind World Heritage Site. Although the real reasons might be a lot more pragmatic, when the forensics have been done and the bodies dusted, it might well have started with the disappearance of a character named Doman, leader of the Goring-haiqua Khoi, who the Dutch called *strandlopers*.

Jan van Riebeeck sent Doman to Batavia to learn the Dutch language and customs so better to serve the fledgling settlement on Table Bay as a go-between. But the plan backfired and Doman, seeing the servitude to which the Dutch put the Indonesians (then known as Malayans), returned with seriously seditious ideas. In 1659 he organised the first uprising against the Dutch at the Cape.

But in 2015 his statue was stolen, his body hacked off just above the feet and spirited out of Groenkloof one dark night. But, theft aside, another and perhaps more pressing reason South Africa's "terracotta army" was moved to the Cradle of Humankind, is that hardly anyone knew it existed. Few people were visiting the National Heritage Monument at Groenkloof, otherwise known as the Long March to Freedom.

The procession echoes various freedom marches during the anti-apartheid era, but this one includes people across five centuries. At its new site it will be much more visible and, being located at a busy tourist focus, is bound to enjoy a growing corpus of admiration.

At the time of researching, the group marching to freedom at Maropeng had one new comrade added, Winnie Madikizela-Mandela, her right hand slotted deftly into Madiba's left that had been left swinging alone behind him back at Groenkloof. Clearly you have to die before convention allows that you be immortalised in heavy metal.

It is envisaged that the cavalcade will eventually number around 400 dissenters, objectors, protestors and other people's champions. The man behind the project is Dali, son of the more famous struggle stalwart Oliver Tambo, and a cultural icon in his own right (remember the scatter cushions he used to cast around the TV studio?).

Tambo Jnr said the idea came to him while visiting his father's grave. He thought: "There isn't a statue of you in this country, but I'm planning to do one." Then, as if from the grave, his father answered (and anyone who has lost a loved one will know how they speak to you from the great void): "Don't do it for me, do it for all of them." Meaning everyone who was involved in the fight for a better covenant for all South Africans.

At the time of their final (we hope) relocation, one news story had the statues made in copper. Another that they had been hewn from bronze. This would have surprised the artists involved, since they are neither made from copper (strictly speaking), nor were they hewn. You cannot carve bronze (from which they are made) into the sensual shapes that you can carve marble. Try to hit a solid block of bronze with a hammer and chisel and it will bounce right off, leaving the would-be sculptor vibrating like a church bell at midnight mass.

Bronze is a combination of copper and other metals, usually tin, which turns the soft base metal into an extremely hard alloy. The invention of making metal alloys ushered in the Bronze Age, characterised not only by sophisticated metallurgy, but also ship building, an effective wheel, writing, the domestication of wild cereals and animals as well as a sudden explosion of trade – and wars – across seas and oceans.

The art of making bronze sculptures also dates back to the Bronze Age, around 6 000 years ago. It is called the lost-wax casting technique, or *cire perdue* if you want to sound poncy. In short, you make a set of two similar moulds, an inner and an outer one, from a material that can withstand the extreme heat of molten bronze. Sounds easy enough, but it is certainly not. The full process consists of between 10 and 12 essential steps.

In the case of the figures marching to freedom at Maropeng, the first thing the artist would have done is to make a scale model, about a quarter of the size, to show the pose and vital details. Once approved by the higher powers of taste and patronage, a full-size model would be made with soft clay showing all the final detail.

The next step would be to coat the clay original with a soft, flexible material to create the inner mould. Today rubber is preferred, but before there was rubber, sculptors such as Michelangelo or Rodin would have used gelatine, tar pitch, resin or even impregnated linen. Whichever, it is applied to the clay model and left to set. That done, around the flexible inner a solid outer mould would be made by dipping it into a plaster-sand slurry.

Once all is dry, the moulds are separated into two parts to give an exact negative copy of the original, releasing the original clay model inside. The inner and outer moulds are rejoined, with keys that slot into one another and with an opening at the bottom. Into this mould molten wax is poured, the mould swirled around to allow the wax to coat the entire inner surface and then excess wax is poured out. The process is repeated until the wax coating is 2–5 millimetres thick for a smaller work and up to 10 millimetres for a larger one.

When cooled, the mould is opened and then you have a hollow wax copy of the original in positive form. Once the wax model has been cleaned up and worked to the artist's satisfaction (using a heat tool), it has sprues attached – a tree-like structure of wax rods that, in the final phase, allow the super-heated liquid metal to flow evenly within the final mould.

With sprues and a cup-shaped nozzle at the bottom in place, the entire thing is dipped repeatedly and alternately into a plaster slurry and sand-silica mixture. Around the wax form an inner and outer layer forms, the outer one between 15 and 25 millimetres thick. Placed in a kiln, the coating bakes to hard ceramic while the wax melts and is lost.

Now comes the time to melt bronze ingots in a furnace, where they melt at around 1 200°C. The ceramic mould also has to be reheated in a kiln so it won't crack when the first liquid metal hits it. When in fiery gold liquid form, the bronze is poured down the hollow cup to fill the vacant space between the inner and outer ceramic surfaces – the figure itself, sprues and cup included.

This all takes place in a foundry and you can imagine the industrial undertaking with furnaces and crucibles, heavy leather aprons and gloves, heat masks and iron clamps; no delicate tinkering in some well-lit and eclectically appointed studio. When the bronze has cooled from its molten state to room temperature, the final bronze form can be released, using a sledgehammer to smash away the stoneware moulds.

Now the artist steps out of his or her health-and-safety heavy gloves, apron and welding helmet and takes up angle grinder, file and sandblaster. The sprues and cup are cut away, the seams filed away and any blemishes filled, then sandblasted and finally polished to full life-size and life-like magnificence.

Lost-wax sculpting is the place where high art meets heavy industry, with techniques and materials varying from place to place. The foundry is like an alchemist's laboratory, all fire, brimstone and molten metal. As they say in the bronze business: if you can't handle the heat, ingot out the forge.

To date around 40 artists have been commissioned to create the phalanx of freedom marchers, with the understanding that they each employ at least one apprentice to teach them the craft of lost-wax casting, and perhaps even the art of model making. Some contributed one figure, others as many as five each.

You'll meet all the usual struggle stalwarts at Maropeng, the parade being led by Nelson Mandela with familiar clenched fist held high, Oliver and Adelaide Tambo, Walter and Albertina Sisulu, Joe Slovo and Ruth First. Among many other familiar figures such as

Steve Biko and Robert Sobukwe are about 20 Xhosa and Zulu leaders of early colonial wars.

Most impressive of these is Maqoma, son of Ngqika, with his royal blue-crane feathers and rifle and cartridge belts slung over his shoulders. He led the Rharhabe (Ciskei) people in the Sixth and Eighth Frontier Wars against the British Army. What impresses most about him is that he is mounted on a charging, palomino-coloured horse.

There are also international figures including Fidel Castro, Olaf Palme, Julius Nyerere, Samora Machel and even the regal Emperor Haile Selassie. Singer Miriam Makeba is there, and it is pleasing to see the writers represented by Alan Paton, Solomon Tshekiso Plaatje and Olive Schreiner.

Most people know Schreiner as the writer of novels like that coming-of-age story about Lyndall on her African farm. But in 1911 she published the extremely outspoken *Woman and Labour*, a surprisingly in-depth look at the role sex and the division of labour, from primitive life forms and primitive societies up to the modern (in her time) place and role of women in society.

Then there is Basil D'Oliveira dressed in his cricket whites, bat raised above his head. Dolly was acknowledged as one of the world's leading batsmen of the 1960s, but this Cape-born sportsman could never play for South Africa in the apartheid days. So, in 1966 he emigrated to England and opened the batting for their test side.

In 1968 the South African government would not allow him entry to represent England in a test series here, so the English team packed their bags and went home. He is regarded as the best South African cricketer never to have played for this country. In 1969 he was awarded the Order of the British Empire and there is an anecdote passed around about that:

When taking his place before Queen Elizabeth, she is supposed to have asked: "Aren't you the one who was blackballed?"

To which he replied: "Yes, ma'am, from birth."

There is a sense of movement and even urgency in the group on the march; Olive Schreiner, with the pages of a book flapping in the wind, her beloved terrier (with whom she was buried) leaping at her side; Sol Plaatje, with one foot on his bike pedal and pushing it forward before mounting; Maqoma on his charger; Oliver Tambo's tie billowing in the breeze; almost all the characters shown in full stride.

They are also all extremely lifelike; it feels like you are standing next to each actual person, what with such attention paid to fine details of clothing, jewellery, spectacles, walking sticks, books, cricket bats, weapons, each and all vital elements revealing the giss[1] of each one.

"We want these freedom fighters to be remembered as real people, not just faces in history books. Our dead are never dead to us until we have forgotten them," notes Dali Tambo.

Among the characters bringing up the rear of the freedom march you'll see the likenesses of Khoi leaders Klaas and his brother Dawid Stuurman, Autshumato and the enigmatic, dishevelled and barefooted missionary Johannes van der Kemp.

Notably absent is Doman whose feet were left dangling, so to say, back at Groenkloof. The floodlights around the park were not working on the night the 148-kilogram figure was carried to a waiting vehicle and rushed away from the scene of the crime (with its feet it would have weighed 150 kilograms). Police suspected an inside job, but to date no arrests have been made.

A spokesperson for the National Heritage Monument said its street value (meaning the price of the metal as scrap) was around R5 000, less a few hundred for those missing feet. That is the same amount they have offered as a reward for information leading to its return.

---

[1] The term "giss" (pronounced "gizz") is used nowadays by birders to explain the recognisable factors of a species in the field. It is often claimed to be an acronym for "general impression, size and shape" that originated during the Second World War for gunners to distinguish friendly from enemy aircraft.

The Johannesburg Museum of Military History
Civil War and Uncivil War: Searching for an Acre Full of Guns and Heroes

For many baby boomers of Johannesburg the "war museum" was a wonderland, if a rather ghoulish one, where bedtime stories told by their fathers and mothers came to life. While the collectve memory of the Second World War is fast fading, this landmark museum is flourishing.

THE STORY OF HUMANKIND is largely the story of war: when the Israelites did smite the Canaanites, the Egyptians did smite the Sumerians, the Assyrians came down like a wolf on the fold, the Greeks sacked Troy, and so on. The story of war is invariably linked to advancing technologies – chariot wheels and recurved bows, siege engines, the trebuchet and gunpowder.

And then there are the heroes and villains – David and Goliath, the Hatfields and McCoys, Churchill and Hitler, Batman and The Joker. Many have, or have had, parents or other relatives who signed up as volunteers to fight in "the war" against the evil that was Hitler's Nazi regime, which spread blood and horror across Europe and beyond in the late 1930s and early 1940s.

My father was one of them. South Africans of the Allied 8th Army were humiliated at Tobruk in Libya by Field Marshal Erwin Rommel. But after their victory at El Alamein they chased the elite of the German army across to Sicily, from there up the twisting mountain roads of Italy, village by village and town by bloody town, all the way to the German border.

Many of us who did (have relatives who served in various wars), grew up fascinated by the stories and the machines that powered them. For us the "war museum" in Saxonwold – it sounds like the place where a wild Germanic army might have ambushed Roman legionnaires – was a kind of dreadful Disneyland.

Things we'd seen only in comic books came almost to life and, we being so small, towered over us. Remember the Messerschmitt 109 with its nose planted in the ground, its props all tangled? That audacious one-man submarine that was so brutal and solid to the touch, the gargantuan Churchill and Sherman tanks, and the one you could climb inside and pretend you were a commander chasing Rommel's desert corps back down the dusty road from El Alamein?

The war museum, now known as the South African National Museum of Military History, was officially opened in 1947 by Prime Minister JC Smuts, hero of three wars and the only field marshal in the British Army not to have been born British. There is a story, apocryphal or otherwise, whereby Winston Churchill had a standing order that if he was to die during the Second World War, Smuts was to take command of the British war effort.

Due to its provenance, it is not surprising that the main focus of the museum was "the war" otherwise known as the Second World War. You approach the museum down a grand avenue of jacaranda trees, which in October radiate in floral showers of the deepest blue. The focal point of the avenue is an impressive four-arched structure surmounted by a winged Angel of Peace. It looks out west over "park" suburbs that are said to be the largest human-planted forest in the world.

If people tell you it was designed by Sir Herbert Baker (as was the monument to the South African fallen at the Battle of Delville Wood in France during the First World War) you can correct them. Actually, it was designed by Baker's associate-turned-adversary Sir Edwin Lutyens, champion of British Empire architecture in the pre-Second World War years.

What is also little known is that the "Angel of Saxonwold" commemorates the British fallen during the Anglo-Boer War, that conflict which so divided our fledgling country and which, in its aftermath, sowed the seeds of the great racial divide of which we now reap the harvest.

Although the two "great wars" have always dominated the collection, and particularly the second, it is satisfying to see the Anglo-Boer and other wars now far better represented than they were in the past. Old Oom Jannie (Smuts) must have called in a lot of favours to get all that hardware shipped over to South Africa in order to build up the embryonic museum's inventory in the years immediately following Victory in Europe Day in 1945. Especially all the German stuff.

Probably the single most valuable item in the entire collection is the Messerschmitt 262 B-1a/U1 night fighter, which you see when you enter the museum complex through the Group Capt. "Sailor" Malan Hall. It is one of only a few of its kind remaining in the world, and was an aircraft far ahead of its time. Of the various German "secret weapons" (*Projekt* 1065) this was the one most likely to have been able to swing the odds in the opposite direction had that lunatic Adolph known anything about military strategy, and praise the gods and dogs of war he did not.

The ME 262 was the world's first jet combat aircraft and could shred the Allies' internal combustion planes. The one in the war museum shows an FuG 218 Neptune radar antenna protruding from its nose cone, indicating this one was one of the night fighters. It was powered by a Heinkel He 178 jet engine, designed by physicist Hans Joachim Pabst von Ohain in 1936.

Adolph Gysbert "Sailor" Malan is considered by many to have been the top Allied fighter pilot of the Second World War; however, he was not esteemed by his Nazi-sympathising *volk* when, after the war, he joined the Torch Commando that was opposed to the Nationalist Government. He was born in Wellington, Western Cape, in 1910 and joined the merchant navy at 17, hence his nickname. When in 1936 Britain started arming for the looming conflict, the sea dog volunteered for the Royal Air Force. There being so few of his kind back then, within a year he had risen to the rank of acting commander of 74th Fighter Squadron.

Once war broke, his heroic deeds mounted along with promotions, medals and swastikas on his fuselage – 35 by war's end. Among his tally of honours were Distinguished Service Order (DSO) and bar, Distinguished Flying Cross (DFC) and bar, Legion of Honour, Croix de Guerre (twice) and War Cross. After the war he became private secretary to Harry Oppenheimer, head of the Anglo American Corporation, as well as president of the Torch Commando. When it became clear that opposition to the Nationalist Party was amounting to little, he retired to a farm near Kimberley where he died in 1963.

Crossing no man's land that is the central courtyard (where the old ME 109 used to stand face-planted but has now been refitted inside the Sailor Malan Hall) brings you to the main GE Brink Hall where, among the attractions, are numerous First and Second World War aeroplanes. For most lovers of war memorabilia it is the de Havilland Mosquito that will get their Avgas pumping. You can climb up a wooden staircase and peer through the armoured glass into the cockpit, as well as swoon over those twin Rolls-Royce engines. The plane was super light and legendarily fast, with a frame constructed entirely of wood.

But you'll find the real connoisseurs of flight staring up at the RAF (Royal Flying Factory) SE 5, the first bi-plane fighter. For its time it was fast, agile and stable (which was rare) and has been described as the Spitfire of the First World War. Problems producing the Hispano-

Suiza H-S 8B engines meant the Sopwith Camel became the most common British aircraft on the Western Front; call the "camel" the Hurricane of WWI if you will.

For the record, General George Edwin Brink was born at Jagersfontein in the year the Anglo-Boer War began. He started off driving tanks and rose to become the second highest ranking officer, after Jan Smuts, in the South African Army. He saw active service in East and North Africa before being injured, and ended the Second World War driving a desk.

The aeroplanes in this hall are all amazing and one of the finest collections outside Britain. But as with all things, it is the stories of the people who made, flew and maintained them that are the most heart-rending. While the name Sailor Malan is still remembered with reverence, that of Pat Pattle is much less so. Yet Marmaduke Thomas St John Pattle, born in the little trading town of Butterworth, was, by some people's estimation, the greatest airman of all time.

During "the war" he flew the less fancied Hawker Hurricane, first against Italians in North Africa and then against far superior German planes over Greece. On 20 April 1941, suffering from battle fatigue and influenza, he was shot down over the sea while diverting an attack from one of his flight commanders (Pattle was squadron commander). The records were lost once German forces took Greece, but it is believed his score of "kills" was around 60 – in only nine months of operational flying.

Other citations in the hall tell of tremendous acts of self-sacrifice and courage by otherwise ordinary people who rose to the challenge when danger and death threatened. These are the South African recipients of the Victoria Cross, including Sergeant Quenton Smythe of the Royal Natal Carbineers, Captain William Faulds and Edwin Swales.

It should be incumbent for every South African to go and read their inscriptions in the museum, to dwell on their deeds and sacrifices, lest today we be goose-stepping around the *platz*. And also, when firebrand politicians demand that public places be renamed to favour their heroes, that they reflect on the bigger picture, because real valour has no political motivation or reward.

Take the case of the SS *Mendi* that was carrying 830 members of the South African Native Contingent to France in 1917. January 16 was a cold and foggy night when, off La Havre, the *Mendi* was T-boned by the much larger troop ship SS *Darro*.

More than 500 people aboard the *Mendi* died that night; some never made it out of their beds and onto the deck while others perished out in the freezing Atlantic waters. But it is the story of the brave men on the deck of the sinking ship that is so uplifting. It goes that the Reverend Wauchope Dyobha entreated them to take off their boots and perform the dance of warriors on the cold steel decking.

"Be quiet and calm my countrymen," he is quoted as calling out, and we can see him there, being thrown about, puffs of condensation bursting from his mouth. "You are going to die, but that is what you came here for. Brothers, we are drilling the drill of death. We are the sons of Africa, raise your war cries …" Chilling stuff.

Then there is, or was, Lucas Majozi, DCM. He was a stretcher bearer, a member of the Native Military Corps of non-armed auxiliaries, on the terrible night of 23–24 October 1942 when the South African forces were being smashed to bits by the German artillery and panzers in the first-wave attack on El Alamein.

Throughout the night, time and again he returned to the areas of heaviest bombardment to carry out wounded soldiers. Even after being wounded he worked on through the night, eventually collapsing from exhaustion and loss of blood in the early morning light. Majozi (he eventually attained the rank of sergeant) was the first – and only – black South African to be awarded the Distinguished Conduct Medal.

The next exhibition space is the FB Adler Hall (FB was a founder of the South African artillery corps) with lots of armour (the insider name for tanks and other big guns on wheels and tracks) and related stuff. If you like firearms, uniforms and associated paraphernalia (the "bags and accessories" department in the war stores), you'll find yourself lingering here.

It also houses Boer and Zulu war exhibits; not as extensive as they might be, given their significance in the collective consciousness of South Africans as well as many people further abroad, but something is better than nothing. There are also small nods to the southern African bush war as well as internal resistance.

A nice hat-doff to modern times and political correctness is the small display on military objectors and dissenters: not just nice white, English-speaking boys who cocked a snook at the SADF's dismal foray into Africa, but others too, like nice Afrikaans-speaking boys who said "*nie 'n vok nie*" to two world wars in Europe on behalf of the *donderse rooinekke*.

Outside is the Dan Pienaar Gun Park that impresses with fearful Russian T32 and T54 tanks captured in Angola, South African jets including a partly cross-sectioned Mirage and the gargantuan G5 and G6 155-mm howitzer guns. But perhaps the most intriguing among them is – and here we break into a mysteries-at-the-museum routine: "It is black with red trim, cigar-shaped, about 1.5 metres high and 11 metres long. It weighs 11 tonnes and has two smaller, similar cigar-shaped protrusions on each side …"

The Molche one-person German mini-submarine was codenamed the Salamander, and it fared about as well as an amphibian in a puff adder's pit. The Molche was the first of its kind in the *Kriegsmarine* (German navy) and, anticipating the assault on Europe, these mini-subs were planned to wreak havoc with Allied shipping around the coast.

But they were extremely complicated for the single crew member to work. On their first sortie in September 1944, 10 of 12 sent out were sunk. Success and survival numbers for the *K-Verband* 411 flotilla of mini-subs steadily worsened, and you can just imagine yourself inside that claustrophobic, cylindrical death trap, all alone, with bombs and depth charges hammering all around you. War, really!

But among all this steel and death, blood and glory, there is one story that stands out, and always has – for me, at least. It is an oil painting, behind glass, and hanging in a dark corner of the Brink Hall. It was painted in Cairo in 1942 by official war artist Neville Lewis. It has preoccupied me since I first saw it as a child on my first visit to the war museum, my eager little hand clutched safely in the hold of my 8th Army veteran Dad's.

It shows the handsome, rugged, dignified face of a man named Job Maseko who had been working for the railways in Springs when war broke out in 1939. He volunteered for the Native Military Corps and soon found himself as a worker for the South African 2nd Infantry

Division in North Africa. When on 21 June 1942, Major-General Hendrik Klopper surrendered to Field Marshal Erwin Rommel at Tobruk, Maseko found himself a prisoner along with 10 772 other British POWs (of whom some 1 200 were members of the Native Military Corps).

While loading German supplies in Tobruk harbour, Job Maseko made a small bomb using a condensed milk tin, cordite and a fuse. With the help of some other of his fellow POWs, he managed to hide it among fuel barrels in the hold of an F-class supply ship. Boom! went the bomb and down went the ship.

Lance Corporal Maseko was recommended for a Victoria Cross but "because he was only an African" he received the Military Medal instead. The King of England's citation reads: "In carrying out this deliberately planned action, Job Masego (sic) displayed ingenuity, determination and complete disregard of personal safety from punishment by the enemy or from the ensuing explosion which set the vessel alight."

The brave man died in a train accident in 1952 and a school in Springs was named in his honour. In 1997 the SA Navy renamed the SAS *Kobie Coetzee* strike craft the SAS *Job Maseko*. One hopes the children at the Job Maseko Primary School in KwaThema are taken on regular trips to the museum.

Mapungubwe

Stone Citadels, Cities of Gold and Protective Spirits: Searching for Ancestral Treasures

Mapungubwe is both a World Heritage Site and National Park in the Limpopo River valley. The eponymous hill is locally a sacred place and focal point of the oldest known Iron Age kingdom in southern Africa.

TREASURE, EVEN THE MEREST whiff of it, can drive people crazy. Probably the most well-documented craziness was the hunt for the fabled "Kruger millions" after the Anglo-Boer War. As the British juggernaut approached Pretoria in early June of 1900, there was a mad rush to get the bullion from the Zuid Afrikaansche Republiek's mint onto the last train departing for Delagoa Bay.

No trace of them was ever found, not officially anyway. As late as 2001 there were ambiguous reports that Kruger pounds had been unearthed on a farm in the Ermelo district. Other famous treasure hunts include the wreck of the *Grosvenor*, the mines of King Solomon and the Queen of Sheba, lost cities of the Kalahari and Monomotapa, often thought to be synonymous with Great Zimbabwe.

Great Zimbabwe was a trading and important gold manufacturing centre from about the ninth to 15th century CE. It controlled around 4 000 gold mines in the region and is thought to have produced around 60 per cent of the world's gold during its time.

The site was sacked first by Portuguese traders and later Boer ivory hunters, but there is absolutely no record of what they might have found there, or taken. Early colonial "archaeologists" intent on proving the stone edifices were built by a power higher and more sophisticated than any African could, did their best to destroy much of what was left.

But Zimbabwe was not the only stone or "zimbabwe" settlement in southern Africa. More abandoned stone cities stand at Khami, Dlo-Dlo and Naletale in western Zimbabwe, at Mmagwa Hill in Botswana's Northern Tuli conservancy, as well as at Thulamela in the northern Kruger National Park. In the Northern Tuli area there is even a natural dolerite dyke that greatly resembles an ancient stone wall and is called Solomon's Wall.

These ruins and rumours of more like them fuelled fortune seekers and deluded swashbucklers for many years. At least one is known to have walked off into the Kalahari wastelands with just one jerry can of water. His skeleton was later found by park rangers.

But not all treasure seekers went home with empty hands. On a hot summer's day in 1932 a young man named Jerry van Graan was hunting in the Limpopo River valley, near its confluence with the Shashe River. He stopped at the hut of an old man to ask for water.

The old black man named Mabina Moribame Mokwena procured for him a calabash of deliciously cool water from inside his hut. Van Graan was delighted and then fascinated by the water, and asked to see where it came from. The man showed him a large clay pot buried up to its neck in his hut floor. The hunter wanted to buy it, suspecting it might be something rare and valuable, but the older man refused.

Van Graan had studied history at the University of Pretoria and knew something about old cultures. He also knew the story about a mysterious Frenchman named Francois Bernhard Lotrie who claimed he had found treasures on a fortress hill in the same area around 1890.

Some months later, Van Graan returned with his father, ESJ, and some friends. This time they asked old man Mokwena to show them where he had found his big water pot, but he declined to. The white hunting party had anticipated this and promptly got a big *shisanyama* going. They produced beer in order to loosen the old man's tongue, but still he would not budge, not even when they offered him a pile of coins. He could not betray the ancestors, he told them, or they would surely punish him.

But Mokwena's son, Jim Chewana, relented when they took him aside and offered him a donkey cart. And so it was that on New Year's Eve in 1932 the young Jim Chewana led the group of white fortune seekers towards a large, flat-topped hill known as Mapungubwe, the place of jackals. Some also called it Thaba ya Badimo, hill of the ancestors.

Once people had lived there but it had been abandoned a very long time before. It was now the domain of the ancestors and no one dared approach it, let alone climb to the summit, lest they be cursed, be blinded or otherwise punished. Young Jim Chewana knew that the hill was sacred and refused to approach too close. Stopping at a shepherd's tree about 50 metres from the base, he turned his back and indicated over his shoulder (neither he nor any other black person would dare point directly at it) that that was the place.

The white party searched the base but could not find a way up, so they called to him. He called back that they should look for a gap behind the big rock fig. Sure enough, they found a crack leading all the way to the top, but it would have been no easy climb. The original inhabitants had chipped holes into the sandstone sides into which would have been driven wooden stakes to act as steps. These were long gone so the white men had to shimmy and claw their way to the summit.

When the Van Graan party reached the top of the hill they found some retaining rock walls, grindstones, dagha surfaces with holes where wooden poles would have been placed, deep grain and water pits dug into the rock, with rocks that could be rolled over to cover them, as well as 24 graves.

Most of the graves were those of children, but others were adults, all buried in upright sitting positions and all facing west. Those of highest rank were buried inside large clay pots. From those graves were recovered glass and gold beads, gold and copper nails, bangles, gold anklets, fine gold chain mail, a golden sceptre as well as a carved wooden bowl and some animals covered in gold foil. One grave contained more than a hundred gold wire bangles and a thousand gold beads. These items now constitute the crown jewels of South Africa and the celebrated Golden Rhino has become our national symbol, replacing the old Dutch castle.

That's what we know they found, but there might have been more. Apparently Jerry had a hard time persuading the rest of the group not to melt down all the gold and flog it. The better person within him contacted his old history professor at Pretoria. In his turn, Leo Fouché contacted the appropriate government people and persuaded them to buy the entire hoard. It now resides in a vault in Pretoria.

It is believed that Bantu-related Kalanga people first crossed the Limpopo from what is now Botswana around 800 CE and set up home and shop – they were Iron Age people – at a place now known as Site K2 or Leopard Koppie. Here they established the first class-based society in South Africa, with the elite living on hilltops and commoners on the plains below. Clay pot shards and glass beads, trade goods from the East African coast, have been recovered there in substantial quantities. They would also have traded ivory with the coast, given that this was then, and still remains, prime big-game and especially elephant country.

Two centuries later a powerful leader established his centre of power on a large, flat-topped hill some way to the north. But this time they were working not only iron but also gold, in fine detail. The "royals" lived in splendour on the top of the hill, while about five thousand "subjects" lived in stockades or kraals down below. The sheer-sided hill was almost inaccessible, but for two natural stairways in the rock face. One is still used to access the summit while the other, the "women's passage", has since been blocked by a rock fall.

The people of both K2 and Mapungubwe exist only in the shady world of prehistory, but the study of bones from skeletons found buried on top of the "hill of jackals" reveals a strong Khoi ancestry. Some archaeologists say it is not beyond the realms of possibility that Khoi-related people were the royalty, and Bantu people the subjugated herders. But we'll never know for sure.

What we do know is this is where dry-packed stone walls were used for the first time in southern Africa to demarcate different living areas, separating a society into different classes. Stone and wood were used together, often with wooden posts and lintels, and stone as space fillers. This is also the known origin of another building material, even more than the stone walls, that is so visually obvious. Some call it clay, some call it *dagha*.

But here it was not simply clay from a river bank. It was termite mound, ground up, mixed with water and re-laid as floors and low walls. When set it would have been as hard as concrete, and in fact much of it survives today. By locating the clay floors it is possible to identify the extent of settlements here as well as other similar "zimbabwe" sites. Which is why some archaeologists call it a dagha culture and not a stone one.

Another unknown is why the site was abandoned less than a century after it was established. The conventional wisdom is that with overgrazing and climate change the area dried up and could no longer support a large cattle population, so the people packed up and moved north and east.

But some researchers refute this. "People adapt," insists young Zimbabwe-born archaeologist Robert Nyamushosho. Which is why people still live in the Sahara Desert, a place that two millennia ago was an important wheat-producing region. There were perpetual tribal disputes, he says, exactly the same as in medieval Europe, when centres of power moved but not the actual people. Just like the people who live in the Limpopo Valley today, as they did back in 1932.

The actual meaning of the name Mapungubwe is in fact lost. Some people in the area have referred to it as "the place where rock becomes liquid". The various names are not so much translations as descriptions of various aspects of the place. Each one of them would have deepened the sense of reverence people in the past had for the place.

The Mapungubwe where rock turns to liquid is believed to signify the place where gold was first smelted in the region. Perhaps not first, but it was certainly the place where it was done on any industrial or commercial scale.

The senior cultural guide at the Mapungubwe Cultural Landscape today is one Kgomotso Phalandwa Johannes Masalesa, a traditional leader and grandson of a tradition healer who had lived in sight of the hill when the Van Graans came a calling. Long before reaching the hill that is the focus of this story, he'll point out another much less significant-looking hill, one that seems much less inviting, almost sinister, with its knobkerrie-shaped summit, surrounded by a dense vegetable moat of mopane thicket and a picket of massive baobab trees.

This is Nyende, the hill of rainmaking. What with their strong Khoi links, it is little wonder that Kalanga, and later Venda, healers in the area learned almost everything they knew about the world of the supernatural from the Bushmen. In an essentially dry place – the Limpopo Valley is today classified as being an extremely arid semi-desert to desert region – having the power to make rain would be a very high order of expertise.

In the book he has written about the place, Kgomotso Masalesa recounts at some length the epic struggle between two traditional healers in the area and the various herbs and spells they used against one another. Some involved destructive thunderstorms, others used the power of animals such as hyenas, crocodiles, owls and black mambas, the same forces, remedies and animal-spirits that today still dog the region. Apparently the droppings of fish eagles, and fat from pythons, are good for chasing away evil spirits, as well as for helping with high blood pressure, lower back pain and various fevers.

But if all the tried and tested remedies of the most powerful medicine men failed to produce the required result, rain, they would resort to the strongest *muti* of all. Another name for Nyende is the "place of sacrifice" – of children in particular. For people living in such a marginal area, with low population numbers, nothing would have been more valuable to them than their children. Today, Masalesa tells his guests, people no longer visit Nyende because of the bad vibes there.

In early 1933 the University of Pretoria set out to examine the hill from which their most recent treasures had come. They employed two local men, Daniel Nalana and his brother, Modiya Mathuncha, to help with excavations. The men later admitted they were terrified at the prospect, and had to consult a traditional healer before approaching it, and to get permission from ancestors to work on the summit tableland.

The prime minister of South Africa at that time, Jan Smuts, took a great interest in the place and visited the site. He managed to persuade his government to conserve the area and so the short-lived Dongola National Park came into being in 1947. The full vision (proposed by a Welsh-born conservationist named Illtyd Buller Pole Evans) was to co-operate with Rhodesia (Zimbabwe) and Bechuanaland (Botswana) in order to create a trans-frontier park that would straddle the Limpopo Valley.

One year later Smut's United Party government was defeated by the Afrikaner Nationalists who immediately set about dismantling all and any of Smuts's work they could, including Dongola. The "Nats" had vehemently attacked it as a case of land expropriation without consent (funny how history repeats itself as tragedy and farce). Today Evans's old conservation blueprint is being dusted off and given new life.

During the 1970s and '80s, some readers might remember, the breathtaking landscape was known as the notorious Greefswald military outpost. It was to this harsh place that drug users, gays and other perceived deviants in the army were sent for "rehabilitation" (read: *opvokkery*). Officers would hunt, actually poach, game here while *troepies* took great delight shooting at, and otherwise defacing, much of the Bushman art in the many rock shelters found in this section of the Limpopo valley.

Much has changed since then. Today school-goers learn about the real historical and cultural significance of the place. It certainly gives a new perspective on South Africa compared to the old one, where Voortrekkers carried the flame of civilisation and overcame "the native problem". In 1998 Mapungubwe once again was designated a national park, then a World Heritage Site in 2003.

In 2007 a lavish ceremony was conducted on top of the eponymous hill, abounding with local luminaries, traditional leaders and traditional healers, VIPs and other grandees. The purpose was to rebury what remained of the skeletons dug up 74 years before, and so still the disturbed spirits at the place of jackals.

Old Mabina Mokwena had worked for Oom Paul Kruger when the Transvaal president came to hunt in the area, and the hirsute Boer leader gave him a pension of a wagon, some horses and money. His son, Jim Chewana, however, was not so lucky. For his role in revealing to white interlopers the hill and the secret way up, the ancestors rewarded him with blindness.

Kruger National Park

*Big Game, Big Trees and a
Ticking Conservation Time Bomb:
Searching for a Game Reserve
That Very Nearly Wasn't*

The Kruger Park needs no introduction. What is does require, however, is to highlight how precarious were its early years, how tentative the creation of our first national park and the uncertain future it now faces.

COULD YOU CONCEIVE OF a South Africa – or a book about its most remarkable places – without a Kruger National Park? The very thought is unsettling. Kruger is not only this country's flagship national park but also one of Africa's top five game reserves, no contest.

The park's north-south distance is matched only by that of Namibia's Namib-Naukluft National Park. But that strip of desert has just two main habitats and precious few large animals; the Kruger has a rude abundance of both. The considerable diversity of landscape and vegetation of the South African Lowveld, which is covered almost entirely by the park, is the result of numerous interacting elements.

To begin are the elevational and latitudinal differences between the relatively high, cool and fertile country around Pretoriuskop in the southwest, to the low, arid, fever-ridden river valleys around Crook's Corner in the extreme northeast. Then there are the soils, and there are few other places, not just in South but all of Africa, with such a varied mixture.

Working backwards on the geological timeline, they begin with the gravelly alluvial soils of the main river valleys, predominantly the Limpopo and its tributaries. Also of relatively recent vintage are the sodic (salty) soils, which cover much of the ground between Punda Maria and Letaba rest camps.

This is the mopane belt that on the surface appears bereft of animals, but in reality is quite the opposite. Most of the reserve's elephants and buffaloes are to be found here, it's just not always easy to see them in among the dense cover.

Stormberg volcanics (Late Karoo period, circa 100 mya) comprise the Lebombo hills all along the park's eastern boundary. These are preceded in time by Early to Middle Karoo sandstones and shales (about 150–250 mya, wherein all that controversial coal is to be found). Most of the park's southern half comprises ancient granite that is about half the age of our planet, two billion years give or take a few hundred million.

Finally, there are the greenstones which, although thinly distributed, are the stars of the geological story. They form the Barberton Mountain Land suite of rocks, our newest World Heritage Site. It's not everywhere you can see and touch antediluvian rocks dating back about three-and-a-half billion years, to the time when the first proto-continents were forming.

Not just that, but what are believed to be the oldest known forms of life have been found in these rocks. You've come a long way, and it's been a rough trip, *Homo sapiens*. Congratulations for making it this far after a shaky start as bacteria and algae.

All this translates into trees. It is the trees, the big ones, that set the Kruger Park apart from any other game reserve in the country. Indeed, there are very few other reserves on our subcontinent that have anything like the variety and scale of trees to be found here – an astonishing 336 species.

To begin an alphabetical liturgy, first come the more than a dozen acacia species (or whatever the botanical knobthorns now want us to call them); following them are the baobab, that titanic succulent of the driest, hottest areas; then buffalo thorn; about a dozen species of bushwillow; boerboon; coral tree; greenthorn; guarri; jackalberry; karee; kiaat; marula; mopane; monkey orange; mountain syringa; nyalaberry; purple-pod terminalia; rain tree; silver tree; sour plum; tamboti; wild figs (several species) and wild pear.

That's around 46 species, 290 to go … On the surface, the Okavango Delta and surrounding arid Kalahari savanna does look like a leafy challenger, but in truth is not that well endowed with different species. The Lowveld is *the* place of big trees and, even without consciously making the connection, trees mean birds and again only the Okavango rivals the Kruger for avian abundance.

Obviously, we go there primarily to see animals large and small, but beneath that is a sense of venturing back in time into a fantastical Pleistocene park where things remain as they were at a time before we humans came along and changed (one is tempted to use the word "ruined", but these things are relative) it all.

This is the Africa we think of when we say we feel we belong there in some visceral way, like we are going back to our primordial home. That we have ingested the red dust of Africa into our bloodstreams and have become intoxicated on the heady infusion.

Not to be outdone by Hollywood's Jurassic fantasyland, the Lowveld of today has its own creatures fantastical and unlikely: lumbering pachyderms, some with unicorn-like horns, others with great tusked teeth and hose-pipe noses; herbivores with necks so long you'd expect them to snap in a strong wind; fearsome toothed and clawed predators that seem to leap out of our nightmares. Sometimes you need to remind yourself just how unlikely it all is.

And then there are the Kruger's rest camps, like no other in this region or any other. The names alone are a poem of Africa from a bygone age: Skukuza and Letaba, Lower Sabie and Satara, Shingwedzi and Punda Maria. Each site was chosen for its natural beauty and tree cover. Some people, mostly long-time visitors, prefer to sit at camp during the middle of the day to just watch the birds and other small critters of these arboreal ecosystems.

At night the rest camps are redolent with the intoxicating aromas of acacia-wood fires and sizzling boerewors. Most of the camps were named for the rivers along whose banks they spread. One exception is Skukuza which reclines under substantial tree cover at the confluence of the Sabie and Sand rivers.

Punda Maria is another, and it was named by the first ranger of the far north, JJ Coetser. He had served in East Africa during the First World War where he'd picked up some Swahili. Clearly, he misheard the local name for zebras and thought that the striped donkeys (*punda miliya*) had an amusing similarity with his wife, Maria's, name (and *punda* being slang for woman).

Early days in the park must have been either heaven or penury for the rangers and their families. There were no proper roads. Most lived in mud huts with no modern conveniences, not even running water. They had to contend with heat, drought, floods, flies, tsetse flies, mosquitoes and attendant malaria, not to mention marauding elephants, sneaking cats and all other things that slither and slide, sting and bite.

From accounts handed down, they do appear to have been a happy and tough band of ranger brothers and their wives, though. In his autobiography, founding warden James Stevenson-Hamilton called the park a Lowveld Cinderella that became a princess, so clearly he liked the place a lot.

When it came time to build rest camps, the warden believed in keeping things Spartan. The first was Pretoriuskop in 1930. He did not want visitors there lolling indoors while all of Africa roared and sang its jungle symphony all around, so he ordered the rondavels to be made cramped, with sparse facilities and pokey windows. Even cooking was to be done outdoors.

The headlong rush to modern conveniences and comfort had been propelled largely by the advent of the automobile. The first visitors had to camp, stretching tarpaulins from their cars to a tree, surround their camp with a thorn screen and were obliged to carry at least one firearm per car. Just three cars entered the park in 1927, the year it was opened to visitors.

How things have changed! For those people who like their game experience served up a bit rarer than what you find in the modern, revamped rest camps, there is Tsendze. This newest of rest camps offers only camping on a bring-all-of-your-own basis. The only head-nod to modern conveniences is solar-heated water and lights in the ablution buildings. The name means "to wander around in the bush as if lost", which seems a fine way to see the wilderness.

The old timers knew not to plonk a camp in the middle of the mopane belt. But modern planners, seeing a large blank area, couldn't resist the urge to fill it. Mopane Camp has a swimming pool (vital for visits during the suicide season when temperatures reach into the upper 40s), and plenty thatch, but about as much appeal as a plate of wors and pap without any gravy.

The park has some 60 marked historic sites that are worth taking the trouble to explore. For example, few people know that in the far north of Kruger is one of South Africa's most important Iron Age archaeological sites; not even the (white) section rangers, until it was "discovered" in the late 1980s. The black rangers, well versed in the world of their ancestors, had kept quiet about it.

The places that will appeal to the younger travellers are those waypoints that mark various adventures of that feisty terrier Jock, the dog made famous by the book that charmed many generations of South African children. Especially if readings round the campfire are part of the daily activities. (Another one to keep the "likkle ones" amused is the Smartie game: you buy a stash and dish out various colours for each of a particular animal or bird spotted by them.)

Jock of the Bushveld was the loyal companion of Percy Fitzpatrick, one of a legion of waggoneers who carried supplies between Delagoa Bay (Maputo) and the Lydenburg gold diggings in the late 1800s. Stories about the fearless dog's exploits were polished through many retellings in the Fitzpatrick household after the man had made his fortune and moved to a mansion on the crest of the Witwatersrand.

Among the rand lord's friends was that champion of imperial Britain Rudyard Kipling, who gave us the *Just So Stories* involving the great, grey-green greasy Limpopo. He encouraged Percy to write down his own "just so stories" of his life on the road and in the bush. That is why, on the title page, you will see it is dedicated to "The Likkle People".

Don't tell the kids but here's a spoiler alert. In the book he wrote about his famous family's coaching company, Harry Zeederberg reckoned there never was a dog named Jock. Harry would have known Percy before he was made a "sir" and reckons the young transport rider made it all up.

Most likely the story of Jock is a compilation of all the dogs and dog tales Fitzpatrick encountered during his time driving wagons. Even today, more than a century later, they ring so true that at the heart of Jock there must be a foundation based in real experience.

Not far off the Doispane Road, the old wagon route to Delagoa Bay, near Crocodile Bridge, stands historical marker number 57. You can get out of your car here to see one example of the Bushman rock art that is scattered around the park. The Stone Age hunter-gatherers, it seems, did not leave any landscape stone unturned in their peregrinations around southern Africa.

In the far northeastern corner of the park, Crook's Corner recalls the shenanigans of the loveable, rogue elephant-hunter Bvekenya or, as would have been written on his birth certificate and numerous arrest warrants, Cecil Barnard.

The corner in question is the meeting of three countries, South Africa, Zimbabwe and Mozambique. This confluence of the Limpopo and Luvuvhu rivers afforded outlaws such as Barnard an escape route from the law no matter from which direction it came for them.

Also up the Luvuvhu way is a site that should be a must on any trip to the park. It is Thulamela (or Thulamala), the Iron Age stronghold referred to earlier, that was occupied between the years 1200 and 1300 CE. This hill location, also marked by an impressive copse of baobab trees, is one of the numerous known stone settlements of people who worked iron and gold, and bartered with first Arab and later Portuguese traders.

On the Iron Age calendar, Thulamela is located between

Mapungubwe and Great Zimbabwe. Out from city states went gold, ivory, game hides and slaves. In came beads, porcelain, cloth and coins. Perhaps most interesting from an anthropological point of view is that all these "zimbabwe" (stone) settlements show a clear class distinction, with an aristocracy living the life of Riley on prominent hilltops and the peasants skoffelling on the plains below.

Another significant place are the ruins of the homestead and store of the intrepid trader and hunter João Albasini, the first white man to call the area home. João was just 18 years old in 1831 when he left Lisbon to join his father at Delagoa Bay to help run a trading post there.

Delagoa Bay was the major slaving entrepôt of the day in southern Africa, a commerce that helped fuel the Difaqane wars that ravaged the region in the early to mid-1800s. At one point, King Dingane ordered an attack on the bay and Albasini was taken prisoner by the Zulu commander Soshangana. He was held captive for about six months but was eventually freed by two black traders who knew him.

When he returned to Delagoa Bay, Albasini decided to diversify the business by following the scent trail of gold and ivory into the interior. When he reached the Lowveld, he conscripted a small army of elephant hunters and became the main trader in the region of ivory and hides (lions, leopards and rhinos mainly).

Around 1846 he built a substantial home at Magashula's Kraal, where today you'll find its ruins just inside the Numbi Gate. This spot became a convenient warehouse for Boers from the higher ground. They would conduct speedy trading sorties in order to outrun the endemic malaria of the area, which also discouraged settlement and farming there.

Business went so well the Portuguese man built two more stores in what would become the Sabie Game Reserve. When gold fever struck the Transvaal Escarpment area, Albasini followed that trail, marrying Gertina van Rensburg of Ohrigstad in 1850.

With wealth and then the status of being appointed Vice-Consul for Portugal in the Transvaal Republic, the Alabasinis moved to the more respectable town of Louis Trichardt. In time the Albasinis married into the Zeederberg clan and today you can still find them living in the area.

All these stories sound extremely romantic and imposing, and it certainly seems like the park has been there forever. Which is not the case at all and its creation was the subject of much dispute.

In the 19th century, ideas about hunting differed between the two settler cultures. At a time when conservation ideas were seeding in the British realm, a hunter was by definition a gentleman (as opposed to a common poacher). Killing for pleasure was considered highly ethical, while shooting for sustenance or commercial gain was deemed to be savage.

The Boers upcountry had a very different relationship with nature. They considered exterminating wildlife to be not only their God-given right, but also their civic duty in order that they might clear the land for agriculture and civilization. The Transvaal (which was originally four separate Voortrekker states) had an economy based on hunting for meat, ivory and hides.

In time the more fertile agricultural areas in the south turned away from hunting and by the mid-1880s around 200 game conservancies had been established there on private farms in the Transvaal. Things in the less fertile north went differently, and ruling over them all stood the indomitable, hugely hirsute and extremely conservative president of the Transvaal or, more formally the Zuid Afrikaansche Republiek, Stephanus Johannes Paulus "Paul" Kruger.

The popular mythology is that Kruger was an early champion of game conservation and was the instigator behind creating reserves around the Boer republic. There are even supposed second-hand accounts published by people who knew people who remember hearing him addressing the Volksraad (parliament) extolling the virtues of and need for creating a "wild kraal" in the Lowveld in order to protect the last, disappearing herds there.

Delving into the actual records paints a rather different picture. Social historian Jane Carruthers reckons that some historical people in this chronicle, particularly Paul Kruger, have been erroneously elevated to conservation heroes. This has led to the repeated telling, retelling and the inevitable adding of embellishments becoming self-perpetuating myths.

In the book *The Conservationists and the Killers*, author John

Pringle records the son of fledgling Sabie Game Reserve ranger Major Robertson recalling a story told by his father of the time when President Kruger had tried to rally his followers with discussions about the necessity for game preservation.

The main problem with Robertson's memory is he (the old ranger) as a junior officer in the British army, and then gold prospector, is unlikely have met Paul Kruger, let alone ever heard him speak. There certainly is no way Paul Kruger could have addressed such an audience around a fire. Kruger skipped out of town on the last midnight train bound for Delagoa Bay in January 1900, en route to exile in Clarens, Switzerland. The Sabie Game Reserve did not start recruiting until 1903.

What the archives actually reveal is that President Kruger was at best a hindrance to the formation of a game reserve in the Lowveld, or anywhere else, and at worst a furtive opponent. He certainly helped to stall the process.

In Kruger's defence some people argue how he pushed for the creation of South Africa's first game reserve on the Pongola River in 1889, the first official game reserve in South Africa. But historians point out that, firstly, it was a tiny parcel of land and, secondly, that it was part of a larger strategy on the part of the Boers. They needed a sea port and Pongolapoort was their first move in trying to secure a land passage through Swaziland to Kosi Bay.

What actually did transpire in the Volksraad in 1884 was that Kruger for the first time voiced his opinion on wildlife and what he did was oppose a motion for tighter hunting controls. The first record of any discussion in the Volksraad about a game reserve in the Lowveld is in 1888.

A commercially minded farmer from the Free State named Williams suggested such a place be established in order that it might be rented to English "sportsmen" for a high price. In 1890 Williams's idea was taken up by two other members, GJ Louw who was Justice of the Peace for Komatipoort, and Abel Erasmus, Native Commissioner for Lydenburg.

They advocated for a "*wildkraal of reserve*" between the Crocodile and Sabie rivers. Erasmus argued that only Africans resided in the area of the proposed reserve so the enterprise would cost only about £420 a year. Kruger and his fundamentalist supporters sat heavily on the idea.

In 1893 and then again in 1895 the subject was raised at successive Volksraad sittings, and again nothing was done. Only after some strongly worded objections did the government eventually agree to vote on the matter and the motion was passed by a majority of one.

But the Volksraad had no executive powers and so the Sabie Game Reserve did not become an immediate reality. Two more years passed and when still nothing was done by Kruger's government, more deputations and protests followed from supporters of the "wildkraal" idea, until eventually the Executive Council issued a proclamation on 26 March 1898.

But even this did not get things moving in the Slowveld. The Executive Council called for more opinions (talk about delaying tactics, you'd almost think Kruger engineered the forthcoming war to side-step the game reserve issue!). Finally, sort of, in September 1898 funds were made available for a warden to be appointed, along with four African (black) policemen.

A year later still no appointments had been made, and then all hell broke loose – the three-year hell that was the Anglo-Boer War. Naturally any talk of game reserves went up in cannon smoke. When Pretoria fell to Lord Roberts's army in 1900, the British, no doubt driven by a healthy dose of guilt, were keen to restore civil law and order in the Boer republics.

And so begins the discussion about the first warden of the still non-existent Sabie Game Reserve. The new administration under Alfred Milner found the minutes proclaiming this Lowveld *wildkraal* and so advertised for a gamekeeper. In October 1900 a Lydenburg farmer and hunter, A Glynn, applied for and was given the posting. However, because Boer guerrilla units were still operating in the area he was not able to report for duty and the initiative stumbled.

A year later Boer commandos had been all but dislodged from the eastern Transvaal. This prompted the Mining Commissioner at Barberton, Tom Casement, to put up his hand. No appointment was made but a general order was issued prohibiting all military personnel from hunting there. Not all obeyed.

In June 1901, finally, Captain HF Francis, a member of the

controversial Steinaecker's Horse outfit (and this term is used about as loosely as the unit was constituted), was appointed "game inspector" of the Sabie Game Reserve. But just a month later Francis was killed in action, so another "reliable man" was sought.

WM Walker turned out to be that man, but again not for long. Although he had worked on gold diggings around Barberton, he turned out to be a dismal failure at the job. (One has to wonder, what with virtually no supervision and not much to do, how bad he could have been.)

By this time peace had been signed and numerous applications were received for a replacement. A Major James Stevenson-Hamilton was appointed and we can be exceedingly grateful for that. He had served with the 6th (Inniskilling) Dragoons and was seeking a civilian position in South Africa.

The stocky, feisty Scottish officer was 34 years old when he was appointed as the reserve's third warden and its first on-the-ground caretaker. It was a position he would retain until retirement in 1946. Another fortuitous appointment was that of the first game ranger.

In his private notes Stevenson-Hamilton reveals much more about the failures and setbacks he encountered than the joys and successes he reveals in his autobiography. One of these is that the park tended to attract the "flotsam and jetsam" of society, people who thought the job there would be one of continual shooting, drinking and lazing around.

Harry Wolhuter was another who had served in the notorious Steinaecker's Horse, but he was no shirker. Three times in his life he was declared dead, twice during the Boer War when he contracted severe malaria, and then after his famous mauling by a very hungry male lion. Nothing seemed to be able to keep him down. Like his boss, Wolhuter remained working for the park until his own retirement.

Close to Letaba rest camp is historical site number 56, which was the northern-most outpost of the curious corps known as Steinaecker's Horse. Colonel Ludwig Steinaecker was a flamboyant German of unknown military provenance who seemed to have washed up in the Colony of Natal some time around 1890.

When war broke out with the Boers to the north, he managed to persuade the British High Command that he be allowed to raise his own regiment. They needed all the hands and arms they could muster and so conceded: raising privately funded regiments had been commonplace in the British Army for years. The colonel apparently designed his own uniforms for the 450-strong mounted regiment.

Their only orders were: keep an eye on the enemy in the Lowveld and try to prevent any Boer artillery escaping eastwards. They did manage to blow up a vital bridge, but only after the Boers had crossed it and vanished into the bush. That in turn delayed the British forces chasing the guns by about a week.

With nothing much left to do they set up guard posts along a 300-kilometre front from Swaziland to the Letaba River. They spent their time searching for Boers to harass, fishing, hunting and drinking rum. The unit not only hunted for food and sport but even entered the trophy market, supplying other army units with curios to take back home.

At the ascension of King Edward VII in January 1901, Colonel Steinaecker presumed he would be automatically put on the guest list and so set sail for England. When he discovered he was not only not on the party list but completely unknown, he protested. This prompted the big wigs of the Home Guard to investigate. Steinaecker's unit was found to be highly irregular; he was stripped of his rank and ordered to disband his regiment.

The fallen officer returned to Komatipoort where he resorted to wandering the streets and haranguing people with his tales of bravado and betrayal. A former subordinate living in Pilgrim's Rest took him in. When Steinaecker attempted to kill his own horse he was arrested but, before he could be brought to trial, he committed suicide with poison he carried in the event that an honourable exit was required.

Once the Sabie reserve became a working reality, the white farmers of the Lowveld started becoming vocally hysterical that the wildlife sanctuary in their bosom was becoming a breeding ground for predators. The Transvaal Game Protection Association, forerunner of the Wildlife Society, urged the authorities to allow them access so that they might exterminate the "vermin".

They need not have worried about it. For the first decade of its existence, the rangers of the reserve shot every large predator on sight

– lions, leopards, cheetahs, hyenas, wild dogs, the lot. They understood their mission was to protect the antelope, or royal game, from predators as was the case in Britain.

When war broke out in Europe in 1914, most of the rangers signed up for service. Fifty-eight-year-old Major AA Fraser, an old India hand, was left to defend the fort. He was an excellent ranger and, since his arrival at the park in 1903, had formed a close bond with the warden. However, by 1914 he had little fight left in him and was unable to hold back the advancing invasion.

Hunters, black and white, sheep grazers and cattle ranchers, mineral prospectors and other fortune seekers very quickly overran the game reserve. After armistice in 1918 it took the returning corps of rangers many years to clear the park again.

It was around that time that Stevenson-Hamilton had the revelation that a game reserve should be for preserving all game, not just antelope, in fact everything within its boundaries whether animal, mineral or vegetable: a reserve for nature's sake. Not everyone agreed with him.

The warden spent the next decade and a half fighting off successive waves of opposition from hunters, farmers, miners and most politicians to see it finally proclaimed the country's first national park in 1926. The battle to push the national parks legislation to its conclusion proved about as arduous as that of the original game reserve.

The so-called Pact Government, with JBM Hertzog as Prime Minister, was in power and it strongly promoted Afrikaner interests. Nature conservation was seen primarily as a British obsession and the idea had only two strong supporters in the cabinet of the day.

Stevenson-Hamilton popped into Komatipoort to do some shopping, and in the hotel there mentioned his woes to its owner. If you propose the name Kruger for your hoped-for park, no Afrikaner politician will vote against it, his hotelier friend advised.

It was this stroke of local genius that won the ayes. That hard-won event was widely celebrated, and the battle for wildlife conservation was won. However, in a chronicle of Kruger National Park it would be disingenuous not to mention the current poaching problems that have gripped it in a grim vice.

The truth is that the park has been beset with similar problems since the day it came into being. Stevenson-Hamilton's first task was to clear the area of human occupation. When he was clearing out the black subsistence farmers and occasional hunters, he had no idea quite what harvest he might be sowing.

Black people had been living there, on and off, for a long time before white people arrived. When they were told it was now a game reserve and they had to pack up home and move out, or else, they were not amused. Skukuza, the main rest camp in the Kruger Park, was the nickname given to Stevenson-Hamilton by those same people; it means "to sweep clean".

For nearly a century, middle-class and, until recently, almost exclusively white, people have enjoyed the wildlife spectacle that the park offers. But part of that experience is also a romanticised notion of how the place was before the world outside became modernised, industrialised, highly regulated and homogenised.

But for the lives of the relatively impoverished people living outside its fences and looking in, all this has little relevance, point out people like Carruthers and other critics. "Many people, particularly those in areas adjoining the Park, who live in extreme poverty, and who have in the past been deliberately excluded from enjoying or sharing in any of the recreational and educational benefits of the Kruger National Park, hold quite different views."

Poaching has been endemic in the park since its inception and in fact well before. In Stevenson-Hamilton's time it was mostly a low-key amateur affair. Today, though, it has turned highly professional and the stakes are more than one of just life and death.

Poaching and the trade in its spoils are today controlled by mainly Asian criminal cartels. They have unlimited funds and can even create markets for their goods, just as they do for the drugs they peddle around the world.

Elephant populations are being slaughtered across the continent north of here, but when those populations are depleted the guns will turn to Botswana and South Africa, where conservation appears still to be holding its own. The price of rhino horn currently exceeds the price per kilogram of any drug, which is why people are killing and dying on both sides of the poaching trenches.

And, just like with the war against drugs, you cannot hope to win the war against poaching with force. It has been tried and it has failed, or is failing, everywhere.

In communities around the park, be they in South Africa, Mozambique or Zimbabwe, poachers are regarded as Robin Hood-style heroes, bringing bags of cash and glamour into otherwise depressed areas. When a rhino poacher is arrested or shot dead the conservation community might celebrate, but the community from which they come most often galvanises around them.

The poaching war will be lost so long as local communities are not working on the side of the law and conservation, so there has to be more carrot offered to them in order to balance the current stick methods. One suggestion of late is that elephants might hold the solution.

Having been protected for more than a century, their numbers are now believed to be about double what the park can support and still maintain a healthy ecosystem. In the past the Kruger and other game reserves such as Hwange where elephant populations cause problems, culling of herds was done. But in recent decades that practice has lost general favour.

No one wants to see the Kruger's sylvan landscape reduced to treeless wasteland as has happened across much of northern Botswana. Then again no one wants to see the elephants being "taken off" in the name of conservation. And yet, it makes sense, to sacrifice some of the resources you have, and share the spoils with your neighbours, in order to turn the tide of the battle.

You wouldn't want to be one of the people who has to make these decisions, but someone has to. It's like when your arm has been trapped by a rock in a lonely canyon for 127 hours, and your life force is ebbing away. You have a pocketknife and the clock is ticking.

With the combined forces of land claims, poaching and radical politics gathering around the perimeter of the park, it takes a bold decision to cut off your arm in order to save yourself – or not to.

Adam's Calendar

Lost Worlds, Celestial Almanacs and Off-World Visitors: Searching for Truth Among Standing and Lying Stones

Stories of the world's oldest purpose-built sundial and celestial calendar have helped boost tourist interest in the hamlet of Kaapsehoop, perched on the lip of the Mpumalanga Escarpment.

MIST-WRAPPED KAAPSEHOOP IS about as small as a place can be and still appear on a road map. It is not so much a town as a hamlet. That's a place with a population too small to have its own church. It rests on the lip of the Mpumalanga Escarpment, and would fall over and become a suburb of Nelspruit in the Lowveld if the Earth gave so much as a burp – as it has been known to do in the past.

The place was originally named Duiwels Kantoor, for the shape of the weirdly weathered rocks in the middle of "town", but was changed to Kaapsehoop in 1885 when it became a gold-rush community. Quite a few buildings from those times survive, although some have fallen into disuse and ruin, which of course adds to the vaporous atmosphere of the place.

Who knows if the good people of the hamlet gather in one of the buildings to commune with their gods? If they did, you suspect at least some would come with wands and strange hats. It's a place surrounded by mainly trees and some grass and where strange things happen. On full-moon nights you might see hatted figures riding horses through the woods; it's that kind of place.

The hamlet has seen a few VIPs, including a house where President Paul Kruger is said to have sojourned. Wherever gold is found you will also find people of high standing, as well as those of low station. It is often hard to tell them apart.

The area also has the largest herd of feral horses in the country. They are called wild, which sounds better, although stretching the truth is not unknown in these parts. Whatever their provenance, the 200-odd wild horses are afforded the same kind of respect as holy cows in India.

There are also VIBs or, more correctly, there used to be. Being correct is the cornerstone of this tale about stones, some standing, others lying, but we'll get to them in good time. The very important birds are the blue swallows that used to be esteemed summer migrants from up-continent. Today they are among the most endangered birds in South Africa.

The high, moist montane grassland here, along with a narrow strip of the KwaZulu-Natal Midlands, is their natural habitat. However, in both areas most of the grass has given way to timber, and now there is precious little grass and few blue swallows left. The last blue swallow seen to nest in old gold diggings along the escarpment edge near Kaapsehoop was around two decades ago. Down south they are also disappearing like grass seeds in the wind. It is thought there are fewer than 120 breeding pairs left in the whole of southern Africa.

To set the lithographic scene (since VISs, or very interesting stones, are the leading characters of this story), the plateau edge here is composed mostly of hard quartzite with scattered outcrops of even harder dolerite boulders. The dolerite dates from the time when Gondwana split apart and Africa was born in great pyroclastic eruptions that also gave us the Lebombo and Drakensberg mountain ranges. The quartzite, which started life as sandstone, is a whole lot older.

Flying over the area one day back in 2003 looking for a downed aircraft, the pilot of one of the search aircraft, Johan Heine, reckoned he'd seen some very suggestively shaped rocks right on that geological lip. While rescuing the injured pilot, he landed near the sticking-up stones about seven kilometres south of the hamlet. They seemed to align with the cardinal compass points, and some looked as though they might have been placed there with purpose.

Heine returned and took photographs, and bearings, and noticed things, like the second largest upright stone had a curved cut-away top as if it might have been carved. If you stood on either side of it, you could get a rising or setting sun to cradle comfortably in its arc. Or a moon if it was nighttime. It looked suspiciously like some sort of giant sundial, even perhaps a celestial observatory.

Turns out that the rescue sortie in '03 wasn't Johan's first flying rodeo. As an airborne firefighter, for years he'd been flying over and photographing mysterious-looking stone circles that lie scattered across the Mpumalanga highlands.

When investigating the stone "kraals", Heine had not been satisfied with the explanations offered by historians who told him they had been built by Iron Age pastoralists who had once lived there. So how come, thought Johan, were they built with stone and not the thorn bushes we see used today? From the air he thought the many stone-circle kraals, or whatever they were, seemed to lie in predetermined patterns and be joined by a geometric network of lines.

Suggestions that the lines were in fact just cattle trails, and the circular and spiral patterns of the macroscale were, if not exactly a trick of the eye, then patterns and shapes that would occur coincidentally, also did not sit well with him. Heine was not convinced, and neither was the man who was soon to become his collaborator in things archaic and metaphysical.

With the find of his huge stone compass, natural or supernatural, he decided to take a different tack. This led him into the welcoming company of Michael Tellinger, noted in places as being an international authority on the origins of humankind. With heads together they laboured and thought and paced and drew and calculated and surmised, and came up with some astonishing conclusions.

The stones near Kaapsehoop had been placed there, a very long time ago, they reckoned. It was all so amazing that Heine and Tellinger were motivated to publish one, and then another and eventually several books about their enigmatic sundial, the stone circles of the Highveld and other seemingly related topics. Believing them to date back to the origins of our species as sentient beings, they named the cluster of upright stones Adam's Calendar.

The assemblage predated both Stonehenge and the Pyramids at Giza, by tens of thousands of years, asserted the authors. "Various astronomical alignments have been identified at the site and it is possibly the only example of a completely functional, mostly intact megalithic stone calendar in the world."

Page after page in their books, supported by diagrams and measurements and lines and angles and circles, and circles within circles, golden ratios and Fibonacci sequences we are told, all point back to a very precise point in time – 75 000 years ago.

This, we are told, had been calculated by calibrating Biblical, historical and forensic reasoning, referencing the "high awareness of astronomy" of the earliest Indian and Chinese cultures, as well as mysterious people-gods whom the ancient Mesopotamians called the Anunakki.

"Mystic investigators" were called in to age the rocks. They all agreed between 75 000 and 80 000 years. That would have been around the time other humans were just beginning to make works showing abstract thought.

We are told by the author that – "with a certain degree of clarity" – the ancient civilisations which he references have been around much longer than anyone else could ever have imagined. It certainly takes resolve not to be hypnotised by all the graphics and arguments and "proof" of things seemingly otherworldly.

What is a layperson to make of it all? If the stones had been placed by hands, human or otherwise – and it is possible they were – the "how" is very much easier to explain than the "who".

The individual stones at what our two authors like to call their African Stonehenge are nothing as big as those standing on the Wiltshire plains. Most are not much more than knee-height, a few are around waist level, one about shoulder height and one about as high as a tall basketball player. The biggest has been estimated to weigh five tonnes: not quite in the league of the 25-tonne blue-stone sarsens of south England.

Working on the "who" yields some likely pointers. The escarpment edge around Kaapsehoop would be a breathtaking place for anyone to watch the sun, or moon, rise out of miles and miles of hazy Lowveld, be they star-crossed lovers or druids of yore. The name Mpumalanga means place of the rising sun.

If anyone was going to move around some veld furniture to make for a more agreeable planetarium, there's hardly a better place to do it. No doubt there is still a lot of mystery to be found here; it does seem to be what some people would call a "place of power".

There certainly is a satisfying symmetry to the place, how some of the stones form a kind of circle and how the several most prominent ones are clearly aligned west to east, which also happens to be the general plane of the ecliptic along which the heavenly bodies seem to move across our sky.

Tellinger tells us the area around Adam's Calendar is known by African elders as *Inzalo y'Langa*, the "birthplace of the sun". We know the people who lived here before it became corporate. plantations were closely connected with the forces of nature and the power of the ancestors. We know also there is, or was, lots of gold in them thar hills, and that black people mined extensively around southern Africa between about 500 and 1 200 years ago. So they look good for early suspects.

Tellinger says it is important to note that the calendar monoliths (consisting of dolerite) *seem* to have been purposefully put in place, in arable soil. Also that they do not *appear* to conform with the layer beneath (Black Reef Quarztite). Geologists have confirmed the two different rock types. A casual observer might conclude it is a normal configuration of erosion in such an environment, but who knows?

Tellinger claims "his" calendar once resembled Stonehenge, while to other eyes it might resemble more of a Hobbit henge, or a mole henge, since it is not very big at all. The two central stones are "said to have been" carved, but by whom, exactly? The central "nativity" stones (my words) "are said to have been" transported from a distant site – just like at Stonehenge then. But why, since there's dolerite all around the place?

Flipping through the pages of Heine and Tellinger's impressive coffee-table books takes you into a theatre of photographs, sketches, diagrams, geometric patterns of connectivity and page after page of a developing argument. On the surface it is a very complicated and compelling drama. Then you start to notice places where the fabric of this worldview is wearing thin. Like the "are said to have been" parts: again, said by whom, exactly?

The two authors' own observations and deductions are, or seem to be, supported by the opinions of numerous experts, which all seem to buttress their arguments. Like one geologist who, we are informed, says the cliff faces are composed mainly of Transvaal Supergroup sandstones which are overlain by a much harder and more erosion-resistant sill of dolerite. To anyone learned in rocky things, it's a bit like arguing for religion on the grounds that the holy scriptures are printed on paper.

There are numerous other similar "are said to have been"s and "seem to be"s. When the person doing the saying and the seeming is the same as the one doing the writing, you might wonder if what is being murdered here is the truth. Empires have been won and lost on less.

If not already alerted, readers with any technical grounding might begin to arch their eyebrows when Tellinger says the latest and most revealing findings about the Mpumalanga stones, that of sounds emanating from the rock formations below. The author (who refers to himself as in the third person, queerly) says he and scientists have detected, and measured, acoustic patterns and electrical currents directly below the calendar stones. Where they reach the surface they form sacred shapes that are suggestive of flowers.

There are repetitive references in the books to experts and technologies which sound awfully like the lady doth protest too much, but that aside. Anyone with a smidgen of high-school physics knows our entire planet is a cosmic electro-magnetic engine, or geodynamo. That's what forms the magnetic poles, the lines of our planet's magnetic field and the polar lights.

Nevertheless, some aspects of the place still provoke. For example, the rocks that seem to have been shaped, or carved, into male and female forms. The most suggestive human-like shape is the menhir that was moved from the escarpment edge to the track near the entrance to the property, on which is fixed a small brass plaque honouring the now missing swallows.

But, just as one swallow does not a summer make, one rock does not a fanciful theory prove. (Tellinger and Heine imply there are many similarly shaped rocks lying all around the property, whereas in fact there are but a few, and none as suggestive as the blue-swallow monolith.)

It seemed the deeper Michael Tellinger (clearly he is the principal author) delved, the more "out of this world" became his observations: some people, he relays, have seen strange lights hovering over the site. Others even suggested that Adam's Calendar was a portal for "off-world" beings to come and go.

In 2009 Tellinger excited the paranormal community with a whole suite of findings about Adam's Calendar. New calculations had "suggested" the age of his treasured sundial was more like 160 000 years old. What were we to make of this? This would have been around the time our heavy-browed forebears were crushing nuts with hefty stone hammers.

There is a philosophical principle known as Ockham's Razor, conceived around 1300 by a man with a blade-sharp mind named William Ockham. He reckoned that, when faced with many conflicting and confusing theories, the one most likely to be correct is the simplest one.

The escarpment around Adam's Calendar is littered with isolated fragments and small outcrops of dolerite. They are the remnants of a hard rock shelf that caused the eastern escarpment to form in the first place. Anyone who knows anything about geology knows that dolerite is a crystalline mineral, that it forms in polygonal columns and then weathers to rounded boulders. Just like the ones around Kaapsehoop.

The problem with the Heine and Tellinger books is that they throw an obfuscating blanket over something that looks very interesting, and once the deception – and maybe self-deception – starts, there's no knowing how deep it goes. The story of the Kaapsehoop stones resonates with one told by the greatest writer on biological sciences in the 20th century, Stephen Jay Gould (professor at Harvard and NYU).

He unpicks the convoluted story of the Lügensteine (Lying Stones) of Würzburg, which started as a student prank to trip up their arrogant professor in 1726 but caused a blot on their profession's landscape for more than 200 years. In summary, they carved some stones into shapes suggestive of fossils and left them dotted in the hills around town for Herr Doktor Professor Johann Bartholomew Adam Beringer to find.

The shapes included shooting stars, letters in Hebrew and those of various familiar creatures. Remember this was at a time when virtually nothing was known about fossils, and the otherwise brainy professor was duly duped. He wrote a famous (now infamous) monogram about them and staked his career on it.

But, as Gould points out, this little ruse ended up causing untold injury to the professor's reputation, as well as that of the students involved, the university, the town and palaeontology. It was in some ways similar to the hoax of Piltdown Man which, more recently, derailed hominin research for half a century. The story of the lying stones and the fake ape-man skull are about tomfoolery progressing through deceit, pride, conceit, deception and self-deception – the entire suite of human folly.

One of Heine and Tellinger's first and most outspoken critics is American Andrew Collins, a big mover in the megalithomania movement that includes some noted authors of the supernatural, paranormal and pseudoscientific, including Graham Hancock (*Chariots of the Gods*), Robert Bauval (*The Orion Mystery*) and Michael Tellinger.

In 2011, Tellinger hosted Collins on a flying visit (with pilot Johan Heine) to see the stone circles and prehistoric calendar sites for himself. But the Yankee big-stone fest fan was not impressed with what he saw and was not shy to say so publicly. Collins begins his diatribe noting how the theories about the Mpumalanga calendar are based on ideas of an alien Sumerian god Anunakki.

But, says Collins: "I can say categorically that in my opinion his translations of the texts are pure fantasy ... I think the problem here is that there is no hard evidence." And of Heine and Tellinger's circles and alignments and golden means relating to Orion and other heavenly bodies: "Such an alignment doesn't work."

"There is no question that Adam's Calendar is a fabulous site that deserves full investigation," Collins notes. To assume the stones have been set upright by ancient hands which go back beyond our present evolutionary cycle is nonsensical, he concludes. He is not the only person to have come to a similar conclusion.

Perhaps the harshest critic is someone who identifies him, or her, self only as Bad Archaeology. He or she begins by informing us that the scientific field in which Tellinger is schooled is pharmacy (lots of drugs there, you are tempted to suggest). We also learn (with a tone of malevolent glee, admittedly) it is only Tellinger himself who claims he is "an international authority on the origins of humankind".

With regard to the Orion alignment theory, Bad Archaeologist (apparently an actual archaeologist) has this to say: "There's [sic] thousands of (visible) stars, of course something lines up. We also cannot treat it as some enormously advanced science to line up stones with stars."

As for the stone circles between Waterval Boven (where Tellinger is based) and Machadadorp, it turns out some smart scientists at Wits University already know about them. They were occupied as recently as 300 years ago, their construction probably began around 200 or 300 years before that we are told by them, and the people who made them and lived there were called the Bakoni.

On first seeing the stones around Adam's Calendar it definitely feels like some supernatural power has been afoot. Then again, we get similar feelings whenever we confront the immense scale and force of nature in spectacular places like this. Which is precisely why we humans developed something called the scientific method, an empirical way to cut the fanciful chaff from the intellectual wheat. It's possibly also intertwined with the origins of religion.

Sitting with your legs dangling over the precipice at Adam's Calendar will get you thinking about the universe, its inner workings and our place within it. We may never find the answers, but it is also our intellectual duty to call out bad science wherever we find it.

Perhaps the one aspect of the Heine-Tellinger theory that balances most uncomfortably is its unapologetic alien-centricity. It goes that, if the stones near Kaapsehoop were indeed placed there for purposes mystical, it had to have been done by anyone other than people who we know lived there in times past, who mined gold and who communed with their ancestors there. This is the same kind of Eurocentric bias that assigned Bushman art to Phoenicians, or Egyptians, or Arabs, or aliens – anyone but indigenous Africans.

The truth is always more interesting than the fable: Adam's Calendar certainly makes you think about things like how the rocks were formed, what the Earth looked like back then and what caused those evocative-looking rocks to look the way they do now. Also, where did all the gold come from, and where did all the blue swallows go?

Kosi Bay

Fish Traps, Turtle Eggs and Skokiaan: Searching for Amphibious Invaders Between the Tides

The spiral fish traps that seem to be stitched into the estuary of the Kosi lake system of far-northern Zululand are the focal point of an iconic South African landscape. But those placid-looking waters obscure a stormy past and possibly a tempestuous future.

WHO DOESN'T LOVE A MAP? Maps talk to you about all manner of things, such as open roads and far-off places. I fell in love with maps in primary school when the wonders of the Mercator projection were unfurled in geography class.

It seemed like a mystery solved to be able to stretch a sphere out across a flat plane. But it did make Greenland and Canada look much bigger than they really are, and the Antarctic a long flat strip. You gain some, you lose some; it's part of growing up. For map fundis, the size distortions of the cylindrical Mercator scale can be largely corrected using an interrupted sinusoidal projection, but it uses more paper and splits some of the continents.

In my travels, few places in this corner of the veld we call South Africa have gone unchecked – except one, Kosi Bay. For years and decades it beckoned. Sometimes the best is indeed left for last. For many years I had flirted around that far-flung spot on the map. On many diving and camping trips I'd visited Sodwana Bay, Cape Vidal, Mapelane, Mabibi and Rocktail Bay.

Kosi is a long way from anywhere. It's like what diarist Samuel Johnson said of the Giant's Causeway in Ireland, when asked by a London acquaintance if he'd enjoyed his visit. "It's a fine thing to see," replied the very urbane man of letters, "but it is not such a fine thing to have to go to see."

Before the twisting, sandy, bumpy, rutted, sometimes flooded access roads were upgraded, one conservationist working in the Kosi area believed the only way to negotiate them was drunk: the local palm wine and mangosteen beer, otherwise known as skokiaan, are legendary. "Only for big men," one informant warned.

There's even an old sea shanty about it:

Oh – take a trip to Africa,
Any ship to Africa,
Come on along and learn the lingo,
Beside a jungle bungalow –
Skokiaan, Skokiaan

Kosi Bay is not only a fine thing to see, but it is a very fine thing to go to see. It is at the very end of the road in South Africa and that alone warrants a close look. Excepting that over the past few years much of the R22 trunk road through Maputaland, as that area is known, has been upgraded to the finest black top complete with more speed bumps than the Eastern Cape has potholes.

That's not all that has changed in the area over the past few decades. Where there used to be sandy roads, beehive huts, cattle and chickens and rickety spaza shops, now there's hardly a hut or cow to be seen. They seem to all have been replaced by a kind of Thongan Tuscan, resplendent with entrance porticos and enough columns to impress a Roman emperor.

You could drive your town cruiser right up to the entrance of Kosi Bay Reserve, but from that point onwards it's low-range 4x4 all the way. The road to Bhanga Nek is something completely different, and an amphibious armoured tank would be your best option there. Apparently, a new road was commissioned and paid for, but the money disappeared; maybe into some local concrete-column-making business or other economic redistribution project.

At the entrance to the Kosi Bay Reserve, part of the larger Kosi Bay lake system, itself part of the even larger Greater St Lucia Wetland Park, which in turn nestles inside the outermost of this conservation Russian doll, the iSimangaliso Wetland Park, sits the comfortable Utshwayelo camp. This is where the rubber meets deep sand.

There is a story that the young Shaka came this way looking for new grazing lands for his cattle. On the trip his mother became seriously ill but was successfully treated by a local sangoma. This greatly endeared the Thonga people to the future warrior-king. Another factor might have been that they were, and largely still are, the only Nguni people who eat mostly fish and vegetables, thereby posing little threat to the otherwise cattle-loving culture.

Entering the park, you crest the highest dune ridge and ahead stretches glittering Lake Kahlu, the lagoon-like mouth of the Kosi estuarine lake system. The metallic sheet of its surface is etched with recurring spiral patterns, each with a ragged edge, as though gouged by an inscriber with a shaky hand.

These are the famous Kosi Bay fish traps, which make this wetland system different from all the others of Maputaland. The region used to be known as Thongaland, where Thonga people have lived for maybe 1 000 years. In 1895 the area was annexed as part of the Colony of Natal, the part between Lake St Lucia and the Kosi lakes declared a nature reserve, and the Thonga people forced into just the Kosi Bay area at its extreme northern end.

Over the generations they perfected the use of fish traps, built in a spiral shape with the entrance facing downstream. This design allowed fish to enter the estuary and swim through the linked waterways without interference. On maturing and heading back out to sea, some fish would be corralled by the curved brushwood palisades bound with palm-leaf ties, and funnelled through a gate of inward-pointing stakes into a central "kraal".

This system ensured that only mature fish were caught. The fish traps were passed down from father to son through the generations. In fact, since colonial times it was more grandfather to father, since recruitment agents typically rounded up the sons and shipped them off to labour in the mines of *eGoli*. While things were not going very well for the Thonga people, the estuarine ecosystem did just fine.

And so things were maintained more or less as they had been for centuries. With the scrapping of the migrant labour system in the 1990s, young men came flooding back to a region with precious little land available and even fewer work prospects. The local chiefs and sub-chiefs suggested the young men go catch fish in the lakes. They did, but they changed things, as young people will.

The new generation of fishers made their fish traps with gum stakes and nylon rope, with few gaps for fingerlings to escape. They also started making them bigger than before and pointing the entrances upstream to catch anything entering the lake system. These were not pensioners adding just a few fish a day to the dinner table, but young entrepreneurs with access to 4x4 bakkies who were shipping out fish on a commercial scale.

This was good for the people inland, but not so good for the estuary. In the past you would see groups of people with long fish spears marching in formation through the shallow lake waters each morning. Now you see only the occasional fisher wading in to check what has been caught, or more likely not, in his or her kraal.

Catches are getting smaller and smaller, they all complain. The fish – mainly grunter and rock cod – are getting smaller and smaller, they agree. Local fish scientists concur: the average size of fish now being caught is around half what it was 20 years ago.

The narrow channel at the mouth is a bottleneck of tide and

current, sweeping swiftly in and out four times a day. To snorkellers it is known as "the aquarium", both for the water clarity and number of tropical fish species that find refuge among the rubble of a collapsed fossil-dune shelf that lies strewn along the channel's outer edge.

You need to keep fingers and toes tucked in here because the large variety of moray eels and stonefishes exceeds that of just about any reef system in the coastal waters offshore. Stonefishes are the ones to be most wary of because they are extremely hard to see (looking just like chunks of rubble) and pack a potent punch of protein toxin from their dorsal spines.

If you want to keep all the bits of your anatomy intact you can opt for a guided turtle walk from Bhanga Nek, about six kilometres south of Kosi Mouth – the challenging hour's drive there and hour back notwithstanding. Tours are dependent on the tides, so could take place at any hour (full moons are best for turtles, particularly lumbering leatherbacks, looking to come ashore to lay).

Although several species of sea turtle (as opposed to the land turtles we call tortoises) occur in the sea here, only two come ashore to drop their clutches: loggerheads and leatherbacks. The loggerhead is a medium-sized marine turtle, attaining a maximum shell (carapace) length of one metre. Their carapace is formed by modified and fused rib bones.

The leatherback is different in a number of respects, the first being that it can achieve a shell length of up to three metres, making it the second largest reptile alive. Also its shell, as the name suggests, is not bone-hard but is composed of many small skin cuticles sutured together. Today these marine visitors are the VIPs of the Maputaland coast and are strictly protected.

However, just one turtle generation ago they were unknown in these parts. A survey conducted along this coastal zone by the Wildlife Society back in 1947 yielded no evidence of sea turtles. In 1963 a report sent from the Department of Bantu Administration to the Natal Parks Board stated that the bleached, bony remains of turtles had been found near Kosi Bay.

One of the big shots on the board at the time happened to be a keen fisher who regularly visited the area. He had never heard of turtles in the area so this sparked his interest. He sent a ranger to Bhanga Nek, on the beach over the dune corridor from Lake Kosi, or Third Lake, to look for any signs of living animals. It is, and remains, about as lonely a spot as you'll find on any map of South Africa.

Thus began the longest-running and one of the most effective turtle monitoring and conservation programmes in the world, and Bhanga Nek, a famous conservation beach bungalow at the end of the road. During the first season 142 loggerhead and 16 leatherback females were recorded visiting the area: numbers so low it was feared both species were headed for local extinction.

It was the age of sailing ships that had the greatest impact on turtle populations around the world. People had been raiding nests since time began, but they were few and they always left enough eggs for turtle numbers to remain stable.

Sailing ships found free, fresh food available mainly on islands but also at turtle rookeries, which were duly logged and visited regularly. But what brought about the near extinction of sea turtles worldwide was the slave trade. You were not going to pay good ducats for food to feed the multitudes chained in misery below decks, so turtles and turtle eggs became their staple diet.

There were even fleets of turtle schooners built to exploit the resource once the upper crusts in Europe and America caught on that the flesh made for a most tasty broth. For centuries Lusty's of London supplied green turtle soup to Fortnum & Mason, grocery purveyors to royalty and aristocracy.

In 1970 Natal Parks Board turtle scientist George Hughes attended a conference in London, where he and some other delegates were invited to the Lord Mayor's annual banquet. On learning that green turtle soup was on the menu, the conservationists informed the mayor's office of the serious survival issues facing the animals. Creamed turtle soup was not served that year, but it was back on the menu the next.

In the 1980s an army colonel holidaying at Sodwana Bay burst into the office of the conservation officer-in-charge, demanding to use his phone. He was in a *toestand* about an amphibian invasion force that had landed during the night, driven up the beach and over the dunes. Pretoria had to be informed immediately! It took the Parks man only a few seconds to realise a nesting leatherback had been the invader responsible.

The process of heaving itself ashore, flippering its way above the high-water mark, digging a nest hole, laying, covering it up and then returning to the ocean can take a mother turtle an hour or more. On land they are extremely vulnerable and even at sea make easy prey (crunchy meal for a hungry tiger shark). Their survival strategy is for females to produce as many eggs as they can, throughout the three-month laying season, for as many years as is biologically possible.

Each season each female can lay as many as 1 000 eggs, losing up to a quarter of her body weight in the process. George Hughes spent a total of 48 years as a "turtle trotter" – the name given to conservationists, researchers and monitors who trudge the deep sands of Maputaland's beaches to track their subjects.

He recalls one night seeing a particularly wrinkled, gaunt female come ashore. It turned out to be a much longer and more emotional episode than he and his colleague could have imagined. On close approach they turned on their torches (turtles almost always come ashore at night) and realised she was a very, very old lady. "Her skin hung in wrinkles of a size and depth that I had never seen before and at every exposed part of the body the skin drooped in long loose folds."

Hughes and his Thonga ranger uMsombululuko sat in awe as they watched the old girl go about her nesting business. After a long wait and watch, they witnessed her drop about 100 eggs into the hole she'd dug. At the very end of the process she did something the rangers had never seen before, or since: she ejected her entire oviduct into the nest. She then covered the hole and, very slowly, made her exhausted way down to the wash zone. She had laid her last egg.

In his autobiography the acclaimed turtle trotter exults in the wonder of being able to walk along lonely beaches on both dark and moonlit nights, a privilege known by few people. "The excitement and wonder of finding, between the tides, sea turtles intent on nesting, is given to even fewer."

Visit Kosi Bay and you could share that privilege.

Isandlwana and Rorke's Drift

Imperial Arrogance, Victorian Pride and African Spartans: Searching for Honour on a Field of Blood

The names Isandlwana and Rorke's Drift, writ to large in the psyches of South Africans and British alike, would not feature on any map of Zululand were it not for the bloody events that occurred there on a hot summer's day 140 years ago.

WHEN ZULU KING CETSHWAYO got wind of a British force heading towards his lands in late 1878, he sent a message to the British High Commissioner Sir Bartle Frere of the Colony of Natal, asking why he was plotting for war. Especially since the Zulus had been British allies after a treaty signed with them in the 1840s.

The Zulu leader famously said that he was nothing but a flea on the blanket of the great white queen (Victoria). He had no argument with the British; however, if it was a fight that Bartle was looking for, then it was a fight he would get. These were Zulus, the Spartans of Africa, for heaven's sake.

The history of South Africa is awash with misunderstandings and misadventures, and the old British Empire can be held accountable for much of the mischief. As it is so often in these cases, Cetshwayo's troubles had started far away, in Canada, some 20 years earlier. Secretary of State for the Colonies Lord Carnarvon had managed to orchestrate a confederation of Canadian territories and was deeply impressed with himself.

He thought a similar arrangement could be made in South Africa and informed the high commissioner there to "look into it". Neither had factored in quite how strongly opposed to such a scheme would be some of the key players, including two Boer republics and the Zulu kingdom.

What so often puts spokes in the wheels of this kind of grand strategising is the implementation of the fine details; there are just so many wheels and so many spokes. Britain certainly never wanted trouble on a grand scale in South Africa. In fact, many of the white-whiskered men in Whitehall didn't even want the colonies there, much less war with any of the local people (although they had by this time reduced the once proud and powerful Xhosa nation to a vassal state).

It was the people they put on the ground who caused most of the mischief. Mostly they were inexperienced in big-picture management and lacked deep knowledge of the place. Largely though, they were bigots and deeply chauvinistic. Britain was in the business of expanding its empire and was at that time getting some serious pushback from its biggest colony across the Atlantic in America.

To South Africa they sent Frere and Frederic Augustus Thesiger, Second Baron and later Lord Chelmsford. Carnarvon did not envisage war; then again, send in a bunch of hammers to sort out an issue and nails are sure to be hit.

Without orders from Whitehall, Frere took it upon himself to turn the great cogs of statesmanship and ordered his all-too-willing commander-in-chief to organise an invasion of Zululand. When Frere asked Chelmsford if he thought he could pull it off, the aristocratic Harry Flashman replied yes, but only if he could get the Zulus to come out and fight.

Frere issued an ultimatum to Cetshwayo with terms he knew could not be met. When the ultimatum expired on 11 January 1879, Chelmsford ordered three armed columns to enter Zululand: one along the coast under Major Pearson, a central one commanded by Colonel Glyn and a third "flying column" under Colonel Wood. Two more units were to be held in reserve under colonels Durnford and Rowlands. Chelmsford decided to accompany Glyn's column and so set in motion a chain of command confusion, the first spoke to break on his war wagon.

The central column entered Zululand by crossing the Mzinyathi (Buffalo) River at the drift just below the trading station operated by the reputedly "crazy" Irish merchant James Rorke. When Rorke saw the trouble coming, he loaded his wife and a few possessions into a Scotch cart and ran for the hills of Natal. His homestead and store were duly commandeered as a field hospital and supply depot.

An army marches on its stomach and Chelmsford's had a large one. It took the train of men, animals and wagons 10 days to get from Rorke's Drift, or *kwaJimu* (the place of Jim) as it was known locally, to its first advance base on the slopes of a prominent rock-crowned hill that resembled a Sphinx just 12 kilometres into Zulu territory. The general decided to ignore his own standing orders and not entrench or otherwise protect the camp: he did not intend to stay there long. That was the second spoke.

The backbone of the central column was around 3 000 infantrymen, accompanied by various mounted units, both British regulars and colonial regiments, as well as a large number of the Natal Native Contingent (NNC). Together with auxiliaries to drive about 300 wagons and the animals that drew them, the camp numbered roughly 5 000 men.

On 21 January a mounted reconnaissance force of about 150 men headed by Major Dartnell rode out in a southeasterly direction. They spent the day chasing various groups of Zulu soldiers, who kept on moving further in that direction. The colonials bivouacked on Hlazakazi Hill, from where they could see the fires of Zulu camps stretching into the distance.

22 January dawned much like it had always done on the gentle folds of hills and dales that lie cradled in the crook of land where the Ngxobongo River meets the Mzinyathi. The British camp on the slope of Isandlwana Hill would have been abuzz with the sounds an army makes on waking up.

As always, Natal spurfowl stridently ushered in their predawn *kak-keek, kak-keek*, followed by the softer but persistent call of red-chested cuckoos, *Piet-my-vrou, Piet-my vrou*, then more compelling calls of Cape turtle doves to *work harder, work harder*. Nguni cows would have been grazing on the lush grasses between clumps of aloes and flowering sweet thorn trees.

Early that morning Dartnell sent two riders back to the main camp to inform Chelmsford that he thought the Zulu army was retreating through a series of valleys to the southeast. It was just what the commander wanted to hear. He quickly rounded up a force of around 2 500 foot and mounted soldiers, regulars, colonials as well as half the NCC and gave chase. That was the third and most vital spoke broken: never split your force when facing an uncertain enemy in unknown territory.

The chase was a decoy planned by the Zulu high command and the British general had taken it far easier and more enthusiastically than they could have hoped. As the famous song says: A vainglorious general with Victorian pride would cost 800 men their lives. Only, Johnny Clegg under-counted the final tally by a factor of about four.

This left just about 1 300 foot soldiers back at main camp, most of them men of the 24th Regiment of Foot (2nd Warwickshire Regiment) who had been conscripted from the Brecon region of Wales. They were supported by six field guns and several Congreve rocket batteries. At around 10:30 Colonel Durnford arrived heading a unit of the Natal Native Horse corps.

The British soldiers were equipped with the latest Martini-Henry breech-loading rifles. The foe they were to face had mainly throwing spears, assegais and cowhide shields, although they also had antiquated muskets and rifles among them. It did prove in the end, though, that you *could* take a spear to a gunfight and win.

Lieutenant Raw was sent out with a small mounted troop to patrol the land to the northeast of Isandlwana, around the Nyoni Heights. They saw a group of armed Zulus disappear over a rise and gave chase. On cresting the ridge they pulled up hard: in the Gwebeni valley below them crouched a virtual sea of black men, sitting in absolute silence. It was said the grass around took an entire season to recover.

This was the main body of the Zulu army, commanded by princes Ntshingwayo kaMahole Khoza and Mavumengwana kaNdlela (a detachment of around 4 000 men commanded by Godide kaNdlela had been sent to cut off Colonel Pearson's column near Eshowe).

They had been gathering there in groups for days, as yet unseen. Their plan had been to fall upon the British Central Column the following day, 23 January. Orders from their king were simple: "March slowly, attack at dawn and eat up the red soldiers."

However, once their cover was broken they rose as one and charged towards the British camp three kilometres away, stamping their feet in unison, hitting their shields and issuing the famous war cry, "*Usuthu!*"

Lieutenant Raw's men wheeled hard around and raced back to camp. They reached it around 12:30 and warned the senior officer Brevet Lt-Colonel Pulleine of the impending attack. And here we stumble over Chelmsford's fourth and final broken spoke: the general did not think to appoint an acting commander for the camp.

When Durnford arrived there, he was the senior officer, but he deferred to the incumbent man. The weakness exposed here was that Pulleine was an army administrator with no previous battlefield experience. Durnford, who did, rushed into the heat of battle as soon as the Zulu army made its first stab and was out of communications to the end.

Pulleine quickly deployed the famous "thin red line" of British riflemen on the higher slope, closest to the expected point of the Zulu approach, but that is not where they struck first. What with their new rifles, backed up by field guns and rockets, no one in the entire empire would have believed that a foe armed with spears could break the famous British line. Even if they numbered a terrifying 24 000.

It took less than half an hour from the time Raw delivered his message to when the first wave of Zulu attackers engaged the British. The Zulu *izinduna* (regimental commanders) had manoeuvred their forces into the equally famous and formidable "head and chest of the bull" formation. And they carried not only spears but, it has been estimated, about one in three also carried a firearm.

The iNgobamakhosi regiment, which formed the tip of the bull's left horn, swung hard around the base of the hill – a completely unexpected manoeuvre. They quickly overran the rocket battery that had been deployed lower down the slope at the Nyokane donga. The British commander had believed it would be the safest place for them.

Colonel Durnford immediately rushed his combined Native Contingent and Carbineer group into the donga to stem the tide of that attack. The Zulu left horn would spend much of the rest of the battle concentrated at this spot. While that was going on, the chest of the bull made for the thin red line and began slogging it out across the intervening grass incline.

After an hour or so of furious fighting, Durnford's men were still holding the British right flank, but their ammunition was running dangerously low. Higher up the superior British firepower was taking a terrible toll on the bull's chest (at this stage the right horn had not entered the fray). Just then – and we now know it was precisely 14:29 – a partial solar eclipse plunged the battlefield into eerie semi darkness, compounded by a pall of grey gunsmoke that sat heavily on the hill.

Many renowned battles in history have teetered on a seesaw, only to see one side gain the upper hand through a single, often seemingly minor event. Like when the British at Waterloo were withering under the barrage of French fire, only for their ally Marshal Blücher to arrive with his Prussian cavalry just as the sun was going down. So it was at Isandlwana on 22 January 1879 when two other events coincided with the eclipse.

The two battalions of black troops under Durnford's command leaped the donga and made a run for their lives. On the face of it that does sound mutinous and cowardly, until you learn that only one in 10 of them had a gun, the rest just spears. Also, if captured, they knew they would be brutally tortured to death as traitors.

Although the white colonial troops could also have run for their horses, they stayed put, but they were each down to their last few rounds. The sight of men fleeing spurred on the bull's left horn and the British right flank quickly buckled and was overwhelmed, every man dead.

In the middle of all this action, however, the Zulu bull's chest was beginning to wither. Seeing their most experienced regiments taking a pounding, the Zulu commanders ordered the *induna* of the senior uMcijo Regiment to fortify them. He was shot dead as he rose to lead the charge, but the momentum was taken up by *induna* Mkhosana Ntshangase of the uKhandampemvu Regiment. He stood up and shouted "*uHlamvana bul' umlilo kahsongo njalo!*" (the little branch that extinguished the fire never gave such an order).

It was a reference to the Battle of Princes at Ndondakusuka in 1856, when Cetshwayo had defeated five of his brothers in a battle for the royal ascendency. The main British line was now also running low on ammunition and was just starting to fall back into tighter groups.

That was enough to invigorate the main body of Zulu impis to rush forward. The left horn closed in and Zulus fell on their foe in vicious hand-to-hand combat. In and out went the Zulu *iklwa* stabbing spears, *ik-lwa, ik-lw*a; their knobkerries came down cracking pale skulls. The British soldiers replied with fixed bayonets and rifle butts.

Things suddenly started looking awfully bad for Colonel Pulleine's men. They started forming tight squares but, with little to fire anymore, they became extremely vulnerable to the Zulus surging around them. After the battle one very impressed Zulu recounted how a man of the 24th Regiment fought to protect the general's flag outside his tent. Using his rifle butt as a club he kept the Zulu spearmen at bay until he resembled a porcupine and sank.

And that was about the time the right horn of the bull swung into action, smashing into the exposed rear left flank of the British encampment. It was all over by 15:00. To this day the old greybeards of Zululand regard that brave band of redcoats as the only worthy opponents the Zulus ever faced.

Around that time Chelmsford was planning the set-up of his next fly camp. When a dispatch rider arrived with the news of the defeat, out of breath and panting, the vainglorious general is recorded as saying: "What! I left more than a thousand men there to defend the place!" (He also got the number wrong, and he of all people should have known better.)

He marched the dejected remaining half of the Central Column back to Isandlwana where they gazed upon the massacre. Of the 1 700-plus force of British troops, the Natal Native Contingent and various auxiliaries, at least 1 300 lay dead, including both field commanders Pulleine and Durnford.

The Zulus had been told not to waste energy killing auxiliaries so many of the mainly African support crew were able to escape back to the army's rear base at Helpmekaar. It is estimated that somewhere between 3 000 and 5 000 Zulus also lay dead on the slopes of Isandlwana.

Historians tell us the last person to die that day was Gabangaye, the portly chief of the amaChunu and an NCO in the NNC. He had been captured and was handed over to the *udibi* or porter boys for the Zulu army, who were told to enjoy their first battlefield kill.

But the day was not over yet. While Chelmsford was licking his wounds and planning his excuses by lamp light at Isandlwana, he and his downhearted men would have heard the gunfire coming from Rorke's Drift. They would have believed the small detachment defending there had no chance of holding out.

When they saw fire lighting up the sky over the depot and smoke filling the air, they must have thought it was indeed over. That was his fifth – and arguably the most heinous – miscalculation of the campaign: while Chelmsford and his men slept, those he abandoned at Rorke's Drift were fighting for their lives.

As soon as they had got the chance, the Undi or reserve corps of 4 000 Zulu impis under the command of Prince Dabulamanzi kaMpande had rushed on to Rorke's Drift, eager to blood their spears on the soft targets there. Dabulamanzi, one of the king's remaining brothers, had been instructed to not engage the enemy unless urgently called to do so, but he was a rash and aggressive man.

Back at the trading store Lieutenant Bromhead had been left

holding the fort with about 150 men, most from B Company, 2nd Battalion, 24th Regiment of Foot, as well as some Royal Engineers under the command of Lieutenant Chard, a bunch of storemen and kitchen staff, some medics and their patients. The medics and patients were placed in the Rorkes' home, a narrow building with small adjoining but not interleading rooms.

They would have heard the frenzy of battle across the river and over the hill, and probably imagined the best of their highly ordered comrades, pride of the British Empire. Around mid-afternoon two survivors from Isandlwana came rushing up with news of the rout. They warned that a large force of Zulus was headed their way. At this juncture Captain Stevenson's colonial company, which had been left to guard the place, jumped on their horses and bolted for Helpmekaar (no irony intended).

So infuriated were some of the remaining Welshmen, frantically preparing defences, that they fired into the fleeing mass and shot dead one of them. Left behind were about 155 men, 39 of whom were sick (mostly with dysentery, the biggest killer of British soldiers in South Africa). The buildings at Rorke's Drift trading station faced a natural terrace with a rock surround, between one and two metres high. Behind it rose up the Oskerberg hill.

The house and store at the trading station stood on a terrace about 30 metres apart, with a stone cattle kraal attached to the far corner of the store. Chard and Bromhead directed the walking to use anything they could to build a defendable yard between the two buildings. Luckily they had mealie bags weighing around 150 kilogrammes each, and large wooden boxes of the army's notoriously resistant biscuits. Walls were hastily thrown up, above head height, with holes for firing.

The medics and a few patients who could stand or sit were given arms and posted to defend various rooms inside the house while the rest took up positions against the walls. The Zulu Undi Corps, comprising the youthful uThulwana and uDloko regiments, reached Rorke's Drift around 16:30. They would spend the next 11-and-a-half hours continuously storming the British defences there.

The combined height of the rock step and bag-and-box wall was too high to scale so the Zulus crouched beneath it, attempting to slash and spear the defending British soldiers through their firing gaps, or grab their rifles. On occasion they clambered over each other's bodies to drive the British off the walls, but each time they were driven back. The Undi impis with firearms had been posted on the Oskerberg and about a quarter of the British dead and wounded were from their fire.

While the red-coated defenders were holding things together behind their walls, inside the hospital it was becoming untenable. After about two hours of pounding and digging at the clay-brick walls, impis managed to gain access to the far northwestern end of the building. By 18:00 Chard ordered the men holding the front rooms of the hospital building to withdraw into the main yard, leaving behind a few infantrymen and medics, a cook and the sick.

When it became clear to those still alive inside that the front rooms had been overrun, they began a slow and desperate retreat. Using bayonets, axes and fingernails they began digging their way out towards the courtyard side, one room at a time. (The smaller back rooms each had a door into one of the larger front rooms, which by then were crowded with Zulus attempting to break into the remaining defended ones.)

The British crawling wounded held off the attackers with fixed bayonets while others dug and clawed through the dividing clay-brick walls. Each time a hole was made the patients had to be dragged through. Some were too weak and refused help so were left to their fates. There was no time for arguing.

Dead Zulus were also piling up, room by room. Privates Hook and two Williams, John and Joseph, were extremely busy inside as they furiously dug, defended and dragged the sick out, one room at a time, stabbing and firing as they hacked and wriggled backwards. In the second-to-last room they met up with patient Private Walters who held off the Zulu storm until they could break through to the final room where they found Privates Robert and William Jones fighting for their lives.

The Zulu force was baying to get at them from all sides. The roof of the hospital had been set ablaze and was starting to collapse. One by one the men crammed into the last safe room of the house. But it had no door to the outside so they had to be fed through a high clerestory window and dropped into the courtyard. Nine patients were shepherded to the safety of the yard. Several of the sick as well as able-bodied defenders died inside.

One Private Waters was not one of them. When he and Private Beckett became isolated inside, they hid in a clothes cupboard. With mayhem all around they made a break for the outside. Beckett was cut down by assegais but Waters, wearing Mrs Rorke's long black cloak, made it out and across the terrace, alive but severely wounded.

As night fell the Zulu attacks became even more urgent. The cattle kraal defence was most vulnerable and so it was evacuated around 22:00. Two more hours of furious fighting ensued, dramatically illuminated by the hospital roof's blaze. Around midnight the Zulu attack began to wane and finally subsided around 02:00 in the morning. However, gunfire from Zulu marksmen on the Oskerberg behind the station kept up for two more hours.

The British defenders had shot off more than 19 000 rounds and had fewer than 900 left. Fourteen British were dead and almost every man left alive inside the barricades was wounded. They were exhausted and did not think they could survive another wave of attack. It never came; the Zulus had also had enough and moved off, leaving between 500 and 800 of their dead behind. They had been on the march for six days prior to this battle and had not eaten anything substantial for two or three days.

Then the sun rose, just like it had the day before, and the day before that. But birds did not sing that morning, so stunned were they, as was everything and everyone else around Rorke's Drift.

Famously, 11 Victoria Crosses were awarded to the defenders of Rorke's Drift, including the two lieutenants and Privates Hook, Jones and John Williams. Private Joseph Williams died inside defending the sick in the hospital. It was stated in dispatches after the event that "had he lived he would have been recommended for the Victoria Cross," since posthumous VCs were not awarded until 1907.

Not bad for two junior officers and a small detachment of foot soldiers, assorted support personnel and the sick who showed up better on the day than the entire senior leadership of Chelmsford's great army.

Many people since have denigrated that handing out of more

Victoria Crosses for just a single, small, one-day engagement than for some entire wars. Even more controversial were the two VCs later awarded posthumously to lieutenants Melvill and Coghill who, when defeat and annihilation were imminent, rode off with Queen's Colour flag towards the Mzinyathi River; protecting the Queen's Colours was considered a matter of life-and-death valour. They were both killed trying to exit the river.

Lord Wolseley who, as we shall see, assumed command in Natal, was not impressed. He believed there should be no honours given to men who had fled the field of battle while their comrades were being slaughtered behind them.

The last word on this is given to the military historian Victor Hanson. He contends that in all the annals of (at least British) military history, you will search hard to find an engagement to match that at Rorke's Drift. Outnumbered something like 40 to one, the defenders killed 20 of the enemy for every one of theirs lost.

But that still was not the end of it. In the aftermath that tumultuous day for the soldiers involved and the reputation of the Empire, conservative Prime Minister Benjamin Disraeli lost the 1880 election to liberal William Gladstone. The new government ordered Sir (later Lord) Garnet Wolseley to Natal in order to relieve the disgraced Frere and Chelmsford of their posts.

Chelmsford, fearing the repercussions of his poor leadership, quickly swung into action. He combined his three columns and marched on the Zulu capital at Ulundi (that took another six months and numerous more furious battles) and razed it. Then he boarded the first ship back to England before Wolseley arrived in South Africa and thereby very likely avoided a court martial.

Back in England he was very quick to put all the blame on Durnford, claiming the colonel had disobeyed orders to fix a proper defensive camp (the colonel arrived only midway through the morning of the battle). Chelmsford then sought an audience with Gladstone to plead his case, but the British prime minister refused to see him: a very public declaration of official disapproval delivered in a typically understated English way.

The reverberations for the local people were far more devastating, though, since virtually every *umuzi* (homestead) between the Mzinyathi and uThukela rivers had at least one person die in the conflict. It was said you could hear wailing carried on the winds, over the green hills, from kraal to kraal, all across Zululand. No one had seen such bloodshed or heard so much wailing since Nandi, King Shaka's mother, had died and her death been requited, in 1827.

With the king dead and the army decimated, Zululand ceased to exist as a political entity. It was reinstated in the 1950s by the white National Party Government in their grand strategy of creating "separate but equal" homeland reservations for the entire black population of South Africa.

Standing on the slopes of Isandlwana, it is hard to stop overwhelmingly deep emotions rising inside you. The main thing that has changed there between that day and this is that where row upon row of white bell tents stood, today rows of white-painted cairns stand to show where the soldiers fell and died on that day in 1879 and were buried in mass graves.

If you have a good guide, one who speaks both isiZulu and English so they can recreate the feeling of the battle, you can hear the vast swarm of impis banging their shields and crying in unison, 20 000 strong, "*Usuthu!*" and "*Bayete!*". You can hear the artillery battery blasting away, the Martini-Henrys popping like pork crackling in a huge red-hot skillet. The sun dims, there is shouting and banging and barging and chaos all round, and smoke fills the atmosphere.

There is also screaming, and blood, and crying. That's when all the smoke causes tears to form in the corners of your eyes. Strong people have stood here, the smoke in their eyes also causing tears to form. Many of them Welsh men and women from the Brecon Beacons.

Mont-aux-Sources and the Amphitheatre

A Vulture-Eagle, a Tsunami in Stone and a Ladder to Heaven: Searching for the Country's Most Amazing Landscape

© Don Hunter

The Amphitheatre is indisputably the most dramatic landscape in South Africa. It stands like a gigantic bookend at the northern end of the Drakensberg mountain range, embraced within the uKhahlamba-Drakensberg World Heritage Site.

WHEN TWO ADVENTUROUS FRENCH missionaries, Thomas Arbousset and Francois Daumas, found themselves at the edge of the Drakensberg Amphitheatre in the autumn of 1836, they were clearly moved. Evidently they dropped to their knees and prayed: one about the destruction of Sodom and Gomorrah, the other about the love of God. It might equally have been the terrifying abyss that floored them.

In 1928, JJ Ross, who was Superintendent of the Witsieshoek Mission Station, said of the place: "With its proud and lofty mountains, clear water and lofty surroundings, is surely one of the most beautiful places in our land." Surely.

It certainly is a place that moves you. Arbousset and Daumas were the first two people whose names we know who stood, or knelt, at the edge of this stunning three-kilometre wide and one-and-a-half-kilometre high curtain of grey basalt that hangs in deep, folded pleats, its hem colour-washed by the greenery of grasses, mosses and ferns. But they could not have been the first.

Before them Bushmen, as well as people of the Amazizi and Amahlube and Amangwane clans, and many others, would have done so for years and decades and centuries; they traversed the area, they just did not write about it. The two missionaries had set off from the Moria Mission Station in the lower lands of Lesotho in early March that year, headed for the Blue Mountains: "Mountains which, so far as we know, no European foot had yet trod."

With their Basuto ponies, or possibly donkeys, they would have followed the valley of the Senqu River almost all the way to reach the "blue mountain" escarpment somewhere between the Rockeries and Mnweni passes, about 15 kilometres south of the Amphitheatre. That is where the Senqu, or Orange, or Gariep River rises in a boggy sump. At that time of the year the area all around it would have been carpeted with the emerald green stalks and red-hot poker inflorescences of kniphofia blooms.

Looking around them (and they did a thorough reconnaissance of the entire area) they reckoned the tent-shaped hill on the high ground behind them must be the highest point in the range. They estimated its height at around 10 000 English feet, or 3 048 metres. Not bad for a couple of proselytisers with no measuring instruments: its summit is in fact 3 282 metres, or 10 768 feet high.

As they watched the placid headwaters of the Thukela River twist through a gully, jump a few pools and then suddenly leap over the rocky lip, they would certainly have had lofty thoughts about angels in their flight attending them.

Had they been admirers of Romantic English poetry, they might have been reminded of that immortal description by William Wordsworth, of the waterfall in the Land of Lotus-eaters which "like a downward smoke, the slender stream, along the cliff to fall and pause and fall 'did seem".

It certainly was very much like Wordsworth's "land of streams". They gave it the name Mont-aux-Sources for the numerous rivers whose headwaters they crossed on their circumnavigation of the area. They did, however, take a small geographical liberty when they claimed that five rivers had their sources on its slopes.

While it is true that the Thukela, the Khubedu and the Namahadi rivers all flow from its slopes, the Senqu does not. But they can be forgiven for thinking the Khubedu was two rivers, when in fact the two uppermost tributaries join before they too take the plunge over into the Free State.

From that time until a few decades ago, generations of South African schoolchildren were taught that Mont-aux-Sources was their country's highest peak. We all now know that the highest peak on the watershed is Thabana Ntlenaya at 3 482 metres, but it lies a few kilometres inside Lesotho. The highest one officially in South Africa is Mafadi, or Injasuti Peak, at 3 459 metres. Mont-aux-Sources is only the seventh highest peak in South Africa.

There are not many places on Earth where you can see a vertical rock wall more than 1 000 metres high. One, in the ferocious Patagonian Andes, climbers have called a scream in stone. The Amphitheatre is more like a giant geological wave moving at a rate of around one centimetre a year – backwards.

A very short history about a very long geological process informs us that the Drakensberg and entire Lesotho highlands are the remaining crown of basalt that poured out of the Earth as molten lava around 100 million years ago. Back then it would have covered a much larger part of southern Africa but, being rather soft, like pumice, it has eroded easily, relatively speaking. Which is also why climbers loathe the stuff.

There are even fewer places where you can see waterfalls flowing over such high rock walls. Auyan-Tepui Mountain in Venezuela's Canaima National Park is one such place. This is where the Rio Kerepakupai Meru, a tributary of the Orinoco River, plummets 979 metres over the edge of the mountain to form what is universally considered to be the world's highest uninterrupted waterfall, the Angel Falls.

The Thukela Falls is the second highest, excepting that on its way down the Amphitheatre wall it hits two small ledges. Altogether it drops 948 meters before disappearing into the dark recesses of the Upper Thukela Gorge. The other rivers that rise on Mont-aux-Sources have drops of between 300 and 500 metres, which would just get them on the list of the world's 20 highest.

Voortrekkers had moved into Natal in the late 1830s but most remained nomads, living in wagons, and only a few built homesteads in the Drakensberg foothills. They found the area to be surprisingly empty of other human occupation; rather strange for such fair and fertile lands. British settlers began arriving a decade later. It did not take the mountaineers long after that to start looking up at the massive walls, turrets, towers and minarets of upward-pointing spears, their fingers and toes tingling.

But it was one young woman who seems to have exhibited the most uninhibited love of the place. When pioneer farmer Fred Kelly asked Edith Pickering to marry him, she replied that she would be most happy to, but only if they could honeymoon in the Drakensberg. Edith had run away from home in England in search of adventure.

And so, in 1878, Fred and Edith trekked by ox wagon into the Mont-aux-Sources area – the first tourists we know of to have holidayed in the area we now call the Royal Natal National Park, where the Thukela River meanders through its braided channel as it exits the gorge.

There, while walking and picking flowers and sitting around a campfire, they came upon a small band of Bushmen, surely the last to ever have occurred there. "Weird-looking creatures," wrote Edith in typical colonial tone, "hardly bigger than a child of 10."

Not long after this, a small band of Norwegian woodcutters arrived at Witsieshoek. They had been fishing at Port Natal but economic depression drove them into the hills. From the moment they started chopping (the area was quite densely forested then), they began working on a single-masted, six-metre-long boat.

It took them three years to complete and in March 1886 they launched the *Homeward Bound*, from the green waves of mountain ridges down towards Port Natal. On 2 May the small boat crossed the bar of Durban harbour and a year later reached Dover. There they were fêted like celebrities. One of the sailors fell in love and married an English lass and stayed, while the other two pushed onwards to "home".

It is by kind convenience that today hikers can get to the top of the most dramatic landscape feature of not only the Drakensberg but all of southern Africa by an easy path, relatively speaking. But that was not always the case. Just like Edith and Fred, early visitors had to visit the 'Berg on horseback or by ox wagon. It's surprising how many did. As far back as the 1850s a guidebook to the region mentioned the Amphitheatre and Tugela (Thukela nowadays) Falls.

In 1898 Walter Coventry visited the upper Thukela area and was entranced. He returned a few years later with a bag of money and a dream of attracting others there. From a Mr van Rooyen of Bergville he bought a chunk of land for £1 an acre. Coventry built a small hostel that was expanded into a hotel, which for decades was a retreat for holidaymakers and mountaineers.

The more active would set off early (including during the Mountain Club's famous winter meets) towards Basuto Gate, an historic crossing point on the ridge that runs down from Sentinel Peak to Witsieshoek. That was where tea would be taken before pressing on down into the Free State and then up Namahadi Pass to the summit plateau. The alternative accommodation was Mount Rydal Hotel, built in the early 1900s much higher up at Witsieshoek.

For many years it was run by eccentric Irishman Tom Casement (his brother, Sir Roger, was hanged by the British Army in 1916 as a traitor). Apparently, Tom's vocabulary was legendary and secretly delighted the lady mountaineers who "were on tenterhooks" as to what he might say next. He would lead guests up the Namahadi, or Eland's Pass, to take in the sensual glories of the summit plateau.

But that route was all but forgotten when Walter Coventry from

Goodoo (now Gudu, in the Royal Natal Park) began to build a road, a rough track and bridle path really, from Basuto Gate up the north flank of the Sentinel. This is the same track and path still used by mountaineers to reach the Chain Ladders. Coventry's plan had been to extend a roadway all the way from Natal, around the northern end of the Drakensberg, into the Free State and Lesotho, but war in 1914 interceded.

In those days, when hikers from the hostel at Goodoo reached Basuto Gate they would find a white table cloth laid out on the ground, with silver cutlery and bone china cups, all set for mid-morning tea. Today that is where you park and heft your pack for the slog up the zigzags, then along the base of the Sentinel to reach the ladders.

There used to be just one two-step set of two iron ladders, installed by the Natal Provincial Administration in 1930 to surmount the final 50-metre rock band, but now there are two. Even though they still present a bit of a challenge, it is very much less than the alternative of ascending The Gully between Sentinel Peak and Beacon Buttress.

Ascending towards the Sentinel, there comes a time when you notice the massive North Wall, or North-East Tower, looming overhead. It is dizzying looking up, and appears like a great tsunami in stone about to break right over you. It is terrifying to think about it, but back in February 1959 Pat and his wife Pam Angus-Leppan stood right there. They appraised the big crack system that runs diagonally across the middle of the North Face and thought they might give it a go.

Nearly 50 years previously, the easier, but not by any means easy, South-West Face – the stepped wall you see on rounding the base of the peak and looking back – was first summited. A friend of Tom Casement, WJ Wybergh, had grown to love the Mont-aux-Sources area and the North-West Tower especially. "A great peak that dominates everything else and invariably draws upon itself the longing gaze of every true mountaineer," he wrote.

In 1910 he found someone willing to join him, NM McLeod, a lieutenant (later brigadier) in the Royal Field Artillery based at Harrismith: "a most sporting companion" Wybergh called him.

They started on the extreme right-hand side and, once they had cleared the first vertical rock band, meandered left across the stepped wall. On reaching the notch high up on the left-hand side, they traversed around to the northwest side where they found a line that took them through the second, and highest, cliff band. From there it was more or less level across the top of the tower to the highest point directly across from Beacon Buttress.

Wybergh remarked that the rocks on the upper crux section were slippery and wet from mist and so they climbed roped together for most of the way. The formidable uppermost cliffs were smooth and nearly vertical, with fearful exposure, but in the end it was "a fine bit of climbing".

An even finer bit of climbing, among the finest ever achieved in the Drakensberg, was the first ascent of the Devil's Tooth, that rock fang that protrudes so suggestively between the Eastern Buttress and Inner Tower. After numerous attempts over the years by the strongest climbers, it was finally crowned in 1950.

In August of that year, after a night spent in the cave at the base of the Tooth, three "hard men" of the day – Ted Scholes, David Bell and Peter Campbell – set out to rub noses with the terrifying column of friable basalt. All through the morning they battled up and around smooth, bulging overhangs, crumbling blocks and slippery chimneys, often using only tiny friction foot and hand holds. It took them five hours to climb the first 50 metres: only a few hundred to go.

At 16:00, with the winter sun having already disappeared behind the Amphitheatre wall, the men crowded onto the summit, barely three metres square. In the custom of their craft they built a stone cairn and decorated it with a tattered pair of pyjama trousers.[2]

Not everyone who has tried has had as much fun. There have been many deaths recorded among climbers and hikers, such as Ross Osbourne who in 1953 fell to his death clutching a chunk of basalt to his chest. Or the man who reached to catch a handkerchief the wind had snatched from the hand of his female companion as they stood near the lip of the Thukela Falls, and down he tumbled.

The last days of April 1959 came with a storm warning in the Berg,

---

[2] I'm guessing they were Ted's: his son Bob would be eternally embarrassed seeing his father set out from winter camps to climb, a pair of pyjama pants under his shorts. Remember though, these were the days of iron pitons and hemp ropes, well before PolarFleece, camming safety devices and dynamic ropes.

but some people, who should have been, were not paying attention. Least of all the group of 15 students from Wits University who left the Royal Natal Hotel at Goodoo on a clear morning. They ascended to Basuto Gate and were making their way up the side of the Sentinel when ominous dark clouds came sweeping over the peaks.

By the time the group reached the bridle path along the base of the Sentinel, the wind was howling, the temperature had plummeted and it had started to rain. Most of the party were dressed in light clothing, and only a few had jackets. Those leading made a dash for the Chain Ladders and eventually made it to the Mountain Club hut on the summit plateau.

The rest were caught out in the open on the lower path when snow began to fall. It would continue falling for the next three days and nights. When night descended three teenagers were trapped on the bridle path. Two were later found comatose by a party of rescuers coming from the Mountain Club hut on the plateau above, in lashing rain and whirling snow. However, young Keith Erasmus, as well as one of the rescue party, Peter Christensen, who set out to find him, froze to death out on the lonely mountain.

But even that was hardly the worst of times in the long drama of the Drakensberg. Things there had been pretty peaceful for the preceding millennia, and probably more. For the Bushmen it had been Heaven on Earth. Several decades before white people arrived, however, small clans of Nguni pastoralists seeking new pastures had begun to push the little hunter-gatherers deeper into the mountains.

Still, things remained tenable up until around 1800. That was the time when those same cattle-herding people began to seriously bump up against one another. Push came to shove came to bludgeoning when the Mfecane (or Difaqane) wars decimated the grassland regions of South Africa.

Those who were left to count the corpses afterwards estimated the KwaZulu-Natal region beyond Zululand had numbered around a million people before the troubles. By the time of Shaka's death in 1828 it was thought there were no more than 3 000. It was said you could easily locate the way south to Pondoland, or north and west over Basuto Gate into Lesotho by white route markers – the bones of all the dead.

Those remaining mostly resorted to cannibalism. Many of the caves previously occupied by Bushmen were appropriated by cannibal clans. The largest of the caves, still known as Cannibal Cave, can be visited near The Cavern, an old-style family hotel. This was where the minor chief Sidinane kept his pot full with human parts. His clan would go out on hunting forays and set upon any stragglers they found. They would not be killed immediately, but strung up to be used as fresh meat when needed.

Apparently they had a song they would sing to the bound victims. This is how the missionaries who encountered them wrote it down:

We are cannibals, we eat people,
We eat thee, we eat people.
We eat the brain of a dog,
And that of a little child.
We eat the fingers of people,
We eat the fat of mankind,
Thou toy of the man-eaters,
Thou delicious morsel –
Strike! Strike him down, my comrades!

Mokapakapa, a Mosotho, told M Arbousset how he, his three wives, their children and their servants had been captured by anthropophagites. His wives were called cattle, the children sheep, the servants were oxen and he was an eland. All but he were killed, butchered and cooked in pieces in pots or over coals. Old Mokapakapa escaped on account of being very skinny.

All those millions of bones would have provided a feast like never before or after for those ossifrages of the mountain skies, the lammergeiers. In the Bible there is a reference to a bird called an ossifrage – a bone breaker, which could be only a lammergeier. It can take juvenile birds up to seven years to master the skill of bone breaking.

The act of dropping bones to crack them open was first described by the Roman writer and naturalist Pliny the Elder. He claimed the Greek poet Aeschylus died when a lammergeier dropped a tortoise onto his bald head. Although their diet consists mainly of carrion, the enormous birds have also been noted to drop tortoises in order to crack them open.

Large parts of the Drakensberg have been conserved as wild areas for as long as a century, which means wildlife has been given a chance to get a good footing. The great topographical step of the huge escarpment wall sets up constant winds, which means it's a great place for soaring birds.

Swifts and swallows dart about like small arrows picking off insects in mid-air; kestrels and lanners speedily patrol the upper slopes for rodents and game birds; buzzards and black eagles scout the high ramparts. But it is the lammergeiers that are the lords of the mountain skies.

Probably due to their formidable appearance, remarkable aerial speed and agility, these "lamb catchers" gained a reputation the world over as aggressive predators. This also led to their persecution in all the high mountain regions of the Old World. Although once fairly common in high mountain regions, during the 20th century their numbers plummeted.

The first time any were photographed in southern Africa was in 1961. A lead from a faded report in a ranger's diary from around 1900 took the small team of photographers deep into the Mokhotlong Valley inside Lesotho. The story is recounted in great detail by Reg Pearse, one of the Mokhotlong party, in his exhaustive book on the Drakensberg, *Barrier of Spears*.

Its scientific name *Gypaetus barbartus*, meaning bearded vulture-eagle, attests to its evolutionary position straddling two branches of the raptor tree. Their common name, "lamb catcher", has led to some very bad press. They very seldom eat anything but bones. Small bones are swallowed whole but large ones are carried aloft. The bird soars high, and then swoops at full speed towards a large rock, known as an ossuary. Approaching at full speed, the bird lets fly like a bomber aircraft. The bone shatters and the lammergeier lands to devour the scraps. Its long, grooved tongue is adapted to scoop out marrow.

These half-vultures, half-eagles spend most of their daylight hours riding the mountain winds, hardly ever flapping. They can be recognised by their very large size, falcon-like flight, golden and charcoal plumage and distinct diamond-shaped tail.

Lammergeiers, and indeed all vulture numbers, are on the decline, in the Drakensberg-Lesotho area and all around the world. The main cause is through feeding on purposefully poisoned carcasses. Elsewhere it is done by farmers who hate all carnivores, predators and scavengers indiscriminately. In Lesotho and South Africa the culprits are mostly different.

There is an estimated R1.5-million a year trade in vulture parts for *muti* here. In local lore a vulture is reputed to have extraordinary powers of sight, as well as foresight and intelligence. If you want your children to do well at school, or you want to better your odds at the horses or in business, you can visit one of around 130 000 *muti* dealers in the region, who between them divvy up around 160 vultures a year of all species.

When the first record was published in *Roberts Birds of Southern Africa* in 1940, the status of this bird (then known as *Gypaetus meridionalis*, alt. *Gypaetus ossifragus*) was given as "a very rare vulture-like eagle, found in only a few mountain fastnesses". In subsequent editions it changed from rare and almost disappeared, to rare and endangered. Its current status is given as critically endangered. There are an estimated 204 pairs in southern Africa, with a 38 per cent decrease "in recent times".

By staying at the Witsieshoek Mountain Lodge you can hit two birds with one hiking boot; first by relishing the comforts of South Africa's highest inn, then by enjoying the sight of lammergeiers coming in to feast on the bones that are put out on the hotel's alpine ridge most mornings.

Kamberg, Game Pass Shelter
The Story of !Xabo, Images of Power and a Secret App: Searching for the Meaning of Bushman Art

There are hundreds of rock shelters in the Little Berg zone of the Drakensberg mountains, between them sheltering thousands of Bushman, or San, rock art images. The area has been called the world's greatest outdoor art gallery. The secret door that led to what those mysterious images mean was unlocked at Kamberg in the southern Drakensberg region.

> Before, the world was like a taut string,
> The world sang in the wind.
> Then the people came and broke that string,
> Now the wind is silent.

No more do we hunt these hills,
The fires have gone cold.
But you can still hear us in the waters,
And see us in the rocks.

A Bushman song – documentary at the Kamberg Rock Art Centre

LONG BEFORE THE SUN rose from its slumber to lay its warm hand upon the land, !Xabo was already up and busy. It was a big day. Even though he was burdened with a heavy hangover after a trance dance, in the stream of water that spilled over the cave overhang he washed off the crusted blood from his torso. The nosebleeds were no problem, but his stomach ached from lack of eating for the past three days. You have to enter God's house with a clean body.

While the rest of his small clan slept on grass gathered on the cave floor, the little club-footed man had constructed a hammock of skins and rope to hang from the trees at one end of the shelter. He liked to keep a bit of distance between himself and the others. His magnificent winter kaross of silver jackal skins, which he had sewn together with antelope sinew, was his palace.

The people had clucked noisily at his folly, warning !Xabo that they had never seen or heard of such a separation, and so obviously no good could come of it. But the mirthful little healer laughed at them. "Aieee, and which of you has seen the great bird that flies under the water?" he mocked them.

"Which of you has spoken with the spirits of my jackals as I skinned them?" Meaning, of course, that they could all sod off. Was it not he, and only he, who went underwater to meet with the animal spirits? Was it not he who came back to share with them knowledge of the world beyond mortal seeing? And was it not he, and only he, who used the power of the otherworld to heal their ailments and answer their questions?

His deformity, along with his epilepsy, gave him special status in the province of healers, having been conferred by the great /Kaggan. But it also meant he could not keep up with the other hunters when they set off after a quarry. In order to earn his place at the table he had become an adept hunter in his own right.

Kamberg, Game Pass Shelter

It was known that !Xabo was working on a secret new vision, in the cave high up in the valley where there was strong eland power and where people gathered in order to consult with the ancestors and to pass through the portals of rights of passage, dance for rain in times of drought, celebrate a birth, coming of age or mourn a death. Each new image painted added to that cave's power.

His people asked over and over when it would be finished. It was very nearly, but he needed to add a bit more blood of the earth before he'd be ready to share it.

!Xabo had instructed the hunters to return only when they had the blood of a freshly killed eland safely inside the vial he provided, a rhebok horn with its tightly fitting wooden stopper. This he would mix with the ground red powder he and only he knew where to collect, high up above the valley of the eland that lay over the pass to the north.

In a twisted leather belt around his waist he carried the tools of his trade. In small oribi horns were the pigments, various ochres from yellow through orange and Sienna to deep brown. In a purse made from a gall bladder he kept eland fat and in another, sap of the milkweed.

When mixed with the ground minerals they made his coloured pastes. White came from kaolin if he could get it, or bird droppings if his supply of fine white clay was used up. Droppings from the *lenong* (Cape vulture) was good, but if he could find that of the mighty *ntsu* (lammergeier), that would be strong energy.

His brushes were either twigs of the bladdernut tree with the ends chewed, or the bristles from the tail of a bushpig he'd trapped. In the shell of a small tortoise he kept small bits of charcoal for rendering the outlines of his subjects. That was fine work, keeping straight lines and flowing forms across the rough crystalline and often broken surface of the cave wall.

With /Kaggan guiding his hand, he was a master of his craft. In his vision the previous night, red had predominated, the special colour, not often used. Not the dark red-brown normally used to paint eland, but bright, bold red, the colour of pure power. !Xabo had a vision where the animal spirit of a dying eland was passing into a human spirit, joined by dotted lines of power.

He remembered the sounds of the dancing, feet beating on the ground and rattles, women singing and clapping until the magic (the !gi:xa – !gi for potency and :xa, to be full) entered his body. Then he remembered the pain, the n/um, in his belly, doubling over, blood streaming from his nose, then ... the visions. He knew many apprentices could not bear the pain and abandoned the quest to master the full power of the spirits and the visions that came with them.

By the time the women were blowing the hearth fire to life and tending the children, the men gathered around sharpening arrow heads, mending their bows and tying new arrow shafts, !Xabo was making his way up the valley of the *nte* (eland) river. They named it after the great antelope that migrated between this valley and the one to the north, and which gave his people their sense of place.

He headed up towards the saddle that was the game passageway, ascending steadily towards the great dominating ridge that formed a corner of the range and which brought rain. It was the giant mountain at which you should never point with a finger, lest you offend its brooding spirit and it sent a violent storm after you.

In his huntings and gatherings the little deformed soothsayer was more gatherer than hunter. Into a large leather bag he tossed all manner of veld food like birds' eggs and the nestlings of lapwings or quails camouflaged in the grass. With a sling he could bring down a scrub hare or fleeing game bird. He would rummage among boulders for dassie burrows, a slow tortoise or sluggish puff adder. He picked berries and any fruit ripening as food for the road, but otherwise left it to the women to bring home the veg and salad.

In the early hours, while surfacing from his trance, !Xabo had heard a pack of hyenas yip-yap-yelping somewhere up in the pass and he set off after their spoor. They were clearly on the hunt. If they made a kill and he found them still on it, he might be able to chase them off with fire and steal whatever meat was left, also possibly the skin and horns if there were any.

The little Bushman shuffled to the summit of the saddle and then continued up to the grassy rump of a spur that was also in the general direction of his special spot for collection of red pigment, hard up against the mighty barrier of the up-standing spears. Only he knew where, and only he know how. It was part of the closely guarded knowledge of sorcery.

It was there that he saw them, off in the distance on the whaleback ridge of a second spur: a grouping of what clearly was hyenas lying around the carcass of a medium-sized antelope. It might be an adult mountain reedbuck, grey rhebok or possibly an oribi, but why were the hyenas asleep before they had eaten?

!Xabo trotted in a long level loop to gain the second ridge, and the closer he got to the perplexing scene the more concerned he became. Was this /Kaggan giving him some kind of warning? Should he run … but then you could not hide from /Kaggan.

The Bushman crept up. The area around the sleeping animals was heavily trampled, much more than it should have been. There was spoor of some very large zebras, as well as other giant two-legged creatures with flat, oval-shaped feet. Then he saw the small red spots on the hyenas. Blood from round wounds about the size of his thumb tip, from a weapon he did not know. !Xabo saw the puff of black powder smoke a second before the thud of lead breaking flesh and bone dropped him.

"It's not exactly the Louvre of Bushman rock art, is it?" remarked my companion, Donald the Astute.

I had to agree, in one sense. That would be Didima Gorge and its side canyons, especially Eland Cave, which shelter many thousands of rock art images. That area has been called the greatest outdoor art gallery in the world. But Eland Cave is a two-day hike in and two days out with wilderness camping en route.

Game Pass Shelter in the Kamberg Nature Reserve, on the other hand, is a mere one-and-a-half to two hours' saunter there, and less on the return trip to the panoramic rest camp. From the camp office and information centre, a long and winding path crosses several streams in the verdant grassland, rises up to Waterfall Cave, then crosses a stick bridge with inviting rock pools.

From there the ascent gets a bit more serious until you reach the band of cream-coloured sandstone that crests the valley. Your guide will unlock the fence gate and then you puff and huff up and over the last few large loose boulders at the expansive maw of Game Pass Shelter.

The shelter is really just that, not a cave at all but a shallow overhang about 25 metres long and not deep enough to afford any real protection from the weather. It was never meant to be a place of lodging.

When we arrive at this or any other rock art site, we bring with us the self-indulgence we are encouraged to cultivate in these selfie times, as well as carrying all the din of the modern world in our heads, which is so at odds with the essence of the place.

The mobile phones we carry are one of the greatest technological inventions of our times: you could take a photograph of the images, send them to a friend, pinpoint your location in the universe and translate your guide's isiZulu into Mandarin. Or phone a friend. What they cannot do, however, is translate Bushman art into any known language.

The images here might not be the Louvre, but they just might be the most important in the entire gallery of Neolithic art. To understand them we need to slow down, look around, take in the grand vista of the abundant Kamberg valley, free our minds, open our hearts and try to imagine the world of people who lived here before we did.

We also need a key to open the door and slip through the crack between their world and ours; a necromancer slipping into a trance, down a cognitive wormhole into the shaman's wonderland. Taking magic mushrooms or LSD might help to give penetrating insights into the secret world, but that alone would not reveal the specific code of the paintings. And you might just get lost down there forever.

The Game Pass Shelter retrospective can be divided into four main groups based on physical separation as well as subject matter. Facing the rock face, the display starts with a set of handprints, the equivalent of signatures on your extreme right. Most extensive and impressive visually is the second panel, which consists of two main divisions, a larger upper panel and lower, narrower one.

There is a parade of eland, each one about 30 centimetres long, above them a group of stick-figure hunters in full stride, each about 10 centimetres high. Then there is a parade of human-animal forms researchers call therianthropes, but what the Bushmen called people who have gone under water, or people who have died. Behind them are the dark, blotchy remains of eland images, each up to a metre long, obviously much older than the superimposed images.

The third and fourth groups are very much more faded than the first two, although no less interesting. But it is the second group that makes this shelter such an amazing place. The panel occupies only the lower, thinner rock band and consists mainly of four therianthrope figures and a dying eland.

One of the "people who has gone under water" is holding onto the eland's tail. The eland has its head lowered, its hair is standing on end, its front legs seem to be buckling and its back legs are crossed. From its nose falls lines of blood (the red colouring has long faded but streaks of the white undercoat remain).

The human-like figures are all, uncharacteristically, rendered in bright red. They all have what the Bushmen called rhebok heads and the one holding on to the eland has its legs crossed and the same hooved feet as the antelope. Another of the figures is doubled over with its arms thrown backwards (this is *n/um*, the pain).

Our guide to the underworld at Kamberg was 20-something Rohan Mweli. He grew up not far from the hamlet of Rosetta, in Tendela, the last village you pass through approaching the gate of the reserve (which is part of the much larger uKhahlamba-Drakensberg Park and World Heritage Site). It must be the best stretch of rural road in South Africa, if only a few kilometres of it.

His people were removed from the park to make way for white farmers back in the bad old pre-rainbow days. But now, in the new political dispensation, they are beneficiaries of funds generated by the reserve. Among the facilities thus provided is the school which sent young Rohan on his journey into the world beyond.

He went on to gain an MSc in Archaeology at Wits University and his next goal, he told us, was to read for a PhD, comparing rock art sites around the world. Rohan was likewise privileged to have as a mentor David Lewis-Williams, Professor of Cognitive Archaeology and Director of the Rock Art Research Unit at Wits University.

Early attempts to genuinely understand ancient rock art – other than dismissing it as the doodles of savages that was pervasive in the colonial mind – were far off the mark. In the early 20th century the paintings were variously attributed to Egyptians, Phoenicians, Arabs, aliens (those weird "spacemen" heads) – anyone excepting the people who actually did create them.

Then came the idea of sympathetic magic, much more credible but still well wide of the mark: the idea that you harnessed the spirit of an animal in a painted image in order to hunt it successfully. This view seemed to be vindicated by the numerous images of stick-figure hunters that are almost universal in the catalogue.

These views held for about a century. Until the 1970s, that is, when a brave new world of archaeologists, led principally by Professor David Lewis-Williams, revisited an old collection of notebooks that had been gathering dust in the central library at University of Cape Town for more than 100 years. They are known as the Bleek-Lloyd collection. Lewis-Williams would need to look not to the future, but into the past in order to find the app he needed ...

Wilhelm Bleek was a German linguist and expert in African languages, particularly those of the Khoi people. In 1855 he was invited to the Colony of Natal in order to compile a written isiZulu grammar (it was here that he met his future wife, Jemima Lloyd). That got the attention of Cape Governor Sir George Grey, and a year later the linguist packed his bags for Cape Town. He was made curator of the governor's private and extensive book collection, which became the core of the National Library of South Africa.

In the late 1850s Bleek got permission from the authorities on Robben Island to conduct interviews with Bushman convicts there and he began compiling a vocabulary, as well as basic sentences (the jackal sat on the kaross, sort of thing) of these indigenous and misunderstood people.

The people whom the Khoi called San (people without property, specifically stock animals) did not abide by notions of private property, whether land or animals. God had given them both as gifts, but the Khoi and later European settlers imprisoned their beasts, and partitioned the land, so the Bushmen took them whenever they pleased. Their lethal poison-tipped arrows did not help to endear them to the newcomers. The Khoi coerced the Dutch in their ongoing battles with the have-nots, and in time conflict became genocide.

Bushmen who did not fall to Dutch firearms, or were starved to death, or abducted into labour on settler farms, were imprisoned and forced into hard labour for the burgeoning colony. As their numbers dwindled, the Bushmen clans organised into often-homicidal cattle raiding parties. They fought literally to the last man, woman and child. From around 1800 the new British colonisers easily adopted the old Dutch bigotry and loathing of the little Late Stone Age hunter-gatherers: vermin to be eradicated.

In the 1860s the arrest of one of these raiding parties in the Cape coincided with the visit of Queen Victoria's son Prince Alfred. He placed the first stone into the shallow waters of Table Bay that became the Victoria and Alfred Basin. Bushman convicts confined in the purpose-built Breakwater Prison provided most of the rest of the labour for the project.

By this time Wilhelm Bleek had married and moved into a large house in Mowbray. His wife, Jemima, was the daughter of the man who later became Archdeacon of Durban. In 1862 Jemima's sister Lucy set sail from Durban in order to attend their wedding. Unfortunately, her ship, the SS *Waldensian*, ran aground at Cape Agulhas and, although she survived, most of her possessions did not.

Lucy, unlucky in love back in Natal, moved in with the Bleeks and in short time was assisting Wilhelm with his linguistic studies. Bleek got permission to take one Bushman from the Breakwater Prison to live at his home in order to better study their language, then two, and in time others along with their various family members. Together Bleek and Lloyd created an extensive account of Bushman language and song, including as much ethnographic and anthropological information as they were able.

They wrote it all down meticulously, but that did not mean they understood it all. But then in 1873 colonial magistrate JM Orpen was sent to apprehend the seditious Zulu Chief Langalibalele in the Drakensberg. Orpen managed to engage the services of a Bushman guide, Qing, who, when relaxed and smoking around the campfire, gave him information about the enigmatic rock paintings in the mountains.

The men with strange horned heads, which Qing described as rhebok heads, were men who had died and gone to live underwater. They had been spoiled by the dances you could see in some paintings (trance dances), the same way an eland is spoiled when shot with a poisoned arrow. Orpen wrote an article about it but understood it literally – they were Bushmen who had died.

For Wilhelm Bleek, when he read Orpen's article, a penny dropped. The paintings illustrated the same Bushman mythology he was busy hearing. "It gives," he noted, "at once to Bushman art a higher character."

Wilhelm Bleek died in Cape Town just two years after the Langalibalele rebellion and, following a codicil in his will, Lucy Lloyd was appointed curator of the National Library, but at half his salary. Lloyd's relationship with the chauvinistic library committee chairman was fraught from the start and she did not last long in the job.

After that she began corresponding with the artist George W Stow (sometime mission teacher, clerk, farmer, book-keeper, trader, wine merchant, diamond dealer, auctioneer, amateur geologist and palaeontologist) about his reproductions of Bushman art. When Stow died in 1882, Lloyd purchased his tracings and copies of his paintings, together with an accompanying manuscript by his wife, Fanny.

Stow, who realised the Bushmen were the oldest known inhabitants of South Africa and the Bantu people relative newcomers, wrote:

"I have been making pilgrimages to the various old Bushman caves among the mountains in this part of the Colony and Kaffraria; and, as their paintings are becoming obliterated very fast, it struck me that it would be well to make copies of them before these interesting relics of an almost extinct race are entirely destroyed."

Lucy Lloyd died at the Bleek family home, Charlton House, in 1914 at age 79. She was buried in the Wynberg cemetery near Wilhelm Bleek. They left 13 000 pages of extensive interviews with mainly six individual Bushmen from the Karoo and Bushmanland areas (with one notebook on the Koranna language contributed by Jemima, who had by that time emigrated to Germany). The notebooks were carefully stored in the main library at the University of Cape Town.

"For many years it was thought that the true meaning of Bushman art was irretrievably lost," archaeologist Lewis-Williams wrote. What he and his team needed was some kind of key, or some other kind of app, in order to unlock the secret language of the paintings. The

Bleek-Lloyd work was known to the experts of his day but no one before had seriously studied them, or linked them to the paintings.

Cross-referencing their penetrating ethnology to the Kamberg paintings afforded the Wits archaeologists their eureka moment. The dying eland frieze there has been called the Rosetta Stone of Bushman art and you could think of Lewis-Williams as the M Bouchard of the Drakensberg.[3]

Studying the Kamberg panels, and the dying eland in particular, a connection was made between the progression of an animal dying after having been shot with a poison arrow, and a shaman going into a trance. Both evinced dying, going into the place of the dead: shuddering, trembling, staggering, lowering of the head, hair standing up, bleeding from the nose. These are animals and men who have been spoiled, have gone under water, sometimes also described as underground, and entered God's house.

Perhaps the central discovery was that all Bushman art was created not merely by artists but very specifically by shaman artists, those and only those who had gone into a trance state, visited the place of the dead and returned to tell their tales. It was realised that all painted images referenced altered states induced during trance dances. This was not art for art's sake, but art with spiritual purpose.

When !Xabo or his doppelganger went into a trance it was akin to Moses going off into the wilderness to hear the word of God. When he went to collect *qhang qhang*, "blood of the earth", it was Moses climbing Mount Sinai to receive the word of God in the tablets. When the little hunter-gatherer returned to his special cave to paint what he had seen in his trance, he was creating the Bushman's own holy scripture.

For !Xabo this was part of the closely guarded knowledge of the sorcerer, turning base metal into golden knowledge. Coincidentally,

---

[3] In 1799 French Egyptologist Pierre-François Bouchard uncovered a large stone fragment, part of a much larger obelisk that has still not been discovered, near the town of Rosetta. When closely studied, it provided the key to reading the ancient hieroglyphics: with a series of hieroglyphics were corresponding texts in Egyptian Demotic script and Greek. It is a fitting geographical double entendre that the nearest town to Kamberg is also named Rosetta; the small inn there serves a fine country-style lunch.

it is believed that the mining of red iron-oxide clay or haematite in southern Africa – where the oldest evidence of mining on the planet has been found – led humans out of the Stone Age and into the Iron Age as they worked out how to render the ore into metal.

In his outstanding work on the Drakensberg, *Barrier of Spears*, author Reg Pearse says that by 1880 there were no Bushmen left living there. However, there is a report that in the first decade of the 20th century a lone Bushman was seen and promptly shot in the area that was soon thereafter to be proclaimed as the Giant's Castle Game Reserve. Around his waist was found a leather belt onto which were fastened several antelope horns, each containing the materials of a Bushman artist. This was !Xabo, although we'll never know his real name.

Equally puzzling to modern researchers were the many depictions of geometric, star-burst and other symmetrical patterns that are widespread in both rock paintings and petroglyphs (rock engravings) across southern Africa. It was experimentation with hallucinogenics, mainly LSD, during the 1950s and 1960s that opened the door on them. In the first stage of induced hallucination the person sees brightly coloured patterns and bursts of light, which were called entoptics.

It is hardly a coincidence that Bushman artists often painted their trance images across a crack in the rock face, or that writer Aldous Huxley described his experiments with hallucinogenic drugs as passing through "the doors of perception".

For a Bushman healer seeing these patterns was also the first sign he was entering the world of the supernatural. Often, they related them to shapes they knew, such as tortoise shells, beehives and honeycombs. So, when you see the image of a tortoise, or beehive, it's not what it at first seems to be.

In the next stage the shaman enters a place where people become animals, often grotesque spirits of lions, or snakes, sometimes stinging and biting insects. Hippies on acid might call it a bad trip but to the Bushman it was an essential part of the spirit journey (users of ayahuasca in the Amazon know this all too well).

Not all the animals there are harmful but in order to survive in God's house, one shaman was recorded saying he needed to become a mamba:

"I see all the people like very small birds and the whole place will be spinning around and that is why we run around. The trees will be circling also." Then, by passing underwater, he leaves the spinning world and enters the spirit world.

Professor Lewis-Williams called Bushman art "images of power", and likened the shelters in which they are found to Bushman cathedrals. Continuing that Catholic metaphor easily leads us to think of the painted images on them as their stained-glass windows.

It seems appropriate that the last words here be those of Diä!kwain, one of Wilhelm Bleek's confidants:

"People do evil and fight when they have grown fat after rain has fallen."

Lambazi Bay, Port Grosvenor

A Lonely Bay, the Wondrously Wild Coast and a Terrible Saga of Castaways: Searching for the Fate of the Grosvenor

Lambazi Bay, on the Pondoland coast about 30 kilometres north of Port St Johns, is also known as Port Grosvenor – but you will find no port there. That name comes from the English East Indiaman that ran aground on a reef there nearly 240 years ago.

THE NATIONAL ROAD BETWEEN Port Edward-Kokstad and East London is avoided by many holidaymakers, which is a bit of a paradox since it is the main access to arguably the best stretch of rustic, seaside holiday land in the known universe, otherwise known as the Wild Coast.

However, once you turn off at a place like Lusikisiki, it's best you have a 4x4 or a tough bakkie. The road to Lambazi Bay, Luphatana and Waterfall Bluff quickly deteriorates, downgrading from tar (with the ubiquitous Transkei speed bumps) to a rolling gravel road replete with goats, pigs, dogs, roaming pedestrians and cyclists, potholes and places where the road seems to go missing entirely, then to a jeep track and that track to a path, sometimes a rockery in places and a quagmire in others, hard clay when dry and soil soup when wet.

It is hard to tell just where peri-urban becomes peri-rural and where all the old Xhosa rondavel huts have gone. In their place are, first, Transkei Tuscan: suburban-style homes complete with faux-classical columns and candy-twist pillars. Then, as you pick your way down towards the coast, modern homes give way to box-like RDP houses topped off by tell-tale solar roof geysers.

This is "old Africa" fast disappearing as our nation somersaults into the global economy. Only when within sight of the sea do traditional, round clay-and-thatch huts make a last stand. Somewhere along here you will think the situation has turned from arduous to desperate (even with GPS or Google Maps you might feel adrift); surely this cannot be the road to a noted holiday resort – but it is. If it has been raining things will be worse and then the getting out will be the trickier (always carry a good tow rope).

Many things in the old "homelands" are changing for the better, but not the roads. Peter and Cher, who run the Drifters Greenfire Lodge at Lambazi Bay, often welcome teary and weak-kneed guests, much like the survivors from the wreck of the East Indiaman who struggled ashore here more than 200 years ago.

All along the Wild Coast there are vaguely recalled accounts of shipwrecks and castaways, white men and more specifically white women who came ashore in the most wretched of circumstances, many of whom threw in their lots with the local people. Some are said to have arrived with and promptly lost hordes of treasure.

Between Port St Johns and Coffee Bay the *amaMolo* are said to be descended in part from "black people" who were shipwreck survivors. Although many shipwreck survivors were of European origin, at least an equal number of their darker-skinned crew and passengers not only survived but thrived by simply staying put where they washed up and setting up home with the indigenous African people.

Further south, between the Nxaxo and Qolora rivers (lots of lateral and guttural clicks there) many of the white stragglers would have begun to give up the hope of ever reaching help or home. Thereabouts are found the *abeLungu*, descended from white people. The "lungu" being a variation of *mlungu or mzungu*, or white, which is said to derive from the foam that gathers along a shoreline after a storm – the white froth, or scum, that comes from the sea.

The "wild coast" did not get its name by happenstance. From the time the *São João* sunk off the mouth of the Mzimvubu River in 1552, ships came to grief there every few decades on average. But one wreck has outplayed all others in the public mind, the *Grosvenor*.

But before we move on to the English shipwreck oeuvre, it is worth taking a short diversion to dwell on just one tale from the Portuguese canon that had a century's jump on the Limeys. Our tragic heroine is the high-born Dona Eleonora Sala. She was one of the "pampered elite" aboard the *São João* who did not do very well for themselves when faced with the realities of being cast ashore in a place where titles meant little.

To begin, she and her two children were carried in litters by willing hands who had been promised substantial rewards. But eventually distance took its toll and after three months' hard walking there was no one left willing to carry her and her litter any further and she was forced to trudge on in her soft pumps across the savage landscape.

Nearing Delagoa Bay the party was robbed time and again, down to the clothes they wore. Dona Eleonora had lost much and now it was her mind. She dug a pit in which she buried her nakedness and refused to go any further. Her husband, the Governor Manuel de Sousa de Sepulveda, left her and her three children buried in the sand somewhere along the coast of Maputaland. He marched off alone into the bush and was never seen again.

Just about every story about every wreck and every castaway who left their DNA on that glorious sun-drenched shore has been ascribed to the *Grosvenor*. There were the Campbell sisters, supposedly the daughters of a Scottish officer doing duty during the Frontier Wars, as well as numerous anonymous others who simply disappeared from the historical record. Then there is Bessie, who seems to have mothered every person of mixed race following every ship wreck over a period of a century or so.

Bessie is something of a mystery, having been found at the age of about seven, maybe less, some days after an unknown wreck, hiding among some boulders on the beach south of Port St Johns (named after the wreck of the *São João*). There is much conjecture that with her were two Indian women, possibly servants or perhaps nannies, whose own African histories are interbraided with that of the white girl.

She married well, becoming the wife of Tshomane, son of Badi, a chief among the Mpondo around the Mngazana River. She was thus accorded high status among the people of the area. But no one has been able to uncover exactly who she was or where she came from. It seems her ship was wrecked about 40 years before the *Grosvenor* came to grief.

When white explorers finally made contact with her children, Bessie's progeny had no knowledge of her birth language or provenance, she having obviously integrated totally into the local culture. Although apparently not entirely so, but we'll get there in time …

Imagine sailing down the east coast of South Africa in a sailing boat and encountering the massive seas and freak waves that are known to build up under "perfect storm" conditions. In many cases the ship would be completely engulfed and simply disappear. Even large ships in fairly modern times have, such as the *Waratah*, a 10 000-tonne luxury steam liner that disappeared without any trace in 1909. People on shore near the Mbashe River mouth reported seeing it around midday and then – nothing.

The many and various wrecks left their marks in as many ways, including the DNA of survivors, flotsam and jetsam, including coins, beads and pottery that still wash up on those lovely beaches and cannons that salvage divers still find. Others are remembered only by their cargoes that washed ashore at places such as Coffee Bay or Mboyti (place of beans). A few left their names, including Port St Johns, Mazeppa Bay and of course Port Grosvenor adjacent to Lambazi Bay.

The remains of the *São Bento* (the sister ship of the *São João* that was wrecked on the same fateful night) were found around mid-last century by recreational diver Geoff Harris while he was wallowing in the waves off Msikaba (just a short way north of Lambazi Bay). He managed to salvage several cannons that now reside in museums around the country. Records say there were 470 or more survivors from the two wrecks, of which 23 eventually made it to Delagoa Bay (Maputo). Dona Sala and her children, as well as her husband, were not among them.

Portuguese wreck survivors typically would head north towards Portuguese East Africa (if you know the area, just imagine trying to walk around St Lucia, the Kosi lakes and malarial swamps, dodging elephants and hippos and crocodiles, and finding enough food along the way), while Dutch and British would try to head for the Cape Colony.

The slaves and Asian servants might well have had mixed feelings: history suggests many of them fancied their chances with the local black people rather than face the uncertain walk and equally onerous lives in servitude back in the colonies.

The *Grosvenor*'s story began well before anyone realised their voyage was doomed. Against good sense and advice, Captain John Coxon pulled anchor in Calcutta (Kolkata), India, very late into the sailing season of 1782. Also, it was a time when the on-off-on-again wars with France were on again and all British ships were required to ply the Indian Ocean in military convoys.

Off Madras (Chennai) the convoy got into a firefight with a French fleet which delayed them off Ceylon (Sri Lanka) until mid-June. Then the main fleet sailed off to engage the French elsewhere, leaving a few merchantmen unguarded.

Following all that, Coxon missed a pre-arranged rendezvous with two other East Indiamen and so set off towards home all alone. The other two ships, *Dartmouth* and *Valentine*, did not fare well either; it was a bad season at sea for the English East India Company. By this time "late" had become dangerously behind schedule.

Throughout July the three-masted ship punched through big seas, squalls and rain. At month's end they sailed into "a hard gale" with lightning and thunder pummelling the ocean around them. The main mast sprung badly and had to be splinted. Then first mate Alexander Logie, the chief navigator upon whom Captain Coxon relied almost entirely for piloting, came down with a severe fever. Everything had been set in place for a tragedy of epic proportions.

In good weather, Lambazi is as delightful a seaside resort as you will find, with a small beach where a stream enters the sea, surrounded by grassy banks and rocky platforms beyond that. Small holiday shacks dot the shore, but two centuries ago there would have been just the humble huts of Mpondo herders.

On the night of 3 August, the sea was a wild cauldron and the sky a torrent of stormy darkness, but things were destined to get even worse. Around midnight the captain calculated they were about 160 nautical miles (300 kilometres) shy of the mainland, then went to bed. With first mate Mr Logie down with fever, that left second mate Mr Shaw officer of the watch.

At dinner that night lots of grog was served for toasts that land would be made soon. Around midnight on the 4th, with a squall blowing from the southwest, 20-year-old seaman William Hubberly reported to the watch, Mr Shaw, that he'd seen "dancing" lights to starboard and that he thought they might be fires on some shore.

At 04:00 Shaw handed over the watch to "oafish" third mate Thomas Beale, instructing him to watch for the reported lights. Beale dismissed them as "lights in the air", trusting his captain's navigation and scoffed, not even bothering to take a look, not even when the sailor Lewis came scooting down the ratlines of the foremast to report they were headed straight for land and it was not far off.

Beale should have done something because those lights were veld fires set by Mpondo herders to ensure the spring rains would herald green grass for their cattle. A few minutes later an inshore reef dug its shale claws deep into the timber guts of the ship.

The first reaction of the crew, once pandemonium had subsided to mere frenzy, was to try to pull the ship off the rocks. But they used too much sail, too late, and managed to break the hull in two, the bow section floating off and sinking almost immediately with many hands on deck and some still below. Two sailors made their own pact with fate; they were last seen breaking into the sinking part of the ship's lazaretto to get at the liquor that was locked inside.

Over the following 12 terrifying and confusing hours, waves lashed the wreck and those still aboard feared the worst for themselves.

Luckily the stern stayed wedged on the reef and from there some very brave sailors swam a hawser rope to shore. It took from dawn to dusk to get 125 people ashore. Those who leaped for bits of wreckage washed up battered, bruised, beaten, some dead. Others, including one John Bryan, had his leg badly gashed by splintered flotsam, and that dictated the rest of his life.

John Coxon, the captain, was an astute trader, a skill which directed his rapid ascendency in the company. But he was not a very good sailor and proved to be a less competent leader on terra firma, worse so on terra incognito. Mostly he seems to have been paralysed by the situation and took his lead from the senior civil servant John Hosea who was typical of his kind – a bigot, a braggart and a blusterer. This greatly weakened the captain's position among his charges, and all of theirs among their surprised hosts.

Among his oversights was not gathering lead shot and gunpowder. They landed with some weapons but the guns were useless and swords and daggers were lost, mostly bartered for food, or stolen along the way. But in retrospect his biggest mistake was not salvaging as much metal from the ship as the survivors could.

From daybreak on the day of the wrecking, and all the while the survivors were making their ways shoreward and merely breathing, the local people were plundering the flotsam and jetsam for whatever metal they could find. Chunks of timber were rendered into firewood, pyres were set to recover all the nails, cleats, fastenings, rings, pins, shackles and every other kind of metal they could. Clearly they had done this before.

Even while bewildered survivors stood on the shore, the Mpondo went among them and relieved them of whatever they could: weapons, broaches, earrings, shoe buckles, anything and everything made of metal. After four days of milling about on shore, with no direction coming from the captain, the group began to break up into smaller parties and set off one at a time for Cape Town. Coxon reckoned the walk would take them 10 days, maybe 17 if things went badly. They did, very.

No sooner had the survivors packed their meagre belongings and begun to wend their ways southwards than they were accosted by locals demanding "*ntsimbi!*" (metal). It turns out they had not thought to repay the locals for the food provided them while they were milling around. When they walked off without offering compensation, it was too much for their hosts.

Few people who know the place would dispute that the Wild Coast is high up on the list of places in South Africa to tick off, but which specific place? The luxury Mngazi River Bungalows, the more rustic Mboyti River Lodge, cosy Trennery's, or no-frills Mazeppa Bay or Kob Inn hotels – any of the dozen or more small old-style family hotels and several smaller backpackers and rustic lodges that are located, conveniently albeit coincidentally, just about one comfortable day's walk apart.

This scenic and dramatic coastline allows for some of the finest hiking and slack-packing, walking or sauntering you'll ever do. Rather than settle for one place, following the story of the straggling and ever-diminishing survivors reveals much about this part of South Africa that retains a kernel of Africa of a bygone age. For them it proved to be no walk in the park, more on the wild side.

To follow the fates – since there were few fortunes – of the survivors, we must turn to the two most reliable historical records because heaven knows there are all too many false accounts flying around. The first is the hand-written diary of William Hubberly, he who first saw the fires of Pondoland and went on to survive the ordeal.

Then there is the official record of the ordeal as laid down by the commission of inquiry appointed by the English East India Company. It was conducted by its principal hydrographer (the man in charge of all seagoing operations) one Alexander Dalrymple, by accounts a "disputatious, cantankerous and formidable Scot".

Theirs is a knotty fabric of threads that tangle and untangle, are torn and sometimes stitched together, each one poignant and harrowing. By following the main characters and groups of stragglers, a patchwork account emerges. At times it can be confusing, but it is never dull. And so, with the trauma of the wreckage now behind, the terrible journey begins …

Once they finally set off from the site of their wretched landfall, you would have thought the first few kilometres would have been easy going as they crossed the beautiful and benign stretch of coast between the Mviti and Mkweni streams. However, clearly it was not because we learn it took them an entire day to make just three to four kilometres.

But it was when they began the strength-sapping ascent of rocky Waterfall Bluff that things really began to deteriorate. The steep-tussocked and boulder-strewn hillside is hardly a doddle, but it is no Matterhorn, or even Ben Nevis. Tiring as they were, though, it was not really the landscape that harassed them.

Somewhere on that grand promontory they were confronted by a horde of warriors complete with spears and shields who came about them, shouting and threatening and stripping them of anything they could. In spite of Captain Coxon's order to offer no resistance, when one of their number was slain, some sailors retaliated.

A running skirmish ensued and when the sailors killed one of the black attackers, things cooled on both sides. It is likely the Mpondo warriors were led by a man known as Bungana. It was he who had arranged to feed the shipwreck survivors while they hung around at Lambazi. When the interlopers left without so much as a cheerio and here's some *ntsimbi* for your troubles, mate, he decided to take vengeance.

Some days later, when two white women were found near starvation hiding in the bush nearby, he took them in. One he chose for his own wife and the other became wife to his brother. Their children, it was told to the Natal settler and trader William Bazley in the mid-1800s, "live among us now".

One benefit of taking a shipwrecked castoff for a wife was that no *lobola* would need to be paid to her family. But the fate of the men who returned to Lambazi was not going to be so welcoming, as we shall see in good time.

As it will in Africa, word of the ungrateful and vulnerable *mzungus* raced ahead of them and so, as they approached kraals hoping to get food, they were most often stoned and chased off. Villagers approached aggressively and ripped whatever they could off the cringing human wash-ups.

All along the way the *Grosvenor* survivors met runaway slaves and various other castaways. At Mboyti – about 18 kilometres south of Waterfall Bluff – they encountered a dark-skinned man who they believed was called Trout. He was Javan born and a former slave of the Dutch; his name likely was Traut. He had a Xhosa wife and children and was on his way to the wreck site to see what he could retrieve. Trout warned the southbound travellers that the Cape was very much further than what they had reckoned.

Captain Coxon and the de facto leader of the group William Hosea (who had bogged down the group at every turn, but not for much longer) begged Trout to guide them and barter on their behalf for food, in exchange for some reward. But the Asian man wanted no part in their pantomime and bade them on their way. The walk from Lambazi over badly broken ground, across beaches and rocky points, foreboding headlands, across rivers and inland around gorges, to Mboyti is not easy. Very soon it was to become even worse.

Immediately south of Lambazi the next significant of many rivers they would have to cross was the Ntafufu. It is not very big, but it seems the travellers had not yet figured out how to work with the tides. The women waded across breast-deep while men carried across the children. It would be the last such act of kindness that would be shown to the group as a whole. And it was here that the wealthy nabob Hosea reached his limit.

The first mate, William Logie, was too sick to walk and was being carried, but only so far. On the north bank of the Ntafufu he was laid down and left with his heavily pregnant wife, Lydia, to fend for themselves. One account has Lydia giving birth in a local *umuzi* or homestead, but dying when she was given unripened corn that brought on dysentery. Another has mother and child surviving and living there "happily ever after".

On the north bank a dishevelled William Hosea sat down "in a state of rigid mortification" while his wife, Mary, holding their baby daughter, Frances, waved – more likely wailed – farewell to the rest. Many years later, an expedition from the Cape Colony believed they had seen Mary and Frances living in a village somewhere in Pondoland.

In the mid-1850s William Bazley was sure he'd met a "very old lady" near Ixopo, with long white hair and speaking isiZulu, who was

Frances Hosea. But the stories are all so tangled it's hard to say, other than that the European and Asian survivors of many shipwrecks along the South African coast enriched local bloodlines.

Just five days into their struggle against the harsh realities of the African mainland, the remainder of the party faced what would be their biggest challenge of the entire saga – the Mzimvubu (hippo) River flanked by the two massive, heavily forested sandstone promontories now known as mounts Thesiger and Sullivan. First, they had to battle upstream to find a place narrow and shallow enough to cross. Along the way they encountered their second most exacting obstacle of the entire homeward journey: a tributary in flood that proved to be the undoing of many more of them.

These were not the gentle woods of England but snake-infested, thorn-armoured, tangled African sub-tropical forest. There were also many strange and terrifying animals, such as elephants much larger and more destructive than the Asian species some of them would have known back in India. Also, brutish rhinos, not to mention angry hippos in just about every river. Also, lions and hyenas and leopards.

At this stage many had lost their "ship" shoes and those who still had any would have found them inappropriate and inadequate for the challenges of the rugged African coastline. *Grosvenor* biographer Stephen Taylor points out that, had the ship been wrecked 50 or 60 kilometres further south, things might have turned out far better for the shipwrecked wretches.

On the bank of the flooding tributary, rafts were made from driftwood (had they reached this spot just a month earlier they could have waded across). The stronger of the swimmers among them made it across under their own steam, or sail, as it were. One lascar is said to have swum across the river pulling with him seven-year-old Mary Wilmot, but that is the last that was heard of her.

One man simply refused to go any further and is said to have expired on the spot. On watching the pandemonium of various attempted crossings, one woman chose to strangle herself with her own silken scarf. All but two of the children and most of the remaining women – including the heavily pregnant Mrs Logie, according to some records – were simply abandoned there. Not knowing what else to do, they turned around and headed back towards the site of the wreck.

While crossing the main Mzimvubu, Captain Coxon's group on a makeshift driftwood raft was upended by an angry hippo and a number of them were killed and drowned. They were still only one week into their trek and the number of the walking fit had been whittled down to about half the original 123 (or 125) souls that were first stranded alive.

Looking on while all the remaining men and a few women went off across the Mzimvubu, young Thomas Law became inconsolable. On the voyage from India he'd become strongly attached to the steward Henry Lilburne. Master Law was one of several children who had boarded the *Grosvenor* in the care of family friends or nannies, sent back "home" for schooling in the more amenable climate of Britain.

A huddle was called and Lilburne and his group agreed they would carry Master Law across with them, come hell or high water. This was the strongest group consisting of 50 or so sailors being led by the ship's carpenter, Mr Page. For them Thomas had become something of a mascot and they looked after him, fed him and carried him when needed. He became their glue. Hazel Crampton, author of the book about the shipwrecks of the Wild Coast, *The Sunburnt Queen*, reckons they conferred on him all the compassion they withheld from one another (rumours of cannibalism included).

Also among the carpenter's original group were four Indian or lascar women, maids of European passengers. Two of them eventually reached the Cape while another two are thought to have settled south of the Mngazana River, possibly the progenitors of the amaMolo, a clan that traces its maternal line back to "black" (Indian) female shipwreck survivors. Although, as Crampton points out, it could have been women from any number of shipwrecks.

Seeing Page and the sailors set off on their own, Captain Coxon promised to pay handsomely anyone who stuck with him. Coxon was one of two men who were known to have got off the ship with sizeable fortunes in uncut diamonds. The other was William Hosea and what happened to his horde is unknown. Coxon's, however, is the subject of much conjecture and possibly the source of the biggest treasure legend to grip South Africa. While the captain was last seen near the Mtata River mouth, his diamonds almost certainly made it further.

On the south bank of the Mzimvubu, where today the lethargic town of Port St Johns slowly abandons its old colonial façade for more ethnic air, another group coalesced around second mate William Shaw. Between the Mngazi and Mngazana rivers they met locals who said they were "people of Bessie". The stragglers had entered Tembu territory and found the local people to be, if not overjoyed to see them, at least not openly hostile.

William Hubberly, the young seaman who had seen "the lights" on the night of the wrecking, was in the group. In his hand-written account that was uncovered in the Durban Museum mid-last century, he notes how different was their reception here (no doubt due to the presence of a white "queen").

They gratefully accepted a bullock offered them, as well as milk. Some of the group made shoes from the hide of the slaughtered animal, but not very long afterwards hunger drove them to literally eat their shoes. From around here the various homebound groups broke up and reformed, but at each waypoint their numbers had dwindled.

Returning briefly to Lambazi … When the regional chief of the area heard that a number of the survivors had returned to the wreck site, he allowed the women and children to remain but ordered that all the men be put to death. When news of the incident reached Bessie, it is said her hair turned snow white overnight. At least one European man avoided the bloodletting, and we'll meet him, John Bryan, in due course.

Having overcome the spiky mangrove fringe of Mngazana, the rivers southwards become generally tamer, smaller and easier to cross, the landscape much less daunting, even though there are more frequent records of encounters with elephants. But one major geographical obstacle lay ahead of the walkers, Brazen Head. It carved its own notch in the tally stick of the *Grosvenor*.

Five of the group expired while surmounting the great promontory. One was the carpenter Page who died here after eating the pods of a poisonous vine (possibly the poison rope, *Strophanthus speciosus*, that is used traditionally for arrow poison).

Beyond Brazen Head the remaining wayfarers noted how the

people in the kraals around present-day Hluleka Nature Reserve looked very different: "they are yellowish and have longer hair (than the Bomvana around Mngazi), which is tightly curled up in the manner of a turban." These were the amaMolo.

Somewhere around here, near the Mpande River, Mr Shaw figured that a more inland route might be easier and that in the higher, more fertile grasslands the local people would be more willing to share their food. This caused another split, with the greater number following Shaw and the rest sticking to the coast under the new leadership of Lilburne, who had taken over from the dead carpenter Thomas Page.

The coastal party made good progress across the rivers by fashioning effective rafts. Meanwhile Shaw's group struggled inland across terrain that proved far more rugged than what he'd hoped for. Anyone who has driven the gravel back roads linking Elliotdale, Willowvale, Centani, up and down, around and over, gorge after gorge such as the spectacular Collywobbles and Cats passes among them, will sympathise. On the other hand, they did find people willing to give up food, but only in exchange for whatever metal objects they still possessed.

On reaching the upper reaches of the Bashee (Mbashe) River, Shaw decided to head back to the coast where they were reunited with those who remained under Lilburne (including Thomas Law). Now they passed into the lands of the Gcaleka people who had no beef with the pale strangers. The walkers were hardly molested, although still offered virtually no food – with the exception of the lad Tom, who Xhosa women singled out and gave milk when they passed villages.

Over the next 10 days Shaw's party, such as it was, lost half its number, even though the terrain offered much less resistance than previously. On 15 September, Shaw had reached the end of his own road. By now they were all on the verge between life and death from exhaustion but mainly due to starvation. For three days and nights "he lay on his back in sand, a pitiful, half-naked scarecrow". Faithful William Habberly stayed with him, feeding him water from mussel shells.

Hubberly records that when they passed the area between the Mtata and Bashee rivers (more or less where the Cwebe and Dwesa nature reserves are found today) it was uninhabited. For three weeks they did not see another person. Now they were approaching the land of the more prosperous Xhosa people which consisted, as it does today, of two main groups: the Rarabe inland, and the Gcaleka along the coast. From here the routes chosen by the various groups of stragglers would have profound effects on their fortunes.

At the Qora River, where today the Kob Inn welcomes the most ardent of fisherfolk, a group stripped to cross. On the far bank a group of Xhosa rifled their belongings before they could dress. The stragglers asked for food and were offered milk, but when they could provide no payment, the milk was given to the Xhosa's dogs.

The next 30 kilometres presented no significant rivers or indeed any other obstacles other than the daily grind of foraging for food – periwinkles, limpets and occasionally mussels and crabs, sometimes berries or washed up items – locating drinking water, collecting firewood and walking, walking, walking. And all along the shoreline they left dead bodies.

On 2 October Lilburne's group reached the Kei River and found the people living there to be neither hostile nor friendly. But once again, because they no longer had any trinkets or brass buttons to trade, the "wretched and despised coastal scavengers" were shown off. The record states that some of them perished there "through great weariness".

However, when a few others reached the same spot some days later, they were set upon with sticks and stones and harshly beaten. There is no record of anyone dying there, but it is possible, even likely in the events that followed, that someone in the party buried something significant.

At the Buffalo River, which runs through modern-day East London, things got even more violent. Hubberly managed to bolt into dense bush but his two remaining companions, Williams and Taylor, were less fortunate. Williams was stabbed to death and thrown into the river. Taylor was also set upon with assegais and left for dead. After dark, Hubberly crawled out of his hiding place and found Taylor alive but only barely.

The unharmed man made the by-then customary driftwood raft and they made it across. Hubberly found a dead turtle washed up with a clutch of eggs inside but Taylor was too weak to eat even a soft egg and died there.

Near Kleinmond's twin lagoons we find Hubberly alone, and his next encounter was symptomatic of the cultural misunderstandings that have dogged this part of the world ever since. He staggered into an *umuzi* of the peaceful Gqunukwebe people who, after initially taking fright, took pity on the wild-looking man: his torso was cadaverous, he was barefoot, wore cut-off trousers, a woman's shawl around his shoulders and a trouser leg on his head.

But he overindulged on their kindness and in the night had to relieve himself. He thought the cattle kraal would be an inoffensive place to let loose, but could hardly have been more mistaken. In Xhosa culture the kraal is a sacred place and burial place of the clan leader. When it was discovered he had defiled this place of the ancestors, he was harshly driven away.

Meanwhile, steward Lilburne's party, bearing along brave Tom Law, was battling on, encountering both elephants and hippos. At the Keiskamma River they had to take evasive action when a herd of elephants came crashing through the dense bush towards the river. Somewhere they met a black man who spoke fluent Portuguese and Dutch. He cooked a meal for the half dozen or so stragglers before seeing them on their way.

When they spotted a scrawny village dog, they managed to catch it, waited until dark, strangled it with a piece of handkerchief, cut it up with mussel shells and cooked it on a fire. It wasn't much for the group; between the Kei and Keiskamma more than a dozen perished.

Still they trudged on, past the modern holiday spots of Morgan Bay, Haga Haga, Chintsa, Port Alfred, Kenton-on-Sea ... They would not have known, firstly, that they were nearing the end of their ordeal or, secondly, that they were approaching what would prove to be the greatest challenge of the entire journey.

Near the mouth of the Bushman's River they came upon a washed-up whale carcass. But it turned out the meat was too far gone, and soon thereafter so was Tom. Uncharacteristically in this tale, instead of just abandoning the lad, the men stayed with him until he died on 2 November.

His death seemed to undo Lilburne's resolve who, only a little way further on, simply fell down, face in the sand, and never rose.

This in turn seemed to take the fight out of a few more of the party who simply "laid themselves down". When the story of young Master Law reached England, it became the stuff of folktale and was told and retold by writers, including Charles Dickens.

At this point those still going had been walking for some three months and were little more than 50 kilometres from the first white settler farms. But the worst tribulations awaited them just around the corner from Cape Padrone where, in 1488, Bart Dias had left his most eastward cross. Ahead of them lay a seemingly endless sand sea: the 40-odd kilometres of shifting, waterless, coastal dunes. (Some sources claim it is the largest such expanse on the planet, but clearly they have never seen the southern Namibian coast.)

Most of the survivors who entered the Alexandria dune field died there. Those who survived did whatever they had to. Accounts show that the ordeal brought out the very finest alongside the most brutish of human nature.

Three of the original carpenter's party reached the Sunday's River, blinded by the glare of the sand, crazed by thirst, hunger and privation. In sight of the green hills beyond the river they thought they saw some birds approaching them. The birds turned out to be the last three survivors from the 50-strong "sailors group" that had been the first to set off from the Mzimvubu.

They helped the new arrivals to a freshwater spring and then went back for one of the party, Wormington, who, in a semi-demented state, had refused to go any further just a few kilometres back. When one of the rescue party heard that one of their number lay in the dunes two days' march back, in a still-fine set of clothing, decided to go back for them. He was never seen again.

The six forlorn men slept next to the spring and in the morning woke to be greeted by a well-clothed and -fed man carrying a musket. They could not understand what he said but understood he worked for a Dutch farmer nearby. And thus did their long walk end at the farm of one Mynheer Christiaan Ferreira (although one source has it as a Christian Roostoff). Names aside, from there they were taken to Swellendam to recuperate and thereafter on to Cape Town.

Accounts of the survivors reached England in fragmentary dispatches.

Newspaper reports there became hysterical about the prospects of British women succumbing to "savage" black men, being dragged ashore only to be thrown into the "vilest brutish prostitution". What they did not mention was that the delicate white women had chosen that course rather than face almost certain death on a homeward march.

This proved too vile for the colonial mind to bear and pressure was put on the Dutch authorities at the Cape to "do something about it". More than four months after the first six survivors were located, a large rescue expedition set out to look for the poor women and children and any other survivors that might be still alive: 47 wagons, more than 800 oxen, about 100 colonists, 200 Khoi servants, about 200 horses as well as slaughter cattle set out.

They managed to gather up a further 12 stragglers, including William Hubberly, who they found hanging on near Kenton-on-Sea, as well as two lascar women. Strangely, though, the expedition got no further north than Coffee Bay, which is far short of the actual wreck site. Then again, pulling wagons over that broken terrain would have been no easy task.

When the full story of the ordeal was published in 1808 it had the effusive title "Affecting Narrative of the Loss of the Grosvenor, Indiaman, Captain Coxon, August 4, 1782; Including the Unparalleled Sufferings and Wonderful Deliverance of Some of the Wretched Survivors, During the Melancholy Period of One Hundred and Seventeen Days, and the Dreadful Fate of the Rest". Indeed.

It was published by Thomas Tegg, Cheapside, London, one sixpence a copy.

Today at Lambazi you will find what is left of not so much the wreck itself, but various attempts to salvage it. Over the course of 200 years, legend had subsumed into myth and myth turned to rumours, rumours to fact and fact to frenzy about the great treasures that were lost when the ship went down. Top of the list was the legendary Peacock Throne which, the wisdom went, had gone missing from India around that time (most common accounts published last century have it pillaged in Persia).

Throughout last century there was a kind of protracted *Grosvenor* treasure rush. Captain Sydney Turner, a trader at Port St Johns, was the first to ... you might say work the site, but what he actually did beggars belief. He arrived at Port Grosvenor aboard the vessel *Adonis* in 1880 and promptly dynamited the wreck site. He managed to retrieve some British, Indian and Venetian coins as well as several of the ship's cannons. But likely he blew much of the rest to smithereens.

During the early 20th century, various salvage operations were floated, such as the Grosvenor Bullion Company. Shares were sold, big monies raised and a circus of fortune seekers descended on the place. Someone tried to build a sort of stone coffer dam around the wreck site, but the wild Indian Ocean was having none of that. Another hauled a steam crane down from the reef by ox wagon with the intention of lifting out the remains of the wreck. Another built floating barges to try to dive the site (see above: wild Indian Ocean).

One bright man with stars in his eyes began digging a tunnel from the shore, hoping to burrow right underneath the wreck. Just what he planned to do with an entire ocean when it poured in is anyone's guess. Fortunes were lost. There are also a few more serious archaeological attempts to "dig" the site.

In the 1990s a large cache of coins was salvaged by professional divers. They also recovered bits of porcelain and other tableware, various brass nautical objects, as well as more cannons. Additional cannons and an anchor were left lodged firmly against the reef.

On a windswept day during a tropical cyclone around 30 years ago, I went sauntering out from Lambazi Bay. On a grassy knoll near Waterfall Bluff I came upon a pile of iron ingots, grass and bush almost concealing them, that were clearly not of recent provenance. I remembered the poem by Mike Kirkwood "Henry Fynn and the Blacksmith of the Grosvenor".

It recounts the story of the *Grosvenor*'s smith who decided to stay put at Lambazi, salvage as much metal as he could and to ply his precious trade among the grateful Mpondo. This would have been John Bryan, not a blacksmith at all but a decommissioned soldier on his way back to Blighty. He had grabbed onto some flotsam and got his leg badly gashed on his way to shore. When the others set off, he told them he was too weak to join them, but some of his colleagues guessed he was bluffing.

In due course he did set himself up as a purveyor of all things metal and his skills were highly regarded by the local populace. In time he took a wife from the local folk and fathered several children. We can conjecture why he was not slain along with the men who found their ways back to wreck site: he had already by then showed his worth in working *ntsimbi*, sore leg or no.

But there are yet a few last twists in the untangled rope-end of this maritime tale. Early last century a farmer of German extraction found a sizeable horde of uncut diamonds on his land close to the Kei ferry crossing. There was a rush to the spot and, when it proved fallow, farmer John Boch was accused of "salting" the ground. He was charged with fraud but his defence argued that the diamonds could not have been of local extraction and must have come from a wrecked ship, most likely the *Grosvenor*.

The judge wasn't buying it, Boch was declared guilty and imprisoned. However, people who have researched the story in depth hold that the diamonds almost certainly had belonged to either Coxon or another of the *Grosvenor*'s wealthy passengers, feeble-bodied William Hosea. The diamonds, about 1 000 in all, disappeared during the trial and have not been heard of since.

About 18 months after the wreck, some Xhosa men who were travelling past Algoa Bay were asked if they knew of any of the survivors who might be still alive. Oh yes, they replied, but their own people were now dying in great numbers. It seems that at least one survivor brought ashore a deadly fever. Within a decade it was reported the region had been decimated by the pox (possibly what had felled first mate Logie on the fated night).

Sitting atop Waterfall Bluff, watching the Mlambomkhulu (big river) dive over the cliffs into the pounding waves below, or nearby at Cathedral Rock where arches, towers and flying buttresses of layered sandstone stand with their foundations in the sea, entreats one to ponder: did any one of those ill-fated shipwreck survivors ever sit down in a place like this and think how lovely it was?

Hogsback

A Place of Waterfalls, Gunsmoke and a Faerie Garden: Searching for a Rare Bird

No one passes through Hogsback, as it is not on the way to anywhere but itself. It's hardly even a place in the sense of a town, or even village. It is a mountain escape set deep in the Amathole Mountains, ancestral refuge of the southern Xhosa people.

WHEN SOMEONE SAYS "HOGSBACK" what is the first thing you think of? Probably Hobbits, Tolkien and faeries? Most people do. Names of places there such as Hobbiton, Tor Doone and Hunterstoun do seem to recall some kind of shire-ish setting, greatly enhanced by the glorious greenery of high, deep and tangled Afro-montane forest, English-style gardens all abloom with roses, azaleas, rhododendrons and lanes of hazelnut and berry trees.

Tolkien's fictional forest of Mirkwood does seem to perfectly describe the magical feelings of the Hogsback village and surrounding mountains, forests, fragrant pine plantations, myriad chattering streams and billowing waterfalls. Many early accounts of the place inform us that the young John Ronald Reuel spent joyous holidays here, running through the woods just as William Wordsworth described his own youth in the Lake District:

When first I came among these hills,
When like a roe
I bounded o'er the mountains, by the sides
Of the deep rivers, and the lonely streams,
Wherever nature led ...

Just about everyone who has ever visited the place over the past century or more has commented on its unfathomable enchantments, whether in summer when the hills and dales are all aflush with wild flowers such as shooting stars, irises, hare bells, watsonias and of course the helichrysums, in which reside the spirits of the dead ancestors. Or in winter when snow lies deep on the sensual folds of the hills, hangs on yellowwood and pine boughs, and icicles cling to cottage eaves.

Of course, every place is unique, and is what it is. But Hogsback is exceptional in a much more special way: the high mountains are the southernmost outlier of the Drakensberg, blanketed under heavy snows in most winters – a high land that is a world apart, like an English village surrounded by pastoral Africa.

But it is very unlikely that Tolkien ever visited Hogsback or, if he did, he would have been very young and baby John would have had absolutely no memory of the place, and certainly would not have run around the place like a deer. His father, Arthur Reuel, was an English banker who was sent with his young wife, Mabel, to run a branch in far-away Bloemfontein, capital of the Orange Free State Republic.

John was born there in 1892. At the age of three, his mother took him and his younger brother, Hilary, on a holiday back to England. While his family was awaiting him, Arthur died in Bloemfontein and Mabel and the children never returned. It is much more likely that the fantastical worlds and characters that JRR created took seed around the Malvern Hills, Moseley Bog, Sarehole Mill and his aunt Jane's farm Bag End in the shire of Worcester, than in any South African Middle Earth.

The first direct Tolkienesque reference we come across high up in the Amathole hills is a holiday farm named Hobbiton. But it seems the place, established in 1947 for underprivileged children, was inspired by Tolkien's first book, *The Hobbit*, published 10 years previously. Anyone reading the book and then exploring the wild African hills, the gnarled forests and bountiful streams would easily have been drawn into a realm of otherworldly sagas and grand, thronely games.

That sorted, next comes the subject of the name. Some references suggest it honours a British officer Hogg who campaigned there during the Frontier Wars. However, more scholarly sources tell us the name is first seen in the diaries of the artist-explorer Thomas Baines who passed that way in the late 1840s. He reckoned it was a reference to the three rocky ridges that rise above the village and resemble the raised hair or razorbacks found on wild pigs.

The approach to Hogsback is up the Tyumie (or Tyume) Valley, refuge of the Rarebe Xhosa and "great place" of Paramount Chief Ngqika. But the colonial map that was drawn up by Eastern Cape Governor and military commander Harry Smith around 1850 cut it in half, the western side for the Colony and the eastern side for Ngqika's people.

You can just image the latter were far from thrilled that white people grazed their herds and trod on the graves of their chiefs and ancestors. This was exacerbated by mounting aggression over strayed cattle: anyone who has driven through Ciskei or Transkei will know the locals there have a rather fluid attitude as to where their cattle, or sheep, wander. In this world view boundaries are not absolute, whether river or road.

Meanwhile, back in Grahamstown, after numerous skirmishes and two genuine wars against the various Xhosa confederations, sometimes allied to disaffected Khoi groups, the settlers' hearts were hardening. From the relatively poor grazing of the Zuurveld, always prone to drought, and the tough thorn thickets known as Eastern Cape valley bushveld, they gazed up towards the distant Amathole

Mountains and dreamed of acquiring more fruitful pastures.

One of them described the far-off mountains so:

"The sides are clothed with noble forests ... Streams without number wind their way through rich fertile valleys. The perpetual verdure, the rich flora, the wildly picturesque view, give an untiring interest to this region of beauty and grandeur."

Stirred up by the unapologetically imperialist and reactionary editor of the *Graham's Town Journal*, Robert Godlonton, right across the Eastern Frontier tensions mounted. The expulsion of chiefs Maqoma and Tyali from first the Kat and later the Tyumie valleys pushed them to breaking strain. Godlonton agitated for all Xhosa lands to be seized and handed over to British settler farmers.

The Sixth (1834–35) and Seventh (1846–47) Frontier Wars had seen the strongest groups of Xhosa under chiefs Maqoma and Sandile pushed back from the Great Fish to the Keiskamma River and then up into the Katberg and Amathole Mountains. To help shore up his line, Smith had built redoubts at King William's Town, his forward base, and from west to east across the south-facing base of the Amathole, forts Beaufort, Hare, Wiltshire, Cox and White.

For three mercilessly hot and dry months towards the end of 1850 Harry Smith's army, commanded in the field by Colonel George MacKinnon – someone history paints only marginally kindlier than the other senior commander, Henry Somerset – battled to force Maqoma out of the rugged Katberg mountains that stand to the immediate west of the Amathole.

They thought they had, and so moved the base of operations from Fort Armstrong eastwards to Fort Cox in order to make a fresh push up into the heart of the Amathole to force Chief Sandile out of there too. On the western front, however, no sooner had MacKinnon's column moved off than Maqoma's men moved right back into the Katberg.

On 24 December a force of 650 men, infantry and cavalry, supported by colonials and "native" troops – again under MacKinnon – made for the base of the Boma (also referred to as Boomah) Pass, then the principal route to the grassy summit grazing plateaus of the Amathole range. The name of this massif means "place of young cattle", meaning a fertile place, or proverbial land of milk and honey.

Hogsback

It was another scorching day, in more ways than one, and it would be remembered as a particularly black one for the British Army. It is largely forgotten now only because it was overshadowed by the day of the dark moon nearly 30 years later on a grassy slope in far-off Zululand.

As background to the Eighth and most violent, unforgiving, bloody and longest of all the Frontier Wars, master historian Noel Mostert piles up the evidence against colonials by referring to the ignorance of Cape Governor Benjamin D'Urban; the incompetence and muddling of Henry Somerset, most senior officer in the Eastern Cape after Harry Smith; the conservative and intolerant attitudes of the Grahamstown population and arrogance of the British settlers in general.

Mostert further discusses general indifference on the British side to the Xhosa plight or suffering (against whom the British Army used scorched-earth tactics), to the Xhosa perspective on the frontier situation and how they had been progressively forced back over several decades. Finally, he throws in the "ruthless deceits" and "connivances" of the Trekboers, ever eager to grab cattle, land, women and labourers, and to seek military recourse to any attempts by the Xhosa to retaliate.

It was a different world back then and people lived by some different rules on the wild frontier. Still, some universal truths do percolate to us through time. One was the Trekboers' thirst for freedom, free land and distance from the British Cape. Then the British settlers, who were dumped in a still mostly untamed landscape and told to just get on with it. And the Xhosa's own issues regarding land, political succession and overcrowding.

As a balance, it is interesting to note the views of a minority of white people in the region at the time, such as governor under Dutch rule Andries Stockenström who attempted to rein in the colonists' rapacious land grabs; the missionaries in general and Charles Lennox Stretch, a philanthropic member of the early Cape Parliament. Stretch had served as a colonel in the Sixth Frontier war so was no stranger to the area and its issues. The Xhosa named him Xolilizwe, the peacemaker.

The summer of 1850–51 was proving to be a hellishly hot and dry one in the Eastern Cape. The British regulars especially, not used to the conditions there, had suffered greatly during the three months they pursued Maqoma's army through the Katberg. On 18 December supreme British commander Harry Smith arrived at Fort Cox. He was happy with the situation as he saw it, finding the country to be "peaceful and contented".

He truly believed the Xhosa people had taken to him like a father. Pushing his luck, he wanted to strip the tribal chiefs of their rank and influence. In this he had some backing from D'Urban back west. He informed the Xhosa that he did not want or intend war and would not send his redcoats after the principle chiefs of that region, Sandile, Ngqika (his oldest foe), Maqoma and Anta … and then sent Colonel MacKinnon out on an "intimidatory expedition" up the Boma Pass.

The column set off in the pre-dawn from Fort Cox, hoping to make it into the high mountains, above forest and crags, by mid-morning. The soldiers were followed by a long train of pack-mules carrying food, ammunition, medical supplies, tents and baggage (a British officer did not want to give up all his comforts and luxuries in the wilds of Africa). One of the biggest problems on the day was the rank-and-file soldiers had not been informed it was supposed to only be a show of strength.

Entering the green gloom of the gorge that forms the headwaters of the Keiskamma River, the stars began to fade (today the pass is mainly covered by Sandile Dam). The experienced Major John Bisset had noticed newly erected stone cairns and informed his fellow officers to keep alert. When the column stopped for breakfast, the vigilant Bisset, scanning the heights with his field glasses, noticed large numbers of Xhosas congregating along the ridges above. MacKinnon refused to believe they had any hostile intentions.

The morning progressed without incident as the British troops slogged in single file up the steep, overgrown path towards Zingcuka Ridge. By the time MacKinnon and Bisset emerged at the head of the pass, their column was spread out in a thin line about three kilometres long. Any attempt at communication could only lead to further confusion, and that was the moment the Xhosa chose to attack.

Ensign Thomas Lucas was riding with the ammunition pack-mules alongside the stream and observed: "What a jolly place it would be for a picnic, with shade and water so close." When the first shot from a

Xhosa or Khoi marksman boomed through the gorge, he remarked that the officers ahead were probably enjoying some game shooting.

"We are the game!" replied Dr William Stuart.

Bugles called up and down the pass, only adding to the confusion: should the troops proceed up, or retreat down the pass? No one was sure. Major Bisset read the situation and, ignoring MacKinnon's instructions to stay put, turned his horse and drove down into the pass in the hope of bringing some order to the inexperienced infantry trapped there. He noticed thousands of Xhosa warriors streaming down the opposite bank. "My God, sir," shouted his orderly, "don't go in there!" He did anyway.

Bisset was wounded almost the minute he joined the fray, the short-range shot hitting him so hard it caused his horse to stagger. He managed to shoot one off from the hip, wounding his assailant.

"I have hit him," shouted the Xhosa.

"I have got it," replied the major.

Bisset found Stuart sitting against a rock, blood streaming from his chest. As the officer bent to attend to the doctor, a second shot struck and blew the doctor's brains over Bisset's face and jacket. And so the day progressed. Bisset managed to lead a large proportion of the infantry to the head of the pass where they were able to make a defensive stand and work their way over to where MacKinnon was waiting out of enemy range. Bisset observed it was so hot the varnish on the peak of his military cap was melting.

This left a Lieutenant Armytage cut off in the pass. He and his troops fought rock to rock, tree to tree. He led them off the path where they were easy targets and into the forest alongside. They were able to hack their way up to reach MacKinnon's position. The pass was littered with the British dead. "As we marched away," recalled Ensign Lucas later, "we could hear the triumphant yells of the enemy, who in a moment seemed to fill the whole bush."

The success gained over the redcoats emboldened the Xhosa chiefs to send their armies down the mountains to attack the British forts and small settlements strung between them. They besieged their ultimate enemy, Harry Smith, inside Fort Cox. The Khoi people of the Blinkwater and Kat River settlements joined the Xhosa struggle en masse. While Smith managed to escape from the fort one night, his reputation did not follow. It was not long before the bigwigs realised it was Smith's ineptitude that had started the war, and he was dismissed.

On a wild and stormy night on 25 February 1852, the troop ship *Birkenhead*, carrying mostly Irish reinforcements that had been requested by Harry Smith immediately following the disastrous Boma Pass incident, wrecked on a rocky reef near the southern tip of Africa. All women and children aboard were saved from the churning, shark-teeming waters; the troops were not.

The Xhosa were slowly driven back, fort by fort, hill by hill and valley by valley but, although they realised the war was lost, their leaders were loath to surrender unconditionally their ancestral lands to white settlers. It took another year of fighting before Chief Sandile and his entourage descended the Amathole heights and down their beloved Tyumie valley, to surrender to the new British commander on the Eastern Frontier, George Cathcart.

The press back in England was scathing of the whole affair. Smith, Somerset and even new Governor George Grey were accused of conduct unbecoming. Of the settlers *The Times of London* said that, if they chose to stay close to the Xhosa people, they should do so at their own risk. Cathcart was of a similar view. Britain did not want a large colony in South Africa, "only a small territory around Cape Town". The settlers, the Trekboers and the British military felt otherwise.

But the end of the war proved to be something of a lose-lose affair. Even Cathcart, who had told the Xhosa chiefs he did not foresee them or their people ever returning to the Amathole, said "It was a peace that, like every South African peace so far, satisfied no one."

Even though the Xhosa people lost the region, no wide-scale white encroachment was permitted. However, although settler enclaves did grow around Fort Beaufort, King William's Town and a few other places, and some choice agricultural land was taken, it was never enough for them. The Xhosa people had lost nearly everything.

It is really hard to believe when you are up there, that this fairy-tale mountainland, high and cool and green and quaint, could in the past have been beset by such violent upheavals. Then again, every place and indeed every person that's been around for a while will have an interesting past. And so it is with Hogsback.

The first white people we find living up there were woodcutters. A growing colony needed timber and these mountains had extensive natural forests. A small settlement took root in a cool valley at the very summit of the Tyumie Valley. Among the first to make crude wattle-and-clay and thatched cottages had the names Booysens and Odendaal. They didn't, but if they had, the sign they painted on the side of their timber shed might have advertised:

B & O Venote/Partners

Yellowwood, ironwood, white and black stinkwood, white and red pear, assegaiwood and many other varieties, finest logs in Kaffraria (that was the name given to the region).

Some Brits, being the odd hatters they are, followed close behind. Notable was Thomas Summerton, who dug a water furrow down the slopes of Tor Doone to the farm he named Cherrie Orchard. He started many of the arboreal avenues and flower gardens around "town". He was a gardener back in Oxford and found the verdant conditions high up in the Eastern Cape mountains much like those of his ancestral home.

A trip to the Hogsback Hydro back in the 1880s must have been an arduous undertaking and anyone arriving there must have seriously wanted to "take the waters". The winding road up from the Tyumie Valley was built only in 1932 when the summit vale became a popular place to build rudimentary mountain cabins. When motor traffic came, the hydro became Hogsback Inn, where weary travellers still warm cold feet by a wood fire and lay their weary heads, although it is hardly the only one.

Another is Arminel, which started life as a wooden shop named the Handy Log Cabin. And Hunterstoun, built in 1910 as the private estate of David Hunter, secretary and treasurer of the Lovedale Institution in Alice, the forerunner of Fort Hare University. Hogsback might well have remained a hamlet had not Kenneth Houghton decided to extend the little chapel he'd built exclusively for his wife in 1935 so anyone could come there to worship. More recent arrivals have built eco-shrines, labyrinths and a very alternative gathering place named Away With The Faeries.

In the mornings, if you are lucky, you will be wakened by the *kok-kok-kok* of Knysna turacos, rather than by those cacophonous Eastern Cape economic refugees, the hadedas. The call of the turaco is not exactly charming, but the birds certainly are. However, they are outranked here by an even nobler VIP, a very important parrot.

Walking up Tor Doone or the Hogsbacks, to the Madonna and Child, Swallowtail, Bridal Veil, or Thirty Nine Steps waterfalls, or deeper into the forest to visit the Big Tree, you'll be surprised at how many large forest colossuses remain, including numerous stately yellowwoods. Fruiting forest species include two types of wild pear, wild peach and others, but it is primarily the yellowwoods which sustain the parrots, as they do the turacos.

There might be fewer than 1 600 Cape parrots left alive in the wilds, their final stronghold being the forests of the Amathole Mountains. The Cape Parrot Project is based in Hogsback, and if you see someone walking at intense pace, carrying electronica and with a busy look about them, it'll likely be one of them – not one of the parrots, but one of the parrot researchers. They are usually only too happy to stop, pant a bit and share with you their latest video or information about where the birds are currently gathering in the evenings; they tend to have favourite roosts depending on what is fruiting and where.

"Excuse me, but we seem to have missed something," said the nice woman striding over to our camper at Swallowtail Country Estate with a look of high expectation. "Where is the 'place', I mean Hogsback, the village? We were expecting something arty and gentrified, like Clarens."

"Well lady, you've sure came a long way to find the wrong place," I informed her … Of course, I didn't actually say that. What I did say was more along the lines of: and that, precisely, is the charm of the place. There is no real *place*, not in the sense of a good old town planning central-place theory.

It's more a motley accumulation of mavericks, eccentrics, recluses, artists and various shades of nonconformists living, not so much in a town, or a village, or even a hamlet, but in cabins in the forest and along back roads and lanes. There are a few stores, and some eating places, but no single focal point.

It's like a secluded, forested Nowhere land where a sign hangs on a tree, informing wayfarers that the inhabitants are "away with the faeries".

The Garden Route

A Post-Apocalyptic Gateway, a Man with a Theodolite Eye and a Very Small Flag: Searching for the Real Garden Route

A "garden route" conjures different mental pictures for different people, but at the very least you would expect a place of untrammelled natural beauty. Yet the area between the Gourits and Storms River bridges is dominated by a multi-lane highway and runaway coastal developments. Whatever happened to the garden?

HAVING DRIVEN THE CELEBRATED Garden Route, visitors from afar often comment that, "Ze route vas very gut, ja, but ver vas ze garten?" Or "Nice highway there, mate, but where's the bleedin' gardin?"

We locals know there is a garden in the route, somewhere.

We've seen it, if only in bits and pieces, mostly in our youths, but it gets harder and harder to find.

Take that grand portal to Mossel Bay, Mossgas. If ever a town had a visible alimentary canal, that has to be it. When they were younger, I used to tell my children that the post-apocalyptic alchemists' cauldron of fire, brimstone and belching smoke was a climate change factory. "They take gas from under the sea, pipe it here and turn it into air pollution."

But indeed there is a garden of many natural earthly delights, moss and fern-frilled forests, rocky points and enticing coves with fine-sand beaches, mountain ranges folding one into the other, little towns clinging like barnacles to the shore and farm stalls where you'll find ambrosial honey and the best fresh-baked pies.

The problem is that it's been substantially obscured by crass runaway holiday towns, roses, azaleas and precision-trimmed kikuyu lawns and spill-over ghettos (which enjoy some of the finest real estate in the country), all stitched together by a double-lane road that perfectly conforms to the government standard national highway protocol.

The secret is to slow down, turn off the air-con, roll down the windows, wind up the road music – a recommended opening track would be Joni Mitchell singing about getting back to the garden in her song 'Woodstock' – and take the first detour that catches your fancy.

There are two options for bypassing Mossgas and Mossel Bay (which has some nice bits but is no parkland), each with its own roadside attractions. The first is to swing north after passing Swellendam, nip through Suurbraak and then over the Tradouw Pass to Barrydale, connect with rolling Route 62 through the Little Karoo, take a right at Oudtshoorn and from there head down to George.

The other is to continue eastwards on the N2, through the lovely wheat and canola fields of the Overberg, where the undulating *rûens* are often alive with steppe buzzards, white storks and those most gracious of all southern African birds, the dancing blue cranes, that have survived the indignity of once being a threatened species.

Swoop over the Gourits River Bridge, avert your gaze to avoid that folly called the Garden Route Game Lodge and then turn off to Herbertsdale. The secret of the trip is to take the less-travelled back roads through mountain and forest wherever a fork beckons.

The Garden Route

From the Oudtshoorn side you want to descend the interior piedmont to reach the coastal plateau via Montagu Pass – and not the Outeniqua Pass which, in spite of having been first constructed by incredible Thomas Bain, today bears about as much resemblance to his original masterpiece as Donald Duck does to *Swan Lake*.

Even though the entire area around the Montagu Pass was burned to charcoal and dust in 2018, including the historic toll house, it remains a driver's delight with 126 bends, twists and turns contained by the hallmark dry-packed stone retaining walls of the old passes.

The fire of 2018 was not the first to have ravaged the Garden Route and no doubt it won't be the last. The "great fire" of 1869 was fanned by a Berg wind that raged like a hurricane and set the mountains ablaze along a front stretching 450 kilometres from Uitenhage to Riversdale. It devastated the farming communities of the region, just to add to the woes of runaway horse sickness and the collapse of the George Divisional Bank.

First you'll come to the tiny settlement of Herold, which might be called a hamlet but for its distinctive Dutch Reformed church. It is the hops-growing centre of South Africa, so say "cheers" and *"rheinheitsgebot"* as you pass. Hops is the herb that gives the distinctive bitter taste to beer and, in the old school of brewing, one of only three ingredients that are permitted along with malted wheat and fresh mountain water.

Montagu is the oldest commissioned mountain pass in the region, having been constructed under the careful eye of one Henry Fancourt White. It took three years to construct the 17 serpentine kilometres from the crest of the Outeniqua range to White's Bridge. In 1848 Cape Colonial Secretary John Montagu cut the tape at the bridge to open it for safe wagon passage.

White's name lives on at the Fancourt luxury hotel and golf course, as well as the area named Blanco. His pass is narrow but safe for any kind of vehicle.

The route via Herbertsdale is all gravel, really a labyrinth of intersecting and interconnecting roads that are not so much winding as winding-winding. Along the way you might get caught up in a cattle drive down the main road. Then, taking a sequence of devious turns, end up in Friemersheim. Who's ever heard of Friemersheim? who has *been* to Friemersheim?

It was started by the Berlin Mission Society in 1869 as an agricultural settlement. In 1872 it passed into the hands of the Dutch Reformed Church and was acquired by the state in the 1960s. Someone well connected in the local district council must like the place because the old mission cottages have almost all been replaced by nice, neat, square, little RDP box homes.

At the Meulrivier intersection you might rub your eyes at the sight of a Disney-like castle, but it's real enough. There are vistas around here so startling they could hurt your eyes, but who knows, you might just meet a princess, or a Minotaur, somewhere along that maze of back roads.

No matter how you get there, the real Garden Route really starts at George – or just outside. The town began as a timber station in 1776. On 23 April, St George's Day, 1811, it was officially declared a town and named after "mad" King George III. Our route into the garden is the old Saasveld Road, now Mandela Road, which allows us to avoid the purgatory of a vast new shopping complex at the eastern end of what is otherwise a rather nice town (it has a surprisingly fine railway museum).

After a short stretch of sylvan suburbia you'll pass the white gates of the old Saasveld Forestry College (now a sub-campus of the Nelson Mandela Metropole University) and suddenly the road plunges steeply down into the cool tunnel of ancient Afro-montane forest. And here all doubters of the magical, of the splendid, of the glories and the power of the supernatural, tremble, oh ye of little faith, for this is where we are inducted into the sacred guild of the Seven Passes Road.

The great age of road building in the Cape began when Charles Cornwallis Michell was Surveyor-General and John Montagu became Colonial Secretary. Together they toured the colony looking for places where passages could be constructed in order to open up the region for agricultural and economic progress.

The real breakthrough came when Montagu cleared the colony's debt and approved the use of convict labour for civil projects. Whatever we might think of the practice today, those labouring on the roads were treated far better than their fellows languishing in hellish prisons. They enjoyed the country air, relaxed discipline, decent health care, a proper diet, even lending libraries, and we got those exquisite roads.

The first new route tackled was Michell's Pass between the Tulbagh Valley and Ceres, built in 1847 by Andrew Geddes Bain with his son Thomas as his apprentice. Next was Henry Fancourt White's Montagu Pass over the Outeniqua Mountains between George and Oudtshoorn.

By 1860 a road was sorely needed to link George with the new timber depot in the heart of the southern Cape forests that was growing on the Knysna River estuary. The emerging timber town was at the time accessible only by sea, and then treacherously so. The man tasked with the job was Thomas Bain, by then the colony's principle road engineer and a man said to have been born with a theodolite eye. It would be of greatest use on this project.

Apart from human power in the form of convicts, the only other technologies available at the time were shovels, crowbars and gunpowder. They worked well enough for moving earth or breaking and moving rock, but, when it came to dealing with the root masses of the giant forest trees, fire, horse power and time would be required in quantities not yet factored in.

At the time, Bain was at the peak of his life and career, having been married for more than a decade, helping to raise a large family (13 children in all), with 20 years' experience building roads and seemingly indefatigable and unbeatable by any physical challenge.

At that time, he was already busy on four other passes (Robinson, Tradouw, Garcia's and Koo), in the early stages of planning a new route through the Swartberg range and surveying two more, as well working on a railway line from Cape Town to Worcester, a canal in Somerset West and various road upgrades throughout the colony.

In 1854 Thomas had married 17-year-old Henrietta, the daughter of the Secretary of the Cape Roads Board, Willem de Smidt, and sister of Adam, a government road engineer. While having been finely tutored at home, apparently Henrietta did not acquire many of the home-making skills so admired in women those days. But Thomas is said to have been quiet, kind, considerate, confident, tolerant and, in private, an extremely funny man, one who was as adept with a shovel as he was with a coal-heated iron. They were, by all accounts, exceedingly happy together.

By 1860 the Bain family was living in Knysna in order that Thomas might oversee the upgrading of numerous elephant migration routes, horse trails and other "Boer roads" – all rough and treacherous bridle paths and wagon tracks – of the area. Then the roads people in Cape Town instructed him to elevate the undertaking.

Bain was already busy forging the Phantom Pass up from the Knysna River Valley to the Zuurvlakte (Rheenendal). In 1867 the decision was made to push a road through the heart of the southern Cape's most formidable forests. A construction base was established at Pampoenkraal under the supervision of his brother-in-law Adam de Smidt. It included a chaplain's house, blacksmith's shop, convict lodgings and a library; the site was to become the Saasveld forestry campus.

De Smidt oversaw work from the western side, but almost from the start they disagreed over the route the convoluted forest road should take. De Smidt was fixed on a course closer to the sea where the river valleys were flat. Bain insisted on one further inland where the rivers were much smaller and would require much less effort to ford (albeit much more to dig into and out of). Due to his superior reputation, Bain got his way, but the two fell out irredeemably and never spoke again.

Imagine walking it today, not along the road but through the dark tangle of steep-sided forest, the gloomy canopy way overhead, and trying to plot a viable passage! Time has shown that just this once the master builder Bain might have misread the landscape, but in the end fate got the better of him and his theodolite-measured plans.

Some years after their fall-out, Adam de Smidt bought Pampoenkraal and covered most of it in pine plantation, the first of many that were to be established in level places that were once islands of fynbos within the temperate forest biome. Then again, we all need toilet paper because, as hikers know, using fynbos is an unpleasantly scratchy business.

At the eastern end Bain continued pushing the Phantom Pass road across the Zuurvlakte where, in those days, the Honourable Henry Frederick Francis Adair Barrington was *baas van die plaas*. At the other end progress was much slower than had been anticipated.

Today you hardly notice crossing the Swart River gorge between George and Saasveld, but it would have presented the road gang with their first serious shoulder-to-the-wheel challenge. Two years later they had managed to cut their way down to, across and up the eastern flank of Kaaimansgat.

The narrow stone bridge that spans the Kaaimans River was built only in 1904. In Bain's day they constructed causeways across the rivers, which were susceptible to being inundated, and even destroyed, by floods. It took another two years to reach Woodville, 26 kilometres from the start and a ways short of the Touw River.

One of the three "big trees" of the Garden Route is found here. It is little visited, though the walk to the many-centuries-old *Podocarpus falcatus* is delightful and delivers all the Garden Route promises. At 33 metres high, and with a bole circumference of 12 metres, it makes you feel very small as an organism standing beside it. The species is the Outeniqua yellowwood, and is distinct from the much more numerous but less impressive real, or common yellowwood, *P latifolius*.

Much timber cutting was done to get this far, with yellowwood, stinkwood, ironwood, witels, Cape beech, rooiels, white pear, mountain pear, wild peach, assegaaiwood and many other Afromontane species burned in camp fires each night. It took a backbreaking 15 years to complete the entire 75-kilometre route, and you can just imagine how many big trees were reduced to ash in order to keep the workers warm and fed.

After Woodville, the next obstacle was the even more challenging decline of the Trek-aan-de-Touw River defile. This was the original name of the Touw (sometimes Touws) River, where waggoneers could be heard bellowing for all hands to "*trek aan de touw!*" (pull on the rope) for all their worth.

That done, the ever-optimistic Bain wrote to the Chief Inspector of Roads, MR Robinson, that he expected it to take 150 men just two more years and £1 000 to be done. That was because a little way further on, after bridging the Hoogekraal River valley, he planned finally to heed his brother-in-law's advice and take his road down to the mercifully flat coast that was covered only in scrub.

Today this stretch between Ruigtevlei and Karatara looks suspiciously like a promised land. The cows look well fed and happy. The neat fields, surrounded by woodlands and framed by mountains, are as deep a green as any you'll see in Switzerland. Scattered around are charming farm cottages, field cottages, forest cottages and garden cottages. However, when you read the realty boards advertising these properties, you realise these are no country bumpkin plots but prime real estate.

Once the Hoogekraal is done and dusted (very dusted), the uncharacteristically orderly settlement of Karatara comes into view, with regulation Dutch Reformed Church steeple prominent. The village was established after the First World War when wildcat logging was finally brought under control and 165 woodcutters and their families were forced out of the forests and into the little box houses. The community was notoriously inbred (cue banjos) and, until opened to all comers two decades ago, something of a curiosity to travellers.

From the outset it had been the Homtini gorge in the upper Goukamma River valley that had most worried Bain. These days, dropping down into its gaping maw, where some of the most impenetrable tracts of indigenous forest fade into a distant haze of saw-tooth mountains to the northeast, you can understand why. From the brim of the western approach, the twisting pass up the other side is revealed only where a few swooshes of gravel road peek out from the green canopy.

Bain planned to avoid it entirely. However, as his workers were battling through the fossil dune fields that flank the lakes between Wilderness and Knysna, pushing around Groenvlei and Ruigtevlei in the expectation of soon reaching the firm, fertile Goukamma River valley, gold was discovered in the Millwood Gully. It is a small tributary in the pleats of the mountain above the Homtini gorge, and it changed everything.

Walking along the tinkling Millwood Stream today, it is hard to imagine the commotion of the place back in 1875 when a booming shack town had all the usual hardware stores, several banks, several more bars, brothels and three competing newspapers. About 400 people lived in the makeshift settlement with a further 600 squatting in the surrounding forest. Unfortunately, the elephants did not fare very well with the onslaught of hungry miners, some unlucky in nuggets but not so in ivory.

In 1886 much bigger gold deposits were located way up north in the Transvaal, just when the Millwood seams and alluvial traces were drying up. The diggers drifted northwards, as did the taverners, journalists and attendant ladies. The forest regained its primordial peace, but went silent without the trumpeting of great pachyderms that had once been numerous. Old tunnels obscured by ferns and shrubs, and some rusting equipment are all that remain. The steam engine standing outside the little museum was dragged there by men "trekking aan de touw".

And so, back into the hills and forest went Thomas Bain and his road. Local self-appointed lord of the manor Henry Barrington had dreamed of a coach route between George and Port Elizabeth that would run past his inn, Portland. At last Bain's road was going to make this dream become reality … but only three years after the haughty innkeeper died. Today Portland Manor is a quaint reminder of those times, and a fine place to stay should you pass this way.

To complete the route into Knysna one really needs to take the gravel Phantom Pass and not the tarred road from Rheenendal to the N2. The pass was named, not after a ghost, but a moth. Barrington got a *kopwurm* that the wild forest mulberries could support a silk industry and so, without any research, brought out 40 families from Italy to work as spinners. The imported silkworms did not like the indigenous wild mulberry trees and died, which left the Italians without silk on their waiting looms, or spaghetti on their tables.

One Italian beauty, Victoria Esposito, stole a horse from Barrington's stables and in the darkness of night made a dash down the pass to Knynsa in the hope of finding passage back home. But there was an electrical storm that night and both the lady and her horse were struck dead. Local legend has it that Victoria was transformed into the endemic moth *Leto venus*.

Today Knysna, with its expansive estuary and grand sandstone "heads" at the river mouth, is the focal point of the Garden Route. The Automobile Association used to run a competition to choose the favourite town in South Africa, but Knysna won so many times the contest was abandoned. It is certainly no longer the charming little timber village that the Thesen family once ran, basically as a fiefdom for more than a century, but it is still an attractive if busy river-and-seaside town.

But reaching Knysna was only the first half of the full extent of the "Tsitsikamma Road" as envisaged by the higher road-building powers. Bain was now tasked with pushing his road from Knysna further eastwards, including tackling four immense chasms between The Crags and Storms River, as well as many more enormous tree stumps.

Today you can race over the Bobbejaans, Groot, Bloukrans and Storms rivers by the most impressive set of single-arch concrete bridges in Africa. It took another century for engineers to attempt to improve on what Thomas Bain left as his legacy, although, to be accurate, the Storms River bridge was opened in 1956 with the others coming only three decades later.

The main road from Knysna to Plettenberg Bay is pleasant enough, passing arty-crafty Harkerville along the way (if you do go this way it is really worth stopping to check out the local crafts and fare, or why bother travelling?). Also, saunter down through the Harkerville Forest to the Kranshoek picnic spot where the drama of the Tsitsikamma's rugged coastline can be enjoyed without the crowds you'll find at the more impressive but also more crowded Storms River Mouth.

It was at Kranshoek where, as a child, Lyall Watson reckons he had an otherworldly experience that propelled him along the path of supernatural fascination. Watson was a mainstream scientist, but between his formal researches on marine mammals he published widely and, some might say, wildly, on things beyond the grasp of rigid methodology.

He spent childhood holidays nearby when the parents encouraged the lads of the tribe to go off on little adventures. While he and some youthful mates were doing their *Lord of the Flies* thing at Harkerville, he records witnessing something astonishing occurring where the picnic spot is now located.

I've seen some pretty otherworldly happenings in my wanderings, so am loathe to dismiss outright what he claims: a bull elephant emerging from the forest and, standing right on the cliff edge, communing with a whale just beyond the breaking swells, by low-frequency rumblings.

Who knows, good Horatio, of all that happens between Heaven and Earth? To experience the deep forest you will want to walk or cycle along the various tracks. The two-day Harkerville Trail is a compressed Otter Trail, if you have the inclination and stamina. It does tend to make you believe in fanciful things.

A much more rewarding (if substantially longer) drive to Plettenberg Bay, however, is to take the detour on top of the hill climbing out of the Knysna valley, to link up with Prince Alfred's Pass. The good people of Knysna Heights insist on stealing the turn-off sign, making as it does a fine waterproof roof or wall for a shack, but the intersection is pretty obvious. Some people contend it is *the* drive of the entire Garden Route.

This route begins by hop-skip-jumping through the township (or whatever we call them these days) and past a quarry (roads must be built) to where tar gives way to gravel and plantation to forest: not just any forest, but Diepwalle, place of legends and unsurpassed beauty. This is "circles in the forest" territory, mythologised by writer Dalene Matthee.

On reaching Ysterhoutrug there are signboards indicating the King Edward VII yellowwood, third largest of the yellowwood "big trees". The ecological role of these big trees is to provide an umbrella for the forest. The temperature on the ground is around 10°C cooler than on the canopy, due both to the shade provided and the refrigeration effect of transpo-evaporation. More than that, though, they are solar panels that convert sunlight and a few basic molecules into batteries of life by the process we call photosynthesis.

The canopy here is typically between 20 and 30 metres high. Destroy the canopy and the high, very moist temperate forest begins to desiccate and wilt. Forest plants do like sunlight, but not too much. Forests are ecosystems driven more by decay than by new growth. When an old big tree dies and falls, it creates a crashing, gaping hole in the vegetal fabric (even if no one hears it).

Sunlight floods in and ferns, herbs and understory shrubs thrive. Tree seedlings germinate and rush for the light ... rushing in the sense of the time it takes for a big tree here to grow to maturity: up to 800 years in the case of the biggest ones. The giants are all – or were – *Podocarpus falcatus*, the Outeniqua yellowwoods or *kalanders*. The word *kalander* is a shortening of Outenikwalander, the name given to the old woodcutters of the region.

Far more common are the real yellowwoods, *Platifolius* (their conifer leaves are about twice as long and wide as the short spiky leaves of the *kalanders*). The female trees produce hard seeds surrounded by a soft, reddish layer called the podocarpium (foot-fruit). Fruit bats, turacos, rameron pigeons and the few Cape parrots left survive largely on these fruits. Down below, bushpigs, porcupines, blue duikers, monkeys and baboons gobble up whatever falls.

Ironwood trees (*Olea capensis*), which comprise about 20 per cent of the tree community around here, provide most of the canopy now. In early summer their blossoms blush powdery white-pink. Here, you feel, nature lives unmolested. The ironwood is the heaviest wood in the world, with a specific gravity of 1.49. By comparison, leadwood, *Combretum imberbe,* has a specific gravity of only 1.215.

The Outeniqua Hiking Trail ends here and people who have undertaken its full six-day odyssey can claim to have become intimate with the ancient forest. Around 30 years ago I came upon fresh elephant dung on the trail. The latest information was that there was (at the time of researching this book) just one left.

In a spasm of colonial enthusiasm the big *Podocarpus* was named the King Edward VII Tree. Perhaps now would be a good time to reconsider it. Since there is already a Daleen Matthee Big Tree at Krisjan-se-Nek near Millwood, how about the Thomas Bain Big Tree after the man who built the road and who did much to ensure that it still stands today?

While working on this side project to the main Tsitsikamma Road, the Bain family decamped to a lovely, tranquil and isolated (even by today's standards) place called De Vlugt, situated in the uppermost valley of the Keurbooms River, between the Tsitsikamma and Langkloof Mountain ranges. Today there is a very alternative "tea garden" there, as well as the original Bain home that can be booked for overnight stays.

In her old age, Bain's daughter Georgina remembered the three years the family lived here (1863–1866) as the happiest of times, walking, horseriding and picnicking, and enjoying the attentions of their polymath father. Excepting for the incident when toddler Alice was knocked off the stoep by a turkey. She died a couple of weeks later from her injuries.

The pass was named in honour of Queen Victoria's son who visited during its construction in order to hunt one of the legendary forest giants. A three-day hunt was arranged (it was really an organised slaughter), and he did eventually get his elephant trophy.

Chief Inspector Robinson reported that the work on the prince's pass was "as formidable and, in places, more formidable than any road yet undertaken in the Colony". When it was eventually completed in September 1866, the chief inspector (earlier a harsh critic of Bain) wrote: "In many places the scenery is grand and the work itself is, I believe, at least equal to work of the kind in any part of the world." All this and Bain's magnum opus, the Swartberg Pass, was still to come.

Whichever way you arrive at Plettenberg Bay it is obvious that the bay which the earliest navigators named Formosa (beautiful), has grown into a fully-fledged town with all the attendant formal sprawl and informal overflow. "Plett" is, like the old joke about the curate's boiled egg being nice in parts, perhaps best passed over for more palatable pickings. Just past The Crags, the R102 allows you to once again abandon the national road, diverge onto the old Tsitsikamma Road and into a wild wood.

No sooner had Thomas Bain linked Knysna with Plettenberg Bay than the Cape roads board wanted him to push on eastwards in the direction of Port Elizabeth. Roads Superintendent Michell was concerned that "there is no practical way – not even a footpath, from Plettenberg Bay through the Tsitsikamma country". At least between George and Knysna there had been paths and tracks to follow.

A few not insignificant obstacles were that the master road builder was still busy getting the last few cuttings cut and fillings filled on the Seven Passes, planning new road projects, as well as repairing older ones damaged during the torrential floods of 1875 (Meiringspoort, for one, had been almost entirely washed away). However, as soon as the words "Tsitsikamma" and "new road" were mentioned, he almost knocked over his boiled egg, along with his theodolite, in his eagerness to bolt from the breakfast table.

It was perhaps inevitable that Bain would be deeply impressed by the mountains, the forests, the fynbos and everything else in the largely untrammelled countryside he roamed. He developed not only a deep affinity with nature, but became a fine artist and naturalist, collecting plants, minerals, antediluvian artefacts and fossils as he went. His sketch maps of the roads he planned, rendered in pen and wash, are in themselves works of a skilled artist.

His love of the forests in particular was sown when he accompanied a Captain Harison (later to become Conservator of Forests) on a reconnaissance of the Tsitsikamma region in 1868, to assess the feasibility of building a road. Harison hoped that a road could help contain the continuing destruction of the forests by linking the logging communities with outside markets, and so offer alternative economic opportunities.

Bain became a believer and thought he would be able to transform his various construction camps along the route, as well as other Crown lands, for farming. Exploitation of the southern Cape's temperate forests had begun back in the early 1770s. When Governor van Plettenberg toured the region at the end of that decade, he was appalled by the level of destruction he saw and attempted to introduce some restrictions.

But the expanding colony needed timber and it was only in 1846 that any real conservation measures were introduced. Those tracts already denuded were sold as agricultural lots and a year later all Crown Forests were declared closed to private logging.

In 1879 Bain established construction camps on either side of each of the major gorges along the 185-kilometre route between Plettenberg Bay and Humansdorp, which enabled work to begin at several points at the same time. Slashing and burning the tall fynbos on the level, wave-cut platform from The Crags to the lip of the Bobbejaans River gorge must have caused Bain to underestimate the hard grind of carving a path through the heavily forested chasms.

The "great jungle" that choked the Bobbejaans, Groot, Bloukrans and Storms river ravines was denser than even those he'd encountered on the Seven Passes. But by this time Bain had learned much about surveying, cutting, blasting and bridging. He wrote to Chief Inspector

Robinson that he expected to complete the job in two years: "The road in general will not be difficult to construct."

It took four years, which is the time he needed to excavate the cuttings into and out of both the Grootrivier and Bloukrans valleys simultaneously. Once again it was not so much the rock cuttings that were the main challenge, but the wood, or roots, of all impeding trees. Up until about 1900 most of the railway sleepers and mine props used in South Africa were yellowwood.

Bain's family was not very happy with his venturing into this gloomy, tangled world, where many dangers lurked; not just everyday accidents like rock falls or flash floods, but elephants, buffaloes and bands of brigands that hid in the murkiness. Yet it seems the man was in his element, and his love of the outdoor life, and the magnificent forests in particular, was inculcated into those around him.

Joseph Storr Lister, who married Bain's daughter Georgina, became Chief Conservator for Crown Forests in the Knysna-Tsitsikamma region. But it was old Hendrick Barnardo who seems to have been most severely bitten by the forest bug. He was foreman of the Grootrivier Pass construction camp and when the road was completed in 1884, he bought a chunk of land at the mouth of the river, without argument one of the most pristine and enchanting tracts of coastal land in South Africa.

But this enigmatic man, who protected the forests with a fanatical fervour, was also an enthusiastic hunter. He and a brother are credited with shooting some of the last big game around there. Barnardo married three times and fathered 19 known children. He named his new home Nature's Valley, and friends were welcomed to vacation there in their wagons so long as they did not disturb anything and took out everything they had brought in with them.

That is why today you can still see several impressive yellowwoods, their canopies festooned with old man's beard lichen, in the fold of Kalander Kloof as you approach the bottom of the Grootrivier Pass, as well as on the riverbank in the De Vasselot campsite. For the record, Comte Médéric de Vasselot de Régné was a French-born and -trained forester who was appointed Superintendent of Woods and Forests for the Cape Colony in 1880.

Where a low bridge crosses the limpid Groot River, the banks are crowded by entangled trees, their crooked limbs festooned with vegetable beards. On the downstream side, some of Bain's original causeway can still be seen. Ascending the pass in spring you should be rewarded by a profusion of sweetly scented, creamy white flowers of the forest boxwoods in full exuberance (for good reason the species name is *floribunda*). In early summer it will be the crinkly pink blooms of Cape chestnuts that brighten the forest canopy.

All too soon you descend the Bloukrans and cross the river by a low concrete bridge. Immediately across the river you know you have entered a different world, one where road maintenance has been neglected for many years. New forest growth and landslides have encroached and the roadway has reverted to single-track width. It seems to hark back to a slower time when the sounds of whips cracking and oxen lowing filled the ravine (warnings that this section is closed, however, need not be taken too seriously).

In her book on Thomas Bain, historian Patricia Storrar writes that the speeding motorist on the N2 is unaware that below them and out of sight is the winding route down to a lovely river, tall forest trees forming an over-arching green tunnel, dappled light tickling mist-festooned fern fronds, along what might well be the loveliest stretch of forest in this entire journey of horticultural rediscovery.

The R102 regains the N2 a short way beyond Coldstream, one of the settlements envisaged by Harison and Bain. It's all plantation around here and, when newly felled with piles of cuttings burning, it's a garden of hell rather than Eden. But take the road down to Storms River Mouth and you'll find what is surely the most dramatically scenic and desirable camping site in the whole country, the jagged shoreline flanked by high, moist forest.

All things change, forest gives way to timber concessions, elephant tracks become wagon roads, which are in turn overridden by byways, and then highways. So too with the biggest of all the big yellowwood trees of the Tsitsikamma. You'll find it in the Plaatbos Forest on the final approach to the Storms River Bridge; and it won't be at all hard to find it.

Not long ago, you could enjoy a transcendent experience walking in the penumbral, liquid green light of Plaatbos, with only fleeting forest birds as companions. Then our parks board went all American and built a large and showy visitor's centre and upped the price to see the old colossus. It is a cause for some regret how we feel compelled to tame the wilderness, even when there is so little left. Then we mitigate it by calling it progress, saying it's good for social transformation and other such obfuscation. And there goes a bit more of the garden.

Still, you cannot diminish the impact of a tree that is reaching towards 1 000 years old, standing 40 metres proud and tall (individuals of 60 metres are believed to have been logged around here). The enormous canopy (about 33 metres in diameter) creates an entwined celestial umbrella way above your head. The walk there and back on timber decking is not long but it is still uplifting, so take your time to absorb the magnificence all around you as nature seems to sing its most inspiring song in leaf notes.

While the Bloukrans, Grootrivier and Bobbejaans bridges were completed in the early 1980s, their groundbreaking engineering was pioneered with the Storms River Bridge that opened to traffic in 1956. The mighty concrete arch was cast in two halves and on the specified day cautiously lowered to meet in mid-air high above the twisting river.

The event was celebrated much like the ceremonial opening of Henry Fancourt White's stone arch bridge on the Montagu Pass back in 1848. One difference, among many, between the two bridges is that the newer one has a thin piece of cardboard in its core.

The story (recounted by a woman from the area) goes that the South African delegation arrived with a flag ready folded to be entombed in the concrete where the two halves met. And where was his flag, they enquired of the Italian chief engineer. In a panic he rushed back to his site caravan and grabbed the only Italian flag he had, the side of one of his imported pasta boxes.

The lady in question must have known her linguine from her ravioli because she married an ill-prepared man and moved back to his home. In Italy the common engineer turned out to be a count, and the Eastern Cape Cinderella ended up living right royally in the country's historic capital.

It's amazing where a bridge can lead you. It has been noted before that all roads lead to Rome.

Nieu Bethesda

An Owl House, a Camel Yard and a Stream of Fossils: Searching for South Africa's Geo-Psychic Centre

A sense of haunted remoteness descends whenever the name Nieu Bethesda is mentioned: most people know about it, but few know it. And yet it could be designated as the belly button of South Africa, a nucleus that is more hole than doughnut, more black hole than supernova.

THERE IS AN APOCRYPHAL story about a leaking roof in Nieu Bethesda. The old NGK building starts leaking like a sieve right above the organ and begins to damage the ceiling and said instrument of the Lord. A nice-seeming *Engelsman* visits the village and offers to fix it, for a fee of course. The *dominee* is desperate that the organ sustains no further damage and so agrees.

The visitor climbs inside the roof beams and emerges some time later, dusting off his clothes and hands and with news that it has all been taken care of. Not so quick, says the wily pastor, and tells the visitor they'll have to wait to see if his handiwork withstands the next big rains before any silver changes hands. No problem, agrees the Englishman.

Rain does eventually come to this arid place, the roof holds and so the man is finally paid. Come the second rainy season and still the roof holds. With the third wet season, however, the ceiling rains down upon the organ so the minister sends a *handlanger* up into the roof. It turns out that the *donderse Engelsman* has tricked them: he simply placed buckets under each hole in the roof which, when eventually filled, overflowed.

It might well have been that old conniver Bonaparte Blenkins who features in the story by Olive Schreiner, he who takes in Tannie Sannie and nearly takes her African farm off her just down the Cradock Road from Nieu Bethesda. You want the roof story to be true as much as not.

Like almost every *dorp* in South Africa, Nieu Bethesda coalesced around an elegant, whitewashed and tall-steepled Dutch Reformed church that here lies in an uncustomary well-watered valley high up in the Sneeuberg Mountains, in the very heart of the arid Karoo. So unexpected is the fertility of the cupped basin that on first cresting the rim of the valley it looks like a South African Shangri-La.

The strictly religious Afrikaans-speaking community had a burning need to meet regularly for the monthly *nagmaal* (communion), and it was around these communion places that the community socialised and that churches and then towns arose. In the high Sneeuberg, originally that place was a humble wagon shed on Uitkyk farm belonging to Barend Pienaar: it gets *bliksems* cold there in winter.

In 1878 the minister of the church in Graaff-Reinet, Charles Murray, solicited successfully to buy a portion of Uitkyk for £4 000, for the purpose of building a church. Until that time Murray or another chosen man of God would have had to travel the long and dusty 50 kilometres from Graaff-Reinet each Sunday and other holy days to conduct services in the shed.

Murray suggested to the newly constituted *dorps comité* that they choose a name for their new settlement from one of four options:

Bethal, Bethalsdal, Bethalstad, or Bethesda, the last meaning "house of goodwill". The committee agreed with their minister-at-large that, since the church was being established in part to help the poor of the Sneeuberg district, Bethesda was a fine choice.

When it came time to say a few words at the foundation ceremony in November that year, the Minister, one of a distinguished line of Scottish Calvinist ministers who preached to the frontier Dutch *volk* in the Cape, said "*Laten wij het nu Bethesda noemen*" (Let us now call it Bethesda). But the scribe on the day wrote it down as "*Laten wij het Nieuw Bethesda noemen*," and so Nieu Bethesda it became.

It is one of many layers of political irony in this country that the church and its pure white congregation should end up denying the very poor for whom it was apparently created: the coloured people of the valley. Anyone from the white side who showed undue empathy for them would likely be ostracised.

The new church could seat 700 faithful but never saw more than 375 inside. Meanwhile, on the eastern slope of the valley, more than 1 000 coloured folk squeezed into five somewhat less grand places of worship. Over time the white community dwindled, as it did in so many similar *platteland* areas mid-last century.

By the 1970s the whites-only school had closed and for a while even a minister did not visit to conduct sermons where, decades earlier, the congregation would gather twice a day on Sundays, while children were also expected to attend a third Sunday School session.

According to Nieu Bethesda authority, writer Sue Ross, the Dutch Reformed Church dominated the valley not only visually but in a manner that informed every thought and action – religious, social, economic and political – of the people who lived in its shadow. It was a place where women did not demonstrate independence of mind or body after marriage.

This was the austere, white male-dominated world into which the shy and reserved Helen Martins was born and in which she was destined to become an outsider from within. Most visitors to the village today come on account of her now-famous creative phantasmagoria, the Owl House.

The controversial woman died in August 1976 after drinking caustic soda. By that time she was going blind, her hands and feet were crippled with arthritis, she was sad, depressed and lonely. But more than all that, her Owl House and Camel Yard were by then full to overflowing, quite literally. Her work here was done.

So much has been said and written about the Owl House, including Athol Fugard's play and movie *The Road to Mecca*, it is hard to do it justice in one essay – you have to see it for yourself. On first entering the Owl House and working your way through its cluttered and jazzy-coloured rooms to the even more overwhelming Camel Yard, many people experience strange reactions ranging through wonder and weird, to bizarre and crude, and sometimes even repulsion.

When all has been seen, said and debated, written and read, you are left with the overwhelming question: Why? Helen was born in 1897 and grew up ostensibly in a typical *platteland* family of that time and place, with several brothers and sisters who did not go *tekere* (crazy). So what led her to flout virtually all the religious, social and moral norms of her community?

She was the youngest of 10 children born to Hester Martins in the last two decades of the 19th century, of whom only six survived. The first clue as to why Helen Elizabeth became such an outsider is her name: she was given the name of an older sibling who died in childhood. Psychologists can tell you that, whenever this happens, the surviving child often fails to develop a full and independent personality. From her earliest days she would have had a looming sense of death, according to biographer Sue Ross.

Although shy, Helen did not display any untoward behaviour while growing up in the village. She attained the top grade then available in the local school, which was Standard Eight. From there she, along with her two surviving sisters and other promising youth of the village who were not tied yoke and chain to a tractor, went on to college in Graaff-Reinet where they trained to become teachers.

We learn that Helen's father, Petrus Jacobus, was a tricky customer. He liked to boast that he'd never attended school and the only book allowed in his house was the Bible – which he thumped continuously. He was also something of a scoundrel: he would skip church services and then drive his sheep onto lands of farmers he knew were congregated in the house of another shepherd.

Once, when he was caught and refused to submit to the law, the local policeman had him manhandled into a wheelbarrow and pushed to the station. You can just imagine how embarrassed his family must have felt. He was also a maverick, maybe even a weirdo. One old villager remembers that Martins would sometimes spend days lying on the *stoep* of the local store with his head in a box.

He could also be outright vindictive, like the times he would tease Helen with letters that had arrived for her then tear them up before she was able to read them. In later life some villagers remembered other incidents relating to his behaviour. He would tell anyone willing to listen that children were a curse: "If a boy is born, it is sad," one remembered old Petrus Jacobus saying, "but if it's a girl, it is worse."

But all this seems not to have had too great an effect on Helen, her two surviving sisters and three brothers. Not, that is, until the age of 23 when she met and married fellow teacher Johannes Pienaar very much against her father's wishes. They up and moved to the Transvaal where they both found jobs and became keenly involved in emerging Afrikaans theatre.

It seemed to suit the dandy Johannes but during this period Helen had her first major setback: she had an abortion. There has been much speculation about why Helen Martins chose to have an abortion in what was at that stage still, apparently, a happy marriage. There is no easy answer provided, other than her sense of not belonging fully to this world, and consequently a deep fear of the burden of parenthood.

After five years together – and very likely as a consequence of the abortion – the couple divorced and Helen moved. She was living in Cape Town when her mother became seriously ill, prompting Helen to return to Nieu Bethesda. She doted on her ailing mother but relations with her father deteriorated.

After her mother's death she confined her by-then feeble father to an outside room. When he eventually died in 1945, Helen began the decoration of the family home by painting that room entirely black. On the step she painted "The Lion's Den". And then her labours took an unexpectedly creative turn, transforming an otherwise standard rural Victorian-era home into an extremely personal and inscrutable dreamscape, not always easy on the eye or the mind.

But this still does not adequately explain her fantastically coloured house, nor the bizarrely decorated garden that leaves your head spinning and has been described by people who know about these things as one, if not *the*, most extraordinary examples of naïve or outsider art in the world.

All her admirers, critics and biographies point to her abortion as being the single most formative incident that informed her later creative life. It led her, we read, into all kinds of psychological entanglements. Another was the relationship she struck up with farmer Johannes Hattingh who moved with his family into the valley in 1939. Within two years they had formed an intimate relationship that would last until his death 24 years later. Even when Hattingh moved back to Peddie with his family, he continued to visit Helen in Nieu Bethesda.

Clearly he was the love of her life, and she his. It was this extra-marital affair that alienated her from her community even more than her weird material works. But by then she seemed not to care much, so driven was she by the creative process, as well as encouragement from the few people at that time who got what she was doing.

What she was doing, to condense a book down to a few paragraphs, was to bring light into an otherwise dark world. She would pay the village children a few pennies apiece to bring her coloured glass bottles. These she would grind up, first with a mortar and pestle and later with an antiquated coffee grinder, and stick the resulting glitter to every surface in the house. Then she filled the walls with mirrors that would reflect sun and moonlight, as well as that from candles and lanterns, from room to room as she moved through the house.

When the house had nothing left to cover, she began creating sculptures in the garden of things she knew and liked, like owls and camels. Most of the wire-and-cement work was done by one of three men from the coloured community, the name Koos Malgas becoming synonymous with the later, more refined pieces. Light and reflection were also the themes, camel trains travelling east to Mecca, moon observatories of coloured bottles and more crushed glass.

Among her sources were some extremely mundane objects, including polish tins and matchboxes. Others were from photographs and postcards sent to her by friends and family. Some were more literary and spiritual, like the extracts from the *Rubáiyát of Omar Khayyám*, which was first shown to her by Eastern Cape bard Don Maclennan. Likely it was also he who revealed to her the mystical world of William Blake.

But there is also much whimsy in this enchanted garden, when you start to look closely at individual pieces. Like the giraffe necks sticking out of the ground. The bodies were still underground, she would tell anyone who asked. Or the figures bending over backwards? That was the best way to worship the moon.

The disconcerting "little devil" figure with one human foot and one cloven hoof which, more than anything else, gives the inside of the house a pervading creepy atmosphere, is thought to be a manifestation of her aborted child. But the Owl House is far from being the beginning or the end of this amazing place.

Take the Kompasberg for instance. Even more domineering than the church steeple, this 2 504-metre high peak lords over the Bethesda Valley and the entire Sneeuberg region. It is the highest mountain in South Africa that is not part of the greater Drakensberg complex and has been a directional waypoint for travellers, including aeroplane pilots and probably animals and birds before that.

The peak was given its name in a map drawn up by Colonel Robert Jacob Gordon, commander of the garrison at the Castle of Good Hope, when he accompanied Cape Governor Joachim van Plettenberg on a tour of the Eastern Frontier in 1778. He spelled it Compassberg, but some locals refer to it as the Karoo Matterhorn, to which it shows a passing resemblance when frequently snow-covered in winter.

In the long grass outside an old farm building on a shoulder of the Kompasberg, you might trip over a commemorative stone with the name GA Watermeyer chiselled into it (as I did once). The poet was born in that building in 1917, but now it is mostly used by hikers. His poem "Oestyd" was for a long time one of my favourite "stories from the veld", long before I discovered the Sneeuberg or Nieu Bethesda.

It is written in the voice of a 12-year-old lad. On Old Year's Eve (it would have been 1929), his father puts a sickle in his hands and tells him, "this summer you will stand bent over, my boy, your sweat upon the land" (my translation).

"Oestyd" is quite a long poem, and quite harrowing too, telling how the farm workers sweat through a blistering summer's day to get the wheat harvested in time. Stanza by stanza we are hauled, hour by hour, through the day's toils as the sun arcs across the sky and the boy struggles to keep up his end of the sacred covenant as son and heir of a poor farmer. It was only after making the connection between the place and the poet that I realised the "Sneeubergkom" on which they sweated was in fact the farm Kompasberg where I had camped as a young mountaineer.

The great volcanic fang has its roots deeply cemented in a matrix of Triassic sedimentary rocks in which reside some truly mind-blowing creatures. They don't actually live there, in a literal sense, although they once did. And there they floundered, and died, their bodies entombed in quickly accumulating debris of floods or in boggy swamplands. Thus encased in their mineral coffins, the flesh (and sometimes feathers, it lately transpires) mostly melted off but the bones were fossilised, transformed to stone.

One of South Africa's earliest fossil collectors was road builder Andrew Geddes Bain, father of the even more prolific Thomas, who built some road passes in the area. One day while holding a fossil in his hands, Bain explained it to sceptical farmers of the district as being the remains of an animal that had jumped off Noah's Ark and sunk into the antediluvian mud.

One of those farmers would not have been Sydney Rubidge, owner of the luxurious oasis and sheep-wool farm Wellwood that is tucked into Rubidge Kloof on one of the two approaches to Nieu Bethesda. His bread and butter, and lamb chops, were Merino sheep, but his dessert was fossils. He was the patriarch of this country's most distinguished lineage of both amateur and professional palaeontologists.

In 1934, the story goes, farmer Sydney had taken the family out for a picnic. At some point he realised he was sitting on a rock that resembled the skull of some huge creature. That epiphany led him to medical doctor Robert Broom in Pearston who was possibly the most avid fossil collector in the land. Rubidge was paid by Broom for each new fossil fragment of a therapsid – the name given to primitive mammal-like reptiles from the Middle Karoo – he brought.

In time, Broom moved off to Pretoria (he was a failure as an MD, giving all his time and money over to his hobby, but was one of South

Africa's greatest ever experts of old bones). But Sydney Rubidge continued with his own collection and today Wellwood has the largest private collection of Karoo fossils known.

Broom ignited the inner fossil hunter in not just the Rubidges but also the three Kitching boys from a poor family in the village. Their father worked as a road gang supervisor and he also collected for Broom. Between the Rubidges and the Kitchings, down the years Nieu Bethesda has produced more eminent palaeontologists than probably any other village, town or city in South Africa.

Today you can visit the Rubidge Fossil Centre in the village, and even take a short walking tour when the river is dry, which it is usually, to see fossilised bones protruding from the riverbed slates of a creature that lived there around 220 million years ago. It makes you think.

Another Eastern Cape poet who captured the spirit of the place is Chris Mann. His poem "Rivers" embeds a multi-layered understanding of natural history in profound literary form:

The rivers of the Eastern Cape lullaby ancient beasts:
rubberflesh reptile, soupblood bird,
leathery mollusk and mouse,
shrug inside black blankets of slate, and shrinkle slowly to stone;
a fossil frosts, fizzles, splits and mammoths strut the human stream.

Sitting in the Two Goats Deli enjoying a ploughman's platter and glass of Andre Cilliers's delicious, chilled Sneeuberg Ale, a woman at a table alongside said she was surprised by how small the place was – not the deli but the village. She had heard so much about it, she imagined it would be much bigger.

It's deceptive, like the Kompasberg that thrusts up at the end of the dirt road outside the deli. There is something in the rocks around here, and possibly the leiwater that delivers pure mountain water from the surrounding Sneeuberge, that seems to infuse the place with a mysterious font of inventive energy.

Swartberg Pass and Die Hel
A Bone-Jarring Passage, Hard People and Harder Wood: Searching Hard for a Forgotten Valley

Many South Africans regard the Swartberg Pass as a devil of a drive. Then there are those who know it is not even half way to hell, with respect to hard-core travel and remote places.

IT IS RECORDED THAT the Frenchman who drove the grader that carved the road from the coast up to Cilaos village on Réunion Island was awarded the Legion of Honour medal. Anyone who has explored South Africa will have ridden over the name Thomas Bain many times. The name Koos van Zyl, however, is not widely, or even narrowly known.

If ever the Order of the Aardvark – named after those most

amazing of natural earth movers – was bestowed for civic honours this side of the Indian Ocean, the builders of the Swartberg Pass and the road through the Gamkasberg down to Die Hel would be contenders. You could have driven any number of passes and *poorts*, highways, byways and goat tracks, but if you have not driven these two you can never claim to be a real hard-travelling, hardwood oke.

Jose Burman, old Cape man of letters, described the "streamlined modern roadways" such as Sir Lowry's, Du Toitskloof and Outeniqua passes as "insipid". For connoisseurs of passes and *poorts*, Burman reckoned the Swartberg (or Zwartbergen as it was known at the time it was opened in the early 1880s) was the "king of passes". That remains as true today as when he wrote it in 1963.

Back in the 1870s the people of the Prince Albert district were displeased with their lot. The roads thus far built through the Zwartbergen proved less than reliable for getting their hard-wrought produce to the bigger market town of Oudtshoorn. Both the Meiringspoort and Seweweekspoort roads were along, as their names suggest, *poorts* (canyons), and were highly susceptible to flash floods, and the roads were passable as often as not.

Both these *poort* roads were the handiwork of Thomas Bain's estranged brother-in-law Adam de Smidt. He had pulled the short straw on these two because their upkeep kept him busy for much of his professional life in the colonial Cape roads department, rather than being remembered for overseeing more illustrious passages, as was Bain.

Through the early 1800s Meiringspoort was the preferred and most direct route through the daunting Swartberg range, containing as it does the highest peaks in the Western Cape. But in 1859 floods obliterated much of the roadway, as they did again in 1865, and then again in 1875. You could almost feel Adam de Smidt wincing.

The Cape Parliament finally and reluctantly agreed to commission Thomas Bain – at the time frantically busy on his Tsitsikamma Road – to report on the possibility of building a road over the Swartberg to link Oudsthoorn with Prince Albert. They thought it could not be done but their attempt might appease the farmers in the Great Karoo.

Thomas plodded the mountains on horseback and foot, reconnoitring four possible routes, until finally announcing that it would be possible to thread a road up, between and over the great peaks and clefts of the range. But it would be steep and it would be hard (in other words costly). He estimated the cost at £40 000.

Because Bain otherwise had his hands full, the project was put out to tender and a certain Mr Tassie of Delagoa Bay got the job. The people of Prince Albert were so thrilled they began building a bridle path from their northern end, through the contorted rock strata of Skotzekloof to help speed up the task. Work on the road proper commenced in November 1881, but after more than a year into the 18-month contract Tassie's team had progressed no more than seven kilometres. At this stage he declared himself insolvent with still about 25 kilometres to go.

The wisdom of the day was, then as now, when you need a big job done well call in the busiest person you can find. That happened to be one Mr T Bain, with his arms shoulder-deep in the Tsitsikamma Forest. He quickly set about doing what he did best: convincing the Cape government that what was needed to get the Swartberg job back on track was free convict labour.

Say what you will about the system, it got the work done. Within a year the road had progressed 15 kilometres on the northern side, including the famous switchbacks that give some motorists, and even more so their passengers, the *grils*. This stretch is supported by some of the finest and highest dry-stone retaining walling to be seen in this country.

On the somewhat less celebrated – but by no means less impressive – southern side, things were progressing more slowly. A bridle path little more than a metre wide and just one and a half kilometres long had been cut and blasted (with gunpowder) into the extremely hard Table Mountain Sandstone base of the mountains.

Poor old Mr Tassie had no clue what he was getting into when he had tendered on this road: it took Bain four years of very hard labour before the first wagon was waved over snaking Swartberg Pass. Although it was steep by standards of the time, with an incline of up to one in eight in places on the steeper northern slope, it was still far better than the one in six of the Montagu Pass. The farmers on the northern side did not complain about their new direct route south over to the Little Karoo.

Road building aside, the Swartberg Pass offers some of the most stupendous mountain scenery travellers are ever likely to see. For starters, crossing the stream in the narrow Skotzekloof side, gorges draw your eye up to where you marvel at what titanic forces must have crumpled a thousand metres of rock layers in tightly folded fibres; it's like seeing the exposed musculature of our planet.

Where the corkscrew gravel road crests the switchbacks and opens out into a vast geomorphological bowl, the all-round views are spellbinding and no single photograph can give the sense of that limitless expanse of jagged mountain ridges and infinite sky that engulfs you. All around stretches the natural wonder that we call fynbos, and very fine it is too.

The Swartberg, being so high and therefore extreme in climate, is a stronghold for these plants that seem to crave a good beating from the elements, and none more so than those crown jewels of the Cape Floral Kingdom, the proteas. Possibly the most attractive is *P aristata*, a tidy shrub distinctive for its chalice-shaped pink-crimson flower heads and pine needle-like leaves. Unlike most other fynbos species, this is one that does not appreciate fire.

P canaliculata is a small shrub with milky white to soft buttery yellow flowers. It is found primarily in rocky places where it is exposed to the most extreme heat and cold of the seasons. Noticeably taller is *P eximia*, which grows in dense stands, has a large pink flower and broad cordate (heart-shaped) leaves.

Another tall-growing species is *P laurifolia*, the leaves of which reminded the naturalist explorer Carl Peter Thunberg (the first traveller to our shores with botanical training) of the leaves of the laurel trees in the Mediterranean region. *P neriifolia* is showier, although the shrubs tend to look rather scruffy. The big oblong heads can be pale pink to deep wine-red, with a fine black beard around the bract tips.

Most widespread of all though is *P repens*, the common sugarbush, its pale-yellow flower bases flushed pink at their tips. The lanky bushes can grow to about four metres high, and their nectar was tapped as *bossiesstroop* to supplement wild honey by people in remote areas like this. Sugarbirds and sunbirds love them, as do baboons, which eat them like ice cream cones.

He did not know it at the time, but this was to be Bain's last pass commission. Soon after the opening of this road, he was called back to Cape Town with the rather mundane but nonetheless important job of managing the Colony's various irrigation projects.

The southern ridge of the Swartberg is substantially higher than the northern one. Cresting either of them, you notice that exalted summit bowl disappearing into a vast horseshoe-shaped canyon: the pale ribbon of road to Prince Albert clings to the side of one arm. Looking west, the breakaway ridge of the Gamkasberg forms an elevated running valley which disappears into the hazy distance.

Right in the heart of the bowl there is a turn-off and a sign that directs you tantalisingly into that foreboding distance. If you have driven or ridden the Swartberg Pass to reach this point, you could be forgiven for thinking you had conquered the worst the Swartberg can throw at you, but you'd be very much mistaken.

The worst thing you could do would be to discount the warning: "Gamkaskloof 37 km – travelling time 2 hours". Two hours, that is, if you have a tough bakkie or 4x4. If not, it could be substantially more, and add another hour to get from the bottom of the Elandspad zigzags that take you down to the floor of the Die Hel valley to the Cape Nature office at Boplaas, 14 kilometres further along.

The conventional story about the place says that the people living in the valley were a lost community that had been cut off from the outside world since the time of the Trekboers. Then, during the late guerrilla phase of the Anglo-Boer War, a Boer force led by General Jan Smuts came upon them while evading the ever-tightening vice of the British army. Which was wrong on two counts.

While it was a Boer commando that chanced upon the "secret" valley, it was led by Deneys Reitz, Smuts's most trusted officer. What is true is that the people and place of Die Hel only became widely known after the incident was described in Reitz's biographical trilogy, *Commando*, published in 1929.

In it, Reitz recounts how his small force came to a very high ridge of the great folded mountains and looked down the precipitous, gnarled slope into a deep cleft. With the British closing in on them they could only go forwards. Deep in the natural gash in the mountains, hidden from time and prying eyes, they spied a dozen or so white-washed cottages.

The commando edged its way down the precipitous slope, their horses' hooves clattering on rocks and skidding on rubble, being clawed by thorn bushes and aloes all the way down. On the shaded valley floor they came upon a man dressed in goat-skin clothes and with a thick Dutch accent who said his name was Cordier.

This wild kloof man took the tired visitors to his home and saw to it that they were fed with goats' meat, milk and wild honey. He told them he did not know much about the goings-on outside the valley, but had heard something about a war. Once they were fed and rested the man led the Boer troops to the far end of the gorge, and out by a safe and easy passage (no doubt the Gamka River gorge).

Many years later, when the provincial administrator Otto du Plessis had occasion to visit the kloof, Piet Cordier told him how during the Boer War they had indeed seen a bit of action themselves. Not the Reitz commando story, but another craftier scheme that he, Cordier, unofficial leader of the community and locally famous as a raconteur, had cooked up.

On one of their forays with a donkey train out of the kloof, up the Gamka and then its tributary the Dwyka River north to Laingsburg, they managed to capture six "khakis". The prisoners were brought back into the kloof and for 14 days were set to work ploughing their fields, after which they were set free.

The second misconception has already been alluded to, that they were a lost community. Of course, as everywhere, the first inhabitants of Gamkaskloof were Bushmen, we just don't know when. The first Trekboers wandered into the valley down the Gamka River gorge in the 1830s while following strayed sheep. The first permanent resident was Pieter Swanepoel, a lease farmer who rented the valley at two and half pennies a morgen (about one hectare).

The valley is 16 kilometres long but nowhere more than 200 metres wide. In order to get a sense of the place, it is necessary to note that the Gamka River Valley and what we nowadays refer to as Gamkaskloof, otherwise Die Hel, are not the same thing. The Gamka River dissects the valley of Die Hel about midway between the Elandspad descent and the terminus at Die Leer. Die Hel is really a deep gash in the greater Swartberg range and not a true river-cut valley at all.

Others followed Swanepoel: Cordiers and Nefdts, Mosterts, Marais, Nels and Snymans – South Africa's archetypal hillbillies. In her delightful book *Diepadkloofin*, author Aletta Hanekom recounts the memories of Susanna Mostert who, as an old woman, allowed that the residents of the kloof did inter-marry, but not necessarily with own family.

The Klowers (as they called themselves) began by raising sheep but were soon carrying vegetables and fruits (mainly dried), herbal teas, some grain, wild honey and tobacco out of the valley to trade. But one product made them famous: their distilled *witblits* (white lightning) which they called *hardehout* (hard wood). You needed hard wood to tell a hard story. In time a small schoolhouse was built where church services were also held.

The living standard was good enough, if simple and undoubtedly tough. There are few places in South Africa that get hotter, or colder, than inside this deep climate intensifier. True, the Klowers led a near-isolated and hard life in their valley (they preferred the name Gamkaskloof). More important was their sense of freedom and dignity, and love of their secret valley. But they had, by their own measure, ample contact with the outside world.

One instance would be when a letter needed to be posted. A Klower would send word up and down the valley letting the small community know there was mail. The next donkey train into town – either Calitzdorp or Prince Albert – would carry mail out along with the other outgoing products. On the return journey they would carry lamp oil, sometimes linen or blankets, Dutch medical remedies to supplement those they prepared themselves and the occasional letter. (Oom Hendrik "Hoed" Mostert was the most famous apothecary of the valley and even wrote a book on their concoctions.)

Susanna Mostert recalled how, as a youngster, when she was allowed, she would wake up at three in the morning to make sure she was ready for the departure of the donkey train at four. She would carry a water bottle, as well as high-heel shoes and silk stockings in her bag. The water was not for drinking, since there were numerous streams along the way, but for washing her hair before entering the town. One had to look one's best for the townsfolk.

But while they greatly valued their freedom, they yearned for a road. Trekking in and out of their kloof was, as one old timer recalled, no fun and games. Floods would often render the usual route either up or down the Gamka River not negotiable. Even when not in flood it was a tortuous and boulder-choked passage that donkeys had trouble negotiating.

No one is sure exactly when or how the process started, but word finally got to district road engineer for Calitzdorp, Louis Terreblanche, about the Klowers' desperate want for a road. He looked into it, but it would need bigger spanners than those he had to get the machinery moving.

Conveniently, the administrator of the Cape Province, Otto du Plessis, was also a member of the Prince Albert district council. He knew about, but had never actually visited Die Hel, so he was charmed by the prospect of a look-see.

As things will when high officialdom is involved, the party of two soon became many, including security and media: *Die Burger* and *Landstem*, as well *SA Panorama* and *African Mirror* (remember those movie news reels!). They were all trucked to the road head at the northern end of Seweweekspoort. From there the going was on horseback up a track into the discouragingly named Bosluiskloof (bush tick gorge) and then down the Gamka River gorge, often having to clamber on foot, heavy old movie cameras and all.

Arriving tired and hot, the administrator and his entourage were entertained by the Klowers for the weekend, with a dance in the schoolhouse on the Saturday night. The Mostert brothers on accordion and guitar provided the *boereorkes*. There are some lovely old photos of Mr Du Plessis dancing with schoolmistress Miss Marina Ehlers, the only unmarried woman present.

Local raconteurs Piet Cordier and Hendrik "Hoed" Mostert had never had such a prestigious audience and the Klowers knew they had just that one opportunity to impress; much was at stake that weekend. The women cooked like Boere sirens and the handmade tables and chairs creaked and groaned.

For breakfast on the morning of his departure we learn that Tant Lenie plied the visitors with coffee, porridge, boerewors, eggs, fresh baked bread and jam. No doubt it would have absorbed the last of the *hardehout* that had been splashed on the administrator, the road engineer and all the other guests. Along with the copious breakfast and memories of their little weekend adventure, they would have dragged out some choice kloof stories.

Like how Gustaf Nefdt Jnr had carried a Dover stove down into the valley. He got his opening when someone complimented the fine milk tart. Yes, answered Nefdt, his wife baked the best *melktert* in the valley in her very fine Number Eight Dover Stove. This was also a bit of a jibe at his own community who otherwise all cooked – and mostly lived – outdoors.

"You see, my family could climb," he explained. And that was a serious understatement, the name Gustaf Nefdt Snr being legendary in the annals of South African mountaineering. The father grew up at the mission station of Amalienstein near Ladismith, in the shadow of the soaring Towerkop peak with its easily distinguished great cleft summit.

As a youngster Gustaf Snr would "walk" the passages of their home by straddling the walls with his feet and hands off the ground. Frequently he had to be called down from the top of the stone church steeple. One day, as a teenager, he returned home after having been missing overnight. He told the anxious townsfolk that he had climbed the Towerkop.

Impossible, liar, only baboons could climb it, they retorted, and suspected him of darker deeds. Hurt by their disbelief, he led a party from Ladismith up the peak, reclimbed his long and technical route to the summit and retrieved the sock he had left there as evidence. At the time, 1885, it was considered the hardest rock climb in the country.

"But where was I again …" teased the storytelling son, "… oh yes, the stove." He bought it, he told the well-oiled audience, in Prince Albert. From there the quickest way back home was via Die Leer (the ladder). It is a vertical face at the western terminus of the valley and can be negotiated only by those with a head for heights.

When the helpers he'd assembled to assist considered the task, they all backed out. So Nefdt disassembled the stove and placed the feet, plates and doors in a bag, which he tied to his back with cattle-hide *riems*, and carried it to the base. He was then able to lower the main body of the stove down the cliff face using his *riems*.

The *hardehout* was by this time taking effect and more hard stories began to flow. "If I could carry in a stove, then why not a tractor," Nefdt thought. At the garage in Prince Albert he put down the deposit on a new Fordson tractor and carried it in, piece by piece. But, while the tractor was working hard in the valley, Nefdt declined to pay any further instalments. If you want your tractor back, he told the agitated salesman, you're welcome to come and fetch it.

Rather than face a formidable foe in his natural castle, the smart town man responded by taking out an advert in the *Landbou Weekblad* farmer's magazine that stated: "Ace Fordson tractor is incomparable: it is one of a kind and ploughs by itself in Die Hel."

A stove, a tractor, so why not a car? In 1958, just one year before the great road indaba was held in the valley, a first-time visitor from Wellington (Cape) was so impressed by the hard work ethic of Martiens Snyman and his seven-year-old daughter Annetjie, he gifted them an old 1938 Morris Eight (without lights or windscreen).

The roof was subsequently cut off and four Klower men somehow got it down Die Leer – vertically. "It was one hell of a business," remembered Ben van Zyl, one of the car carriers. Luckily they had remembered to take with them some "strengthening water".

Snyman, who had driven trucks in the army during the Second World War (patently word of that war did reach the Klowers), nevertheless took some time to get the hang of driving again. Thereafter the car was used basically for joy rides up and down the valley's main track. But the extremely rough and rocky track took its toll and the remains of the old Morris were laid to rest in the veld outside Hendrik Mostert's cottage – one of several cottages in the valley that can be hired for stayovers now.

Meanwhile, things beyond the valley were moving apace. The administrator had not spent all his time there just partying. While daylight persisted, on the Saturday he had sat down in the schoolhouse with road supervisor Terreblanche. Together they had pored over maps and considered the various options.

First and most obvious were the routes in via the Gamka River valley, from Prince Albert in the north, or from Calitzdorp in the south. However, river courses were the least favoured options given bad flood experiences with the Seweweekspoort and Meiringspoort roads. Also, a dam was being planned somewhere along the Gamka River, so that ruled it out.

Direct routes – north over the Swartberg to Prince Albert, or directly south to Calitzdorp – were discussed but quickly rejected on the grounds of the frightening terrain and implicit costs. On the map, the way to the west, joining the head of the Seweweekspoort Pass and then directly to Laingsburg, looked promising. But that was only till Du Plessis saw Die Leer, the crux to that route.

Given that not even donkeys could negotiate its particularly steep and arduous heights, and that the extremely hard Table Mountain quartzitic sandstone would have to be extensively blasted, clearly that would be the hardest of all. Which left only one option: the eastern one from the summit plateau of the Swartberg Pass.

The biggest plus for this route was that the underlying geology was mostly forgiving Witteberg sandstones and Bokkeveld shales, with substantially harder Table Mountain group rocks below that. This meant that most of the R30 000 eventually allocated in 1961 for the building of the road could be spent on a new road grader and its driver (the rand unit of currency was introduced to South Africa in the same year.)

The grader chosen for the task was a tomato-red Allis-Chalmers HD II that was duly named Rooibul (red bull). It did not have a closed cab so the driver allocated by the Cape Roads Department, 23-year-old Koos van Zyl, had to sit in an open seat that could have doubled as a compartment seat on the Octopus ride at the village fair. The Klowers took both their shiny new red bull and its driver into their hearts. From the time it started work early in 1962 they tracked its progress daily.

They became experts in the audial aspect of the job. As the road scraper went *knaag-knaag* (as one described its "voice"), they would immediately recognise it as the blade biting into Witteberg sandstone or Bokkeveld shale; sometimes they heard *knaag-knaag-knaag* as it hit hard Table Mountain substrate. Occasionally it would hit a pocket of Old Cape Granite and then it was more *knaaag-knaaag-knaaag*.

The first 14 kilometres were the easiest, and led everyone to hope the road would not take very long. But then came 26 kilometres of convoluted descents and ascents, going down then up, down then up, 500 metres at a time, the rock changing characters like a chameleon dodging around the hooves of a big bull. The final long haul up to the summit of the Elandspad snaked like a sidewinding adder, 10 left curves each followed by 10 right sweeps. And then there was the descent into the valley proper.

There are a few roads in our "world in one country" that so test machine and driver, and passengers. The road through the Gamka Mountains will shake you with the best martinis, it will rattle you and, should you lose concentration or nerve, it will surely roll you.

But if you have been to Die Hel and back you get a gold aardvark badge. If you have ridden there on a bicycle (and each year a bunch of crazies do just that), then you are genuinely *hardehout*.

Cape Point

A Fearsome Wind, a Ghost Ship and a Bay of Plenty: Searching for a Paradise, Almost-Lost

The sharp promontory of sandstone that forms the southwest corner of Africa juts into the southern Atlantic and is a catcher's glove for all the weather that passes. It is a wild, windswept place that for centuries was both beacon and ill omen for sailors. It is also, arguably, and biologically speaking, the most diverse place on our planet.

IN THE CIRCUMNAVIGATION OF the oceans chasing the fabled white whale Moby Dick (which is, incidentally, based on a true story), this is how author Herman Melville described our little corner of the world:

"The Cape of Good Hope, and all the watery region round about there, is much like some noted four corners of a great highway, where you meet more travellers than in any other part."

Cape Point is indeed a corner of four great highways, but more in a natural than any human sense. It is the meeting place not only of travellers, but also of the very elements themselves. The entire Cape Peninsula – its petrified head Table Mountain and the Point its dragon-like tail that dips into the ocean – is not only informed, but actually formed by earth, water, fire and wind.

Standing on the crest of that blade of sandstone, which drops vertically into deep churning waters, you get a sense of a place that is imbued with a wild spirit. It is a raw, wind-thrashed and wave-beaten slab of Palaeozoic-era rock jutting into the southern Atlantic Ocean, but it also shelters the largest bay in Africa that provides safe haven for the oceanic wonderland that is False Bay.

There are four or more species of whales, some migratory others resident; at least seven species of sharks, including the famous aerial great whites around Seal Island; roving pods of dolphins sometimes up to several thousand strong; orcas on occasion; cormorants in their thousands; terns; gulls; skuas; and of course those comics of Boulders Beach, the African penguins, all getting fat on the bounteous fish and shellfish population of the bay – as do the crayfish and abalone poachers.

Earth: The sandstone layers which comprise the Point were once connected to a great slab of land that is now visible only as the Falkland Islands. The ragged eastern side of the point looks like it was sliced off by the titan Atlas's sword, and in a sense it was. The truncated flying buttresses of rock once arced all the way over False Bay to join the Hottentots Holland Mountains on the other side, rising in great contorted folds, three or more times higher than they are today.

All these mountains were once beach deposits of the Agulhas Sea that existed in times of Gondwana. When they started eroding after the break-up of that supercontinent, they created the sandy, nutrient-poor soils which so bedevil horticulturalists on the Cape Flats trying to grow lush gardens. For the natural coastal fynbos that evolved in this environment, however, it is home.

Many visitors to the Point believe they are standing at the southern tip of Africa, which is just one of the misconceptions about the place that seems to persist no matter how much information you throw at it. It is not that, but what it is rather is a giant geological exclamation mark that bookends the southwestern corner of the continent. The actual southernmost point, Cape Agulhas some 200 kilometres to the southeast, is by comparison a rather drab, flat expanse of coastline.

Water: Probably the most pervasive misconception about Cape Point is that it separates the Atlantic Ocean on the western side from the Indian to the east. Oceans never really meet, they are just convenient geographical boundaries – like country borders. Even ocean currents don't meet, but they swirl around one another in a great liquid dance, driven mainly by the Earth's rotation and differences in water temperature between the tropics and poles.

The wash of foamy water just off the point, to which people often gesture from the high viewpoint of the old lighthouse and exclaim: "Oh look, that's where the oceans are meeting!" is really just a rocky outcrop known as Bellows Reef. It has been the undoing of many a ship and the main reason a lighthouse was first constructed there in 1859.

A not so small issue was that it did not completely solve the problem and ships continued to wreck themselves whenever the lighthouse was shrouded in low cloud, as it so often is. That rusting lighthouse has not shone since 1919, when the current beacon of hope in the night was switched on lower down. The new one is the most powerful light around the South African coast and its 100 megacandelas flashes can be seen up to 100 kilometres out to sea.

What Cape Point is, oceanically speaking, is the wedge that separates the flow of the warm Agulhas Current that courses down the east coast of southern Africa, from the cold Benguela Current that drives nutrient-rich, sub-polar waters up the west coast.

Fire: The Cape Floral Kingdom, that scrubby-looking vegetation of the region, is no stranger to the great restorative element of rebirth and renewal, new hope and sometimes blackened dreams. In fact, they are inseparable; there could be no, or very little, fynbos without fire. Over the past five million years fynbos has evolved to respond to the frequent fires that are fanned by the region's relentless winds.

Many of the 9 000-odd known species will germinate only after immersion in smoke rather than the flames themselves. Fire also clears out the dry, dense, senescent old growth of this rapid-growing vegetation type and opens it up for new life. After long and hot blazes, which seem to be on the increase, it appears that large areas have been reduced to post-holocaust ash and sand from which the vegetation could never recover.

But it does, and following the next rainy season hundreds of species of bulbous plants, annuals and small herbs, as well as bracken fronds emerge as a new green weave of biological colonisers. But it will not be the same, especially if one fire follows too closely on a previous one.

While fynbos needs fire to regenerate and remain healthy, the ideal time between burns is more than about seven years. This is how long it takes the larger woody species, which includes most of the proteas, to reach seeding maturity. Burn the veld in less time than that and you start saying goodbye to species.

What makes the Cape Floristic Region even more special is not only the total number of plant species in a relatively very small area, but the number of endemic and rare species. Burn them too often and they too start disappearing: ericas, irises, orchids, pincushions and conebushes, the marsh rose, blushing bride, painted lady ... as many as 1 700 species in the biome are currently threatened with extinction.

Wind: *Ruh* in Arabic, *pneuma* in Greek, *animus* in Latin, *imoya* in several South African dialects – breath, spirit. Even inspiration means to be infused with the breath of the divine spirit. For birds and butterflies it is their element. Sailors love it most of the time, curse it at others but always depend on it, as do we all.

While ocean currents influence our climate in long-term, annual cycles, wind does so daily. Wind balances the energy of our world, taking hot air from the tropics to the temperate regions, and cold from there back towards the equator. It also works in three dimensions, so the warm autumn breeze you might enjoy in Kathmandu will not be the same life-or-death jet stream that batters climbers in the high Himalayas within sight on the same day.

Author of the supernatural aspects of our world, Lyall Watson, called it "heaven's breath": without wind there would be virtually no rain on land, only over the oceans. The tropics would fry and everything beyond the tropics would freeze. Our planet would be uninhabitable by all but marine creatures (which might not be a bad thing, given that things have gone steadily downhill since the emergence of life on land).

Following the fall of the Eastern Roman Empire at Constantinople in 1453 and subsequent closure of the Silk Road to them, for European sailors seeking a maritime passage to the East the winds of the south Atlantic were as much a gift as the cause of much grief.

When the flat-topped mountain that guards the passage around Africa was spied by sailing ships of old, there would have been cause for celebration. After months at sea, with little or no fresh water left, food all gone, or gone rancid and mouldy, bodies wracked by scurvy, the sight of Table Mountain meant they would probably live a while longer.

But sometimes summer's prevailing southeast wind would deal them an Ace of Spades, or the Joker. There are accounts of sailing ships battling their way against a ferocious wind into Table Bay, only to be wrecked within sight of land. Worse still are accounts of ship's crews, too ravaged by sickness to work the sails, dying within sight of the mountain.

Making its way around Cape Point meant the ship would soon be able to change sail configuration, from beating on a close-hauled course very close to the wind, to a more comfortable reach with land to portside and wind to starboard. There is a belief that people in Brazil speak Portuguese because the early navigators worked out they could more easily reach the Cape by taking a long tack across the Atlantic to South America, turn once and then make one long tack back again.

The Portuguese word *agulhas* means needles, and there are various versions about how it came to be the name of the southern tip of Africa. The one most likely to be true is that was where their compass needles would, God-be-praised, turn favourably for them (they were deeply religious and placed stone crosses to give thanks for safe deliverance wherever they made landfall).

While foreign visitors are often disappointed when told that no ocean currents meet at Cape Point, the more cultured ones are surprised to learn it is the setting of the famous opera *Der Fliegende Holländer*. On wild and stormy days it is said you can see that ghostly ship, its timbers rotting and its sails shredded, battling the fates and sirens far out to sea. The future King George V of England was one of about a dozen on board the HMS *Inconstant* who thought they had seen it back in 1880.

Sighting the fated ship was taken as a bad omen. The ship's log noted:

"July 11th. At 4 a.m. the *Flying Dutchman* crossed our bows. A strange red light as of a phantom ship all aglow, in the midst of which light the masts, spars and sails of a brig 200 yards distant stood out in strong relief as she came up on the port bow, where also the officer of the watch from the bridge clearly saw her, as did the quarterdeck midshipman." The entry ends with the sad news that "At 10.45 a.m. the ordinary seaman who had this morning reported the *Flying Dutchman* fell from the foretopmast crosstrees on to the topgallant forecastle and was smashed to atoms."

The anti-hero captain of Richard Wagner's opera is named Van der Decken, and is thought to have been modelled on an actual 17th-century seaman, Captain Bernard Fokke. During the heydays of the Dutch East India Company, Fokke became legendary himself: some thought his extremely swift journeys around the Cape between Holland and Java could be accounted for only if he had made some sort of deal with the Devil.

Van der Decken's story goes that his Dutch East Indiaman could not make headway into a fearsome wind around Cape Point. With his crew suffering and dying and threatening mutiny, the captain cursed God for delivering them into such a terrible situation. God returned the compliment by dooming him to forever sail the southern sea, never able to make progress or port.

The Portuguese, who had an even harder time of the elements on their earlier voyages around the Cape in flimsy caravels, had their own myths about the place. Who knows where the stories all started, but out at sea on dark and stormy nights would be a safe bet. Theirs is the story of Adamastor, first penned by the mighty scribe Luís Vaz de Camões in his epic poem "Os Lusíadas" that celebrated the Portuguese "voyages of discovery".

In the story Adamastor is banished to the south for the kind of convoluted transgressions you find in Greek legends, where he takes the physical form of the cliffs of Cape Point. There he becomes the embodiment of the forces of nature that the early Portuguese sailors had to contend with.

The Indian Ocean was his domain and he dared anyone brave or foolish enough to try to unlock its secrets. In the poem's Canto V, he appears to Vasco da Gama (the first European to successfully round the Cape and reach India) as a formidable storm cloud:

> *Even as I spoke, an immense shape*
> *Materialised in the night air,*
> *Grotesque and enormous stature*
> *With heavy jowls, and an unkempt beard*
> *Scowling from shrunken, hollow eyes*
> *Its complexion earthy and pale,*
> *Its hair grizzled and matted with clay,*
> *Its mouth coal black, teeth yellow with decay.*

The first written name we have for the place is Cabo de Tormentosa, the cape of torment, or storms, which returned with the small fleet that had been commanded by Bartolomeu Dias. Dias did not make it back to Portugal, but the news that he had rounded Africa in 1488 was game-changing: without trade with the East, Europe faced economic meltdown.

Back in Lisbon, Prince Henry the Navigator was thrilled with the news, but not the name. In a deft cartographical sleight of hand he had it changed to Cabo da Boa Esperança, cape of good hope. That was much more likely to spur future fortune-seeking sailors to dare the elements, Adamastor and *terra incognita*.

In the mythology of the indigenous Khoi people, the Peninsula mountain chain is Hoerikwaggo – the mountain of the sea. In spite of the tricky pronunciation, theirs is perhaps the best description given: that it was born of the sea around 400 million years ago, from every aspect is bathed by ocean and in an estimated 10 million years or so will return to the sea.

How you see and experience the Cape depends very largely on the weather of the day. In summer it can attain sweltering temperatures, so much so you pray for the southeaster to blow as hard as it wishes. When it obliges, it can be for weeks at a time until you want to jump overboard, or off the planet. As much as it bathes the Peninsula in cooling air, it drives some people mad. To the coughing colonials who were sent out here in the 19th century to cure their tuberculosis, it was the Cape Doctor.

In winter the heathlands of the Cape Point nature reserve are lashed by rains that, like the desiccating wind in summer, can rage for weeks at a time. It makes Scottish people feel at home, and to those from the frigid Falkland Islands a bad day at Cape Point is a fine one. Yet, in between, the Cape bathes in Champagne weather (which is a bit of a mixed metaphor; given its Mediterranean climate it is more southern Rhône than Champagne, if we are going to make a wine comparison here).

Another early name for the Cape was the "tavern of the seas", since it was the first port out of Europe that had a distinct European character, and was rich in fresh food, inns, taverns and willing women. Early circumnavigator, privateer and slave trader Francis Drake had been given fearsome warnings about the "cape of storms" but he happened to visit the "cape of good hope" during a spell of glorious southern Rhône weather in 1580.

Of it he wrote the most oft-repeated marketing blurb about the place, that: "This Cape is the stateliest thing, and the fairest cape we saw in the whole circumference of the earth." It's all about timing, and at that time he was on the final leg of his continual voyage around the world, only the second person after Ferdinand Magellan to do so. There is no record of what the earlier Spaniard had to say about the place; maybe he passed it in a squall.

The wind that drove sailing ships around Cape Point also drives the terrestrial and the marine ecosystems there. The climate of harsh, hot and dry summers followed by cold and wet winters has created a vegetation type described by botanists as "*sclerophyllus* Mediterranean shrublands", or what the early Dutch settlers called *fijnbos*.

In botanical terms the fynbos biome is just a short hop-skip from desert: rain does not fall when plants need it, then buckets down all through winter when most of them are dormant. Every aspect of the fine-leaved plants is designed to prevent water loss in summer when the searing southeaster howls and fans fires from the merest rock strike or flicked *stompie.*

The leaves of most ericaceous plants, including the true ericas, buchu and other aromatic shrubs, look like needles but are in fact tightly rolled. Protea leaves mostly have a leathery texture and often waxy or hairy coatings. The reed-like restios, the most diagnostic of all plants in the fynbos biome, have no leaves at all and so experience negligible water loss. There are only a few trees found in the fynbos, mainly coastal dune types, other than the Afro-montane species that still cling inside shady, damp south-facing ravines.

This stressed environment, compounded by very nutrient-poor and acidic soils, means the plants have to work hard to procreate. It's a numbers game, which accounts for the celebrated seasonal floral extravaganzas. Every month the Peninsula has its types and colours: mostly red proteas and green-yellow conebushes in winter; woolly-white *blombos* and many pink or red ericas in spring; white and yellow everlastings in early summer; chrome yellow pincushions and bitou bushes in late summer; mauve and blue senecio and Felicia daisies, ice plants, as well as a host of irises and other flowering bulbs proliferate in spring.

Talking of numbers, the fynbos biome, otherwise known as the Cape Floristic Region or Cape Floral Kingdom, is unchallenged in the world for the number of plant species by the square metre. It is the only vegetation type, rather than a specific place, on Earth that has been accorded World Heritage Site status. The number of indigenous plants occurring from Table Mountain to Cape Point is comparable to the total count for the United Kingdom.

Correspondingly, the number of animal species in the kelp forests that fringe the Point are thought to be comparable to that of the Great Barrier Reef, although the count is still in its early stages. On any day, in any weather, standing on a cliff edge looking out across the Point lighthouse, you can feel the energy percolating like few other places on Earth. Consciously or subconsciously, it is the incredible diversity of both marine and terrestrial ecosystems that underpins this profusion.

The same wind that is the engine behind the flowering abundance of the fynbos also drives the richness of the sea. Anyone wishing to swim in Cape Town had best not visit any west-facing beach (which locals call the Atlantic side), powder-white sands notwithstanding. There is a phenomenon here called upwelling, whereby surface water along the western side is blown away from the shore by the southeaster.

As the relatively warm water moves offshore, it is replaced by cold bottom water. The harder the wind blows, the more inshore water is displaced and the more cold water wells up to take its place. This process of upwelling can drop the sea temperature from a balmy 23°C to just 8°C, and in some cases 6°C overnight – in the middle of summer when the land temperatures can touch 40°C. At the same time, the temperature inside False Bay, where the water is trapped by the wind, remains in the pleasant low 20s.

Another aspect of upwelling is that it brings with it a soup of nutrients from the lower reaches of the water column. This is the food that feeds the kelp forests and other algal plants, which in turn feed the huge biomass of creatures that at first glance might not look overly impressive – sea lice, limpets, urchins, abalone, rock lobster, whelks, mussels, barnacles – but, as has been alluded to already, equals any other marine system of our blue planet.

In a type of vision quest to understand the kelp forests, Cape Town photographer Craig Foster pledged to dive them at least once every day for a year, which became two, and then eight and then, around the eight-and-a-half-year mark, the bar was raised to 10 years. If he misses a day he tries to get in two dives the next. Not scuba diving but snorkelling, and not in the thick wetsuits used by all other divers around here: when he says he "skin dives" he means exactly that.

Overcoming the one or sometimes two hours' immersion in the often icy waters leads, he discovered, to a kind of hallucinatory experience that he first encountered while filming Bushman shamans and hunters in the Kalahari. Breaking through to the other side, to use an old Doors lyric, has led him to discover animal behaviour that has never before been seen. Also, in his submersed meditations, he has discovered some new species.

In his breathtaking (in all senses) book *Sea Change*, Foster charts the path down which he was taken by an octopus, in a kelp garden within sight of Cape Point. Once the human had spent sufficient time to allow the vulnerable cephalopod to take Foster into its confidence, it took him literally by the hand to reveal a secret underwater octopus world.

Octopus intelligence has been fairly widely documented, but what Craig witnessed impressed even that sage man of the planet David Attenborough, to the extent that the Capetonian's octopus adventures made up an entire episode of the *Blue Planet II* series. All the sea around Cape Point is really just part of one ocean, but it is an extremely fertile one, and one that is only just beginning to be more widely appreciated.

It would be useful if the powers that be in the world of marine biology could tap into the knowledge being accumulated by the most ardent of divers in the area: the abalone poachers. Abalone diving and abalone poaching are Cape traditions as entrenched as the self-declared *Tweede Nuwejaar* holiday (second New Year, when the locals are customarily still too hung over to operate machinery heavy or light).

Until about 20 or so years ago, poachers were few and the abalone was plentiful in the extreme: five species of *Haliotis* occur in Cape waters, but bulky *H midae* is the prize. Put your head into a kelp forest and the amount of abalone the size of rugby balls was staggering. But that was then.

With the lifting of apartheid laws came a flood of Chinese business people into the region and they wanted one thing only a little bit less than rhino horn, and that was perlemoen, as the protein packages inside their spiral shells are called in these murky waters. Most people will recognise the mother-of-pearl shells that are often used as ashtrays.

In centuries past, *bao* (abalone, but it can also be bread, a steamed bun or slang for vagina) was served to Chinese royalty as an exotic treat. Then it was more or less forgotten as anything other than a braai titbit in fishing communities where it occurs naturally, like Australia and Japan, but mainly South Africa. When China's pre-eminent chef of the new free-market era began cooking *bao* as a banquet delicacy for Chairman Deng Xiaoping, the shellfish became a must-have for the Chinese aspiring classes.

Said chef noted that the best *bao* comes from Japan, somewhat smaller than the South African giants, but more attractive, sweeter and tastier. Using a motoring comparison, he explains that the superior Japanese product is the Mercedes of China's seafood buffet, while the "reliable" *H midae* is a Honda.

Marine biologist and co-author of *Poacher*, Kimon de Greef, figures that between the years 2000 and 2016 around 36 000 tonnes of perlemoen was poached from South African waters, most of it between Langebaan up the west coast to Hermanus on the south coast, with Cape Point as the fulcrum of operations. The tonnage amounts to around 100 million individual *bao*, most of it headed directly to Hong Kong.

The Chinese traders were paying top dollar for the shucked and cleaned gastropod flesh, but the ghetto gangs of the Cape Flats that controlled the poaching would not allow them in. In truth the Chinese, all connected to international crime cartels, were terrified of the Cape gangsters. In order to keep them under control they introduced a perlemoen-for-drugs system, which was incredibly lucrative in both directions – other than for the larger Cape Town society and the health of the marine ecosystem.

Over the past two decades the once over-abundant perlemoen has reached that rare status of being critically endangered. At the same time, the grip the drug gangs have managed to extend over the coloured communities – which make up around 60 per cent of the provincial total – is staggering. What happens when the abalone is indeed extinct in local waters and the drugs stop flowing in from Chinese triads is anyone's guess, but it won't be pretty out on the Cape Flats.

When the heartless planners of the apartheid state uprooted established coloured communities from places like Simon's Town, District Six and just about every suburb of old Cape Town, and dumped them into dreary under-serviced ghettos, they were planting the seeds of social disharmony and environmental destruction.

The Cape of Good Hope has turned, for many, into a Bay of False Hope. On the brighter – or at least it's a dull glow – side, the demise of *Haliotis midae* from our seas might just be what it takes to stem the tide of drug-fuelled lawlessness in our communities. And if that's what it takes, so be it, *inshallah*.

In classical literature there can be found numerous references to a second Garden of Eden, or earthly paradise, somewhere in the southern hemisphere. The idea took root in ancient Greek literature, whereby everything in the universe had to balance. Whatever was found in the northern hemisphere had to have its equivalent in the south: hence Arctic and Antarctic.

Having struggled down the desolate and waterless Skeleton and Namaqua coastlines, on reaching verdant Table Bay early sailors must have thought they had indeed reached a lost Garden. "Paradiso" was the final part of Dante's trilogy *The Divine Comedy*, the first two being "Inferno" and "Purgatorio". In it he wrote: "Upon this promontory (Table Mountain), Nature hath formed here a great plain, pleasant in situation, which with the fragrant herbs, variety of flowers, and flourishing verdure of all things, seems like a terrestrial paradise."

Carl Linnaeus (1707–1778), the Swedish father of ecology and modern taxonomy, never visited the Cape but was overwhelmed by the botanical riches sent to him by collectors of the time. In a letter to Cape Governor Ryk Tulbagh he wrote: "May you be fully aware of your fortunate lot, to enjoy that Paradise on Earth, the Cape of Good Hope, which the beneficent Creator has enriched with his choicest wonders."

The Cape is a natural Elysium, abode of the blessed, yet for some of its less fortunate residents it has been rendered an earthly purgatory and even an inferno. But even in the fiercest storms we can look around at our gracious mountain and our plentiful sea, and perceive that a Cape paradise is not all lost.

West Coast Fossil Park
Four-Tusked Elephants, Giant Giraffes and an African Bear: Searching for a Paradise Lost

Humans generally do not like change much. We tend to perceive that the world around us is much the same as it always has been, whereas in fact it is in a state of perpetual flux. Take the southwestern Cape for instance: 10 million years ago it was a tropical forest with all kinds of fantastical creatures. You can go and see them right where they lay down to die.

THERE IS BEWILDERING CLAMOUR about climate change, whether the doomsday predictions are on the money or whether it's all just a snowflake conspiracy. Spoiler alert: it's true and it's accelerating, but it's complicated.

Meteorological data from many sources over a substantial time (including atmospheric, ocean floor and glacial samples) show clearly that harmful carbon in the atmosphere has increased alarmingly over the past 200 years, a phenomenon that can be attributed only to our burning of fossil fuels.

This pollution – and all other kinds – is pushing the climate to an extreme over a time period seldom seen other than in times of catastrophic change. It happens, but it's seldom comfortable for living creatures when it does, like when giant meteors strike our planet. The world's climate is never static and it is driven over long time periods by the simple observation that the continents as we know them just won't stay put.

Take the Cape west coast, for example. Around 10 million years ago (mya) it was covered by dense lowland tropical forest much like that which today covers the Congo Basin. Then things started to cool down and by five mya the area was a grassland-woodland mosaic with the forerunners of fynbos flora becoming established.

The single main cause of this enormous change was the final separation and moving apart of South America and Antarctica, a process that had started about 100 million years previously, when supercontinent Gondwana began to fracture.

"What is a fossil?" asked Nicolas Engelbrecht, a gardener at the Chemfos phosphate mine at Langebaanweg on the Cape west coast.

It was not an easy question for a young researcher to answer, even though Pippa Haarhoff was at that time working on the dig site at the Chemfos mine. As the earth-moving machinery cleared tens of metres of overburden to reveal the phosphate layer that was their pay-dirt, they uncovered old bones by the score. From the time the mine opened in the 1950s the managers just ignored and crushed them into the phosphate fertilizer mix.

Even to mention the word "fossil" could lose you your job, recalls Nicolas now with a chuckle. But the bones just kept on coming and eventually they could no longer be ignored. In 1958 scientists got wind of something unusual going on in that *nek* of the veld. Professor Ronald Singer from the University of Cape Town's medical school visited the place and was shown some of the old bones: one was a tooth fragment from some sort of elephant and another the ankle bone of a giraffid.

These two inauspicious-looking fossil fragments turned out to be the foundation specimens of the Iziko South African Museum's largest collection of fossils from any one site, and one of the largest in the world of its kind.

When Pippa explained, Nicolas said he wanted to work with her. But first he had to learn human anatomy: "We did not learn this at school," he recalls, "femur, tibia, fibula …" he recites. Then came learning relative anatomy. When you picked up a fragment of old bone, you needed to recognise if it was part of an amphibian, avian, marine or terrestrial creature, and then which part.

That was some decades ago and today he is a lab technician and tour guide at the West Coast Fossil Park where Pippa is the park manager. When not taking tours to the dig site, Nicolas spends most of his time sorting out bones.

Most of the big bones found to date have been sorted and identified – mammals, birds, marine animals. He works with magnifying glasses, emptying plastic packets of soil, sifting for fragments and sorting tiny bones into trays. The vast majority are frog bones, tiny leg bones, scapulas and vertebrae, each the size of a lentil.

This suggests the main E Quarry dig site was once a pond or backwater of a large river, an estuary of a large river cut off from the sea by a sand bar, very much like the Berg River that today empties its load into the Atlantic Ocean some way to the north.

Lucky for Nicolas, he was working at what would become recognised as one of the richest fossil sites in the world, and only one of four places on the planet where you can come and see exactly where the creatures fell, decomposed, their hard parts turned to stone and later exposed by mining machinery and then the trowels, brushes and dental picks of palaeontologists.

The mine eventually closed in 1993 and the land was transferred to a trust to administer and develop the site. Money had to come from private funding, but more recently it has support from another somewhat unexpected source due to its potential for job creation, education of the local populace and ecotourism.

Another good question to ask would be, what did the west coast look like between 10 and five mya (what bio-nerds know as the Late Miocene and Early Pliocene Epochs of the Late Tertiary Period)? Firstly, the sea level was much higher than it is today, by some 90 metres, and the coast was 20 kilometres further inland.

Tropical forests covered the area (as it did most of Africa beyond, excepting for the mountains). We can tell this from the microscopic pollen fossils found at the site. Pollen and their receptors are like keys and locks; each kind is unique and fits only into its own kind.

The oldest fossils found at Langebaanweg are those of forest animals, including ancestral musk oxen, wolverines, a bear-dog, a three-toed horse, dwarf deer or chevrotain much like those still found in the Congo rainforests, and deer-like ruminants.

Then something profound happened: South America completely separated from Antarctica, the southern ocean gyre got into motion, the south polar ice cap grew enormously, temperatures fell along with sea level and southern Africa got colder and drier.

Forest gave way to woodland and grassland and the very first mountain colonisers appeared along the west coast around five mya, what today we would call fynbos. Along with this, forest animals either moved north or went extinct where they stayed.

Teeth can tell an awful lot about the creature that used them. From a single tooth you can tell immediately how big the creature was, how old, what it ate, and that in turn can tell you a whole lot about its lifestyle and life cycle. Like, did it live in forest, woodland or grassland, and was it a grazer, a browser or a carnivore. And that would tell you a whole lot more about the environment in which it had lived, and died.

Take the sabre-toothed cats, for example, which are the dominant predators of the E Quarry remains – the largest was an African bear *Agriotherium africanum*, significantly larger than today's polar bears. Although the African bear almost certainly arrived at the Cape from its original home in Eurasia, what makes it remarkable is that the Langebaan fossils represent more *Agriotherium* specimens than the rest of the world together.

A surprising aspect to this site is that one third of all mammals found are carnivores, most notably two species of sabre-tooths. They and the African bear could eat only the softer parts of their prey. This left a big niche for scavengers such as five species of now-extinct hyenas which fed off the fat of the land; by comparison there are only four species of hyena in the whole world these days.

At the time, civets were much more numerous and dominant than they are today, and back then filled the role later taken over by jackals. When the larger-brained jackals arrived on the scene, civets survived by becoming retiring, solitary, nocturnal and omnivorous.

However, when more modern big cats appeared on the scene (lions, leopards, cheetahs) newer smaller species of hyenas had to learn not only how to duck and dive, but also how to hunt for themselves or be left with just gristle and bone. This was also the time when the first two-legged creatures swung down from the disappearing trees and posed a new threat to the hyenas, stealing meat from predators. In time they would wreak destruction with all creatures on the planet, large and small.

But the stars of the fossil park are those creatures whose bones were first identified from the E Quarry fossil pit, the antediluvian giraffes and elephants. There are three species of giraffe represented in the park, one not so much different from today's species, while another resembled the okapis that today are found in central Africa. But it was the sivathere that was most impressive, and numerous of the three.

The sivathere is an extinct short-necked, long-horned giraffid that was about the size of a modern elephant. The remains of 517 individuals retrieved from E Quarry tell us they were very numerous, but there is much more to the story. For a fuller picture we need to turn to the finer points of taphonomy, or the science of how things died and were then preserved.

The sivathere fossils of E Quarry represent individuals spread fairly evenly across the age groups. Normally it is the fossils of young and old animals that are most commonly found at a site. This is called an "attritional mortality" pattern, which mirrors the normal death ratio in a population.

But at Langebaanweg we see a "catastrophic mortality" pattern. So while the sivatheres were common herbivores, they also died more than any other large animals, in events we can categorise as catastrophic, like major floods in a big river system. And that matches precisely with what the balance of the evidence suggests.

The other big guys were the proto-elephants, of which four species have been identified. One was a true elephant from which all modern species descended, as well as the mammoths. The other three were gomphotheres which became extinct around two million years ago, having first appeared in Africa some 40 mya. The gomphothere named *Anacus* was particularly impressive, sporting two upper as well as two lower-jaw tusks.

The largest grazer was *Ceratotherium praecox*, ancestor of the white rhino. Its existence alongside the common three-toed horse *Hipparion*, as well as numerous alcephalines or grazing antelope (early kin to modern hartebeest, wildebeest, blesbok, tsessebe and impala), indicates the area had good grass cover by Early Pliocene times.

A first-time visit to the E Quarry dig site with one of the park guides is a real eye-opener, but each time you return you discover new things – as do the guides at this active palaeontological locale. Helping to make more sense of this "animal soup" is a brand new visitor and exhibition centre (it was under development when this book was being researched). And it promises to be brilliant when complete.

The interpretation iconography is so modern and radical some "head in the ground" scientists stare at the diagrams and scratch their heads; but kids seem to get it somewhat more quickly and intuitively, which is exactly the impact chief exhibition developer Joanne Duggan planned.

While I was there, I watched as Stellenbosch-based sculptor Egon Tania used a chainsaw and other power tools to fit the jigsaw pieces of timber (all repurposed old bits and pieces) to his family of life-size sivatheres – call them giraffes when scientists are around and they'll correct you most emphatically – that grace the main hall space.

They have a real primitive power and energy that is awesome. But the "underground" space is possibly even more intriguing, as you hurtle down an illusionary wormhole into another unexpected world. Once you acclimatise to the whimsical penumbral world, you see in the suffused half-light a collection of subterranean creatures one seldom sees out and about in the sunlight. You'll feel like a miniaturised Alice in Gondwanaland who has fallen inside a termitarium where everything is magnified 150 times.

There is also a lovely dimension of natural witticism: a family of wire-moulded mole rats scuttling along a tunnel, tail-to-teeth, with a black rubber mole snake in hot pursuit. Also a metal-and-leather dung beetle with dung ball in its burial chamber. But centrepiece is an aardvark snozzle with its sticky tongue protruding deep inside the termite mound replete with termites sticking to it.

"You have to mute the old-style museum environment in order to tell the story of this place," says Joanne. "It must feel calm if you want people to engage with the story." It is that, and highly informative and entertaining too. The new-look park is as much about job creation, ecotourism and general education as it is about scientific research.

For funding all this we can thank the national Lotto. The wheel of chance that picks a winner each week out of millions of players gives about the same odds as does nature in turning a dead animal into stone, and that fossil ever being unearthed. But sometimes you get lucky.

The Heerenlogement

A Cave, a Chisel and a Wagon Road: Searching for Fabled Kingdoms

Imagine what the first European residents of the Cape thought of their new abode, confronted as they were by wild weather and mountains, strange people and even wilder animals. Yet they had to be brave and adventurous to have made the move in the first place, and they were eager – if fearful – to explore their new home.

IT WAS A COOL DAY in August 1685 when Simon van der Stel, governor of the Dutch East India Company (VOC) settlement at the Cape, led a stately procession out of the sturdy wooden and iron-studded gates of the Castle of Good Hope. Seated in his personal horse carriage, he was trailed by 56 company employees, five slaves – three of whom were the governor's personal attendants – and an unrecorded number of Khoi interpreters, *voorlaers* and guides.

They were headed north, in search of a southern African El Dorado that had been beckoning for decades, if not centuries. In the caravan were eight carts and seven wagons pulled by 289 oxen, 13 horses and eight donkeys. For not only did they have to take ample food and water for themselves – given the aridity of the lands towards which they ventured – they had to carry the same for the animals.

It must have been quite a spectacle and certainly the most impressive expedition to ever set out from Table Bay. They even hauled a boat, for who knew what mighty rivers they might have to cross. But it would not have been the first time the people tilling the gardens behind the fort (because, let's be honest, it's not really a castle) had seen a similar parade headed for who knew where. For the chattering classes it would certainly have alleviated the burden of labour for a while.

From their deeds and the reports they wrote, it is hard to figure out the frame of mind of people more than 300 years ago. We do, however, learn that the Cape's first shogun, Commander Jan van Riebeeck, was not the most adventurous person to wield pen and sword at the Cape.

The commander was clearly a company man through and through and everything he did, or said he did, was for the benefit and profit of his employer, the Verenigde Oostindische Compagnie. The company wanted profits and in order to spread their enormous risks they invented the share certificate whereby anyone could buy shares in a trading voyage.

Very often the ship or fleet thus floated financially was lost at sea and you lost your investment. On the other hand, if your ship came in, the payout could be enormous. For 200 years the VOC paid a dividend of around 20 per cent per annum; that is the best investment opportunity that ever existed.

For millennia Africa had delivered fortunes in gold, ivory, animal skins and other riches to the world – all that gold leaf on the pharaohs' sarcophaguses and the gold adornments of Solomon's Temple – and yet the source or sources remained a mystery to the world beyond. For centuries the legend of Prester John persisted. It was said he ruled over a Christian kingdom of Vigita Magna and that was where much of the wealth of the continent could be found.

The Heerenlogement

Van Riebeeck had no urge to go exploring the vast land that confronted him, what with all those jagged mountains that spread right across the eastern horizon full of dangerous beasts and even more dangerous people with their strange ways and poisoned arrows and such. But it was his duty as a company man to at least try to locate that wealth and divert it into the company coffers.

Van Riebeeck and his fellows saw that the Khoi, who they called Hottentots (*Hottentoten*), sported copper ornaments. When they inquired where the metal came from, they were told about a place far to the north, in the home of the Namaquas. Surely this must be their Vigita Magna, Monomotapa, El Dorado.

Rather than venture beyond the pale himself, though, the commander of the fort sent out small expeditionary parties to scout the land and even sent a ship up to Saldahna Bay in an attempt to trade with the locals for copper and whatever other values they could find. They were, or course, all dreaming of gold. But the going was tough and they had limited success.

The way north consisted of rugged hills and mountains to the east and northeast while due north it was all deep sand that sucked the wheels of the wagons and tested the draught animals to the extreme. They fretted continuously about fresh water, which became increasingly scarce the further north they went. One place in particular became well known as the best shelter to be found on the entire journey northwards. The first white travellers known to seek shelter there named it the Dassenberg.

Paved roads and regular towns now allow travellers to cover the vast distances with regular comforts. But for about 250 years this small shelter, located about 15 kilometres down a rutted gravel road north of Graafwater, was an outspan celebrated by some of the most famous people to ever venture out from Cape Town.

We know this primarily because they carved, or some painted, their names on the natural wall of the "inn". Unfortunately, the popular historical literature is riddled with more holes than a Swiss cheese or that coarse sandstone face. The fundamental slip-up is to assume that everyone who ventured north from the settlement at the Cape of Good Hope decamped and left their name for posterity there.

If you do a Google search you will learn that the first date given for a visit by any person is 1650, said to have been carved into the rock face by a Jan Danckert. The indigenous people had been using the place for a long-time before that (which is how the colonists found it) and also left their marks on the granular canvas. They acted as guides for the colonial travellers and led them from water point to water point. Unfortunately, although images of elephant and ostrich are mentioned in some early writings, they are no longer discernible.

From the archival documents we know Danckert was dispatched by Van Riebeeck to reconnoitre the lands beyond the fort. But he could not have at the dates given because that would mean he set out a few years before Van Riebeeck arrived at the Cape.

In fact, the first expedition sanctioned by Van Riebeeck was led by one Jan Wintervogel. They headed out of the Cape settlement in 1655. The popular history books tell that his was the second name to be inscribed on the walls of the famous shelter, but both claims do not tally with reality; no matter how hard you search you will not find them there.

We learn from the official records that Wintervogel progressed only as far as the "Zwartland" around present-day Malmesbury. That would pin his furthest waypoint only about halfway to the shelter that is the pivot of this story.

Other expedition leaders sent out by Van Riebeeck to test the figurative waters inland included the Danish surgeon and adventurer Pieter van Meerhof (the same man who married Eva, otherwise known as the Khoi woman Krotoa) and Pieter Cruythoff. They got as far as present-day Piketberg and named a prominent peak nearby Meerhof Kasteel, but this was later changed to Riebeeck Kasteel.

A much more likely first date for Danckert would be 1660. Late in 1659 he and Van Meerhof reached a wide river where they saw a large herd of elephants and duly named it the Olifants (the Khoi called it Tharrakamma). Danckert was convinced they had reached the mythical Rio de Infante and that they must be very close to the golden kingdom of Vigiti Magna.

But any further exploration was cut short when many of the party came down with some severe illness, which forced them to turn their train around here and head back to the safety of the fort under Table

Mountain. So once again this is a false start for the famous visitors' book at the historical bivouac.

Danckert, Van Meerhof and Cruythoff aside, the majority sources assert that it was Olof Bergh who began the tradition of carving his name on the cave wall. And, I must confess, that when I first visited the place as an inchoate travel journalist, I accepted the popular record on face value and regurgitated the fake news.

While it is evident Bergh used the place as an outspan in his journeys north in 1682 and '83, he did not in fact leave any mark there of his passing. The inducement for these two excursions was the arrival at the Cape settlement in December 1681 of a deputation of Namaqua Khoi chiefs bearing gifts for the new governor, Simon van der Stel, that included exceptionally high-grade copper ore.

Van Riebeeck had departed the Cape after 10 years' service, establishing a garden, getting a wooden fort built but not much more. Over the next 17 years there was a rather quick succession of seven governors, none of whom accounted for much ink in the history books. But when Van der Stel set his buckled shoes ashore in 1779 he proved to be an entirely different shipload of enthusiasm and initiative.

He set about expanding the colony, setting up new farming enterprises and preparing to properly explore his domain. Greatly impressed by the copper ingots he saw, he sent out his personal favourite, the complex Swedish character Olof Bergh, to locate their source.

In time Bergh would earn honours, be convicted of fraud against the company, be exiled first to Robben Island then Ceylon, return to the Cape and accumulate great wealth. But in 1682, as a lowly soldier, Bergh set out from the Castle with a mandate to forge trading relations with the Namaqua Khoi and also to seek their help in locating what they were already calling the Copper Mountains. Early in November he stopped at a spring on the Sandveld plain which he named Berghfontein.

His next outspan was at a spring above which there was a sandstone ridge with a shallow cave inset near the summit. He named the place Dassenberg due to numerous dassies, or rock hyraxes, found there. In his diary he wrote the place "surpassed others in verdure and was moistened by diverse and quickly flowing springs providing most sweet and agreeable water". (Unfortunately, these springs have long since been depleted by farming activities.)

But Bergh did not carve his name there, nor when he returned a year later. Neither did Isaq Schrijver who led an expedition north in the same year (1683) and stayed in the shelter that was fast – for the times that is – gaining a reputation as the most congenial of resting places on the hard road northwards. Shrijver returned with some medium-high-grade copper ore he'd dug up from somewhere well south of where the main copper deposits were finally located, near the present-day town of Garies.

What Bergh did do, though, was carve his name on a rock at the spring he'd named after himself. Today the place can be reached by heeding a signpost on the Graafwater-Ratelfontein road that indicates the turnoff to the Olof Bergh Rock.

The catalyst for the big adventure north in 1685 was almost certainly the arrival at the Cape of a Friederich Mathias van Werlinckhof, mineralogist for the VOC on his way to take up the post of chief mining engineer of Sumatra. On route he was to stop over at the Cape and make a report back to HQ in Amsterdam on the mining prospects there.

This was all the motivation Van der Stel needed and the spirited governor set about planning "his" grand expedition. They moved out from the fort on 25 August and two months later arrived where the copper mining boomtown of Springbok would later be established. They found the granitic hills all around to be stained green with copper oxide, or verdigris.

Holes were dug and when they yielded some results, shafts were sunk; the deeper they went the richer was the ore they hauled out. But it was not long before reality deflated the initial euphoria. Copper in great quality and quantity clearly was there for the taking. Excepting they were a very long way from home, in a region almost entirely devoid of fresh water and the multitude of life it might sustain. Of stones and scorpions, however, there were plenty.

The cost of exploiting the resource for commercial gain would be prohibitive. It would take another 200 years before, with the advent of a railway line from there to the coast at Port Nolloth where a harbour was established, that the Springbok-O'Kiep area would emerge as the world's richest copper mines of the time.

Official records of Van der Stel's trip reveal the party stayed at "Dassenberg" on both the outward and homeward journeys, given the limitation of comforts in the region. The governor's name is not to be found inscribed on the cave wall, nor that of anyone else in the group. It was, however, from this time that it gained its current name of "heerenlogement": what was good enough for a governor was surely good enough for a gentleman's lodging.

What they did leave behind was a heavy iron casket that can be seen there still today. They probably hoped it would be full of rich copper ore (or better) on their return trip, but once lugged up to the cave it was likely they had no heart to drag it down the hill and heave it all the way back to Cape Town empty.

The task of finding the earliest names there was made all the harder when a fence was erected some time in the early 2000s to keep naughty hands well away from the estimable doodles.

And so we arrive at the answer to the central question of the story: Who did first leave their name chiselled into the walls of what today is a national monument? The answer is provided by no less credible a source than the Van Riebeeck Society, self-appointed keepers of early Cape history. The answer is KJ – Kaje Jesse – Slotsbo, although he wrote it K.I. SLOTfSBO in the typographical style of the day.

It seems that, following the commercial and psychological failure of the Van der Stel venture, the appetite for further exploration at the Cape subsided for some years. New developments were afoot in Europe and all too soon the governor was busy preparing for the arrival of shiploads of religious refugees from France, the Huguenots. If he is not remembered for copper, he certainly is for turning the paltry Cape settlement into a thriving and prosperous agricultural colony.

Whether it was a coincidence or by some contrivance, it was the year of Van der Stel's death that saw the next substantial expedition venture northwards beyond the Cape and its vineyards flourishing in the valleys radiating out from the Boland mountains.

That was the year when ensign Kaje Jesse Slotsbo led a military expedition consisting of 180 soldiers, civilian commandos and Cape Hottentot or Pandour Corps and goodness knows how many animals on a tour of the interior. Its purpose was no more or less grand than reinforcing the VOC's authority over the Khoi people of the region. The most dramatic event recorded from the trip was the drowning of one soldier, Matthys Indsidlaar, at a place they named Ongeluckigen Vaalej (unlucky valley).

Slotsbo's troop stopped over at the *logement* but it's likely only the more senior among them would have been billeted within the relative comfort of the shelter: if not for reasons of protocol then at least for the more practical one that space was limited. But it was the leader who decided, perhaps taking his cue from Olof Bergh's name that he would have seen on the rock at nearby Berghfontein, to carve his here. Underneath his name, in a smaller size, he left the date 1712.

Over the next 50 years some 15 more names were added to the Heerenlogement's interior adornment, mostly company men and soldiers who otherwise did not leave much of a mark on history. Other than one, that is, Sergeant IP Giebeler who passed that way in September of 1739. A fine combing through the historical record opens a dark window into the nature of the military expeditions of the day.

The archives reveal that "Sergeant Kiweler" (sic), postholder of the Groote Schuur estate, rode out at the head of a commando consisting of 40 company soldiers and an unspecified number of "Baster-Hottentots" – people who in time would give rise to the Cape coloured or mixed-race people.

Their primary purpose was to barter trade with the "Namacquas". The scribe of the journey noted these Khoi people were found in groups of between 100 and 200 souls living in kraals two or three days' journey apart but, it was written, "if a tree stand here, & a quarter of a mile farther there is a 2nd, one cannot call the place a wood." Does not this sound suspiciously like the company justifying its increasing claims to the land?

Of the Bushmen they had somewhat lower views. They were disorganised, destitute, irresponsible and living like wild animals, "here to day and there tomorrow. They are, indeed, the slyest, most rapacious & most to be feared on account of their savagery."

These commandos always felt they were being watched as they progressed, because "as may well be imagined they can see very far into the plains from the high mountains". And they were. At some point the report of the expedition, as written by OF Mentzel, states they were swarmed by as many as 1 000 Bushmen (*bosjemans*), men, women and children, who seemed to be threatening attack.

The sergeant sent out a platoon of Bastard-Hottentots to confront them and find out what their beef was. With an insolent manner they demanded brandy and tobacco ("dagga"). These were provided on the condition that the Bushmen keep their distance; the colonials were as fearful of the Bushmen's poisoned arrows as the hunter-gatherers were of the settler's guns.

Giebeler set up a defensive position while the Bushmen squabbled over their windfall, demanding more brandy when the few bottles they had been given were all too quickly consumed. The commandant feared his position was being threatened and ordered that his field cannon fire grapeshot into the encroaching crowd while his musketeers let fly in volleys of 10, "thereby killing & wounding a considerable number of men & women".

When the "enemy" fled in wild panic, some of the soldiers gave chase, to quote the report. "Some of the most brutal ones seized the small children by the legs and crushed their heads against the stones. Others killed the wounded women and cut off their long breasts, afterwards making themselves tobacco pouches from these as tokens of their heroism."

Some three decades later the San had fled much further into the arid interior and the plains of Namaqualand were crawling, quite literally, with a new kind of visitor, these ones on their hands and knees searching for "*planten, gewassen, kruijden, insecten, ens*". The grand era of the European naturalist-explorer had reached the Cape.

First of this strange kind of creature was the Swedish naturalist Carl Peter Thunberg. He arrived at the Cape as the surgeon aboard the VOC vessel *Schoonzicht*. The only way officially to visit the colony was as an employee of the Company and Thunberg's real job was to collect specimens for the botanical gardens at Leiden. He undertook several trips through the Cape with various similarly minded companions.

On one of them he was accompanied by the superintendent of the gardens in Holland, Johan Andreas Auge. They bivouacked at the

Heerenlogement (1774), made their way on an arc to the northeast and east to intersect with the Breede River. This they followed to its mouth at Cape Infanta, and from there progressed further east through the Little Karoo and Langkloof as far as the Gamtoos River where it flows into Algoa Bay.

On his next trip Thunberg was accompanied by the British gardener Francis Mason who was collecting plants for Kew. On one trip Thunberg was accompanied by Robert Jacob Gordon, on leave from his regiment back in Holland. Gordon was a senior Scottish officer in the employ of the VOC who was later posted to the Cape.

While holding the office of acting governor he had the indignity of surrendering the territory to an overwhelming British expeditionary force that landed in False Bay in 1795, and shortly thereafter took his life in shame. Gordon's Bay and the region of Gordonia, or Bushmanland, are his legacy here.

My favourite naturalist of the early Cape is François … his name is spelled variously Vaillant, Le Vaillant and Levaillant (the double "l" in French being pronounced as a "y"). But at Heerenlogement he wrote it Le Vailant (1783), just one "l" and there's no knowing how he pronounced that.

Not only was he a keen explorer, naturalist, zoological collector, ethnologist, cartographer and author, he was also this country's first serious (albeit devious) ornithologist and bird artist. While most of his work is true to life and science, he compiled at least 10 species from an amalgamation of avian types and another 50 which he described from the Cape but do not occur there now any more than they would have then.

His official posting was as a gunner in the VOC forces, but that was just a cover to go exploring and collecting for the treasurer-general of the company, Jacob Temminck. This explains why numerous of our birds bear his name in either their common or scientific nomenclature.

During his travels the Frenchman fell hopelessly in love with a comely Gonaqua (Khoi) "princess" whom he named Narina after an attractive lily. He proposed to her, but she spurned him. He named the most beautiful bird he saw on all his wanderings after her, the Narina trogon, an iridescent emerald-gold resident of the Afro-montane forests. He also named an emerald-green and white cuckoo after his favoured camp helper, Klaas.

Le Vaillant, however you choose to pronounce it, was a free thinker in the tradition of the French laissez faire school. He described and treated indigenous people as equals, castigated the Dutch settlers for their bigotry and one time even allowed an indigenous healer to diagnose and treat him when he fell ill (he writes the treatment was successful and he recovered).

From his three expeditions he produced an impressively comprehensive map of South Africa and gifted it to the King of France, Louis XVI. The now-famous "King's Map" measures about two metres high by two-and-a-half wide. The artistic cartography is further enhanced by 62 illustrations of plants, birds and animals including the soon to go extinct blueback.

In spite of his scientific contrivances, and the fact that he rejected the Linnean binomial naming system, species which later birders named in his honour include a barbet, a cisticola, a cuckoo, a parrot, a tchagra and a woodpecker.

The next visitor of note to the Heerenlogement was the German botanist Karl Ludwig Phillip Zeyher (1829). He travelled extensively around the northern Cape and collected many rare plants. Together with Danish botanist Christian Ecklon, he produced a three-volume catalogue of South African plants.

Zeyher suffered the setbacks that so dogged naturalists in faraway lands during the era of sailing ships: having valuable collections lost at sea. Then, back home in Hamburg, a warehouse housing his main collection went up in flames. But his legacy lives on in one genera of tropical plants (*Zeyheria*) and an impressive number of individual species that bear his name.

Andrew Geddes Bain laid his no doubt weary body on the cave floor in 1854. Most South African travellers will recognise his name and even know something about his life, including the fact that Bain's Kloof Pass celebrates his pioneering road-building career. Bain was born in Scotland and came to the Cape in 1816 at the age of 19 with no training. At 21 he married an "Afrikander" woman, Maria Elizabeth von Backstrom. They settled in Graaff-Reinet where they raised three sons and seven daughters.

By the time of his visit to the famous shelter on the southern boundary of Namaqualand, he had worked as a saddler, failed as a farmer, gone on trading expeditions deep into southern Africa, had to flee black armies during the Difaqane wars, was a correspondent for the *South African Commercial Advertiser*, served as a captain of the Beaufort Levies during the Eastern Cape Frontier Wars, worked on the construction of the Ecca Pass and Fish River Bridge (then the largest in the country), become Surveyor of Military Roads for the Corps of Royal Engineers, then Engineering Inspector of the Cape Roads Board. He had overseen the building of Michell's Pass, the Queen's Road between Grahamstown and Fort Beaufort and recently completed Bain's Kloof Pass.

So with some level of certainty we can say he was weary, in some sense at least. And yet he was only in mid-stride career-wise. He was the engineer in charge of many more roads and mountain passes, became a famous fossil collector and serious geologist. In 1852 he produced the first comprehensive geological map of South Africa. But for all this, he is probably best remembered as the father of road-builder Thomas Bain (not to be confused with Thomas Baines, another famous traveller but one who used his hands for painting mountains rather than moving them).

The majority of the names to be seen on the cave wall date from the first two decades of the 20th century, with a disproportional number dated 1921. Which begs the question: When does historical documentation become vandalism?

For reasons of decimal standardisation we tend to set the cut-off point of these things at 100 years. Which implies that in 100 years from now any names written on the wall in current times (there are a few of course) will be of historical significance, which somehow does not seem right. Maybe it should be confined to only famous people, excepting how would anyone other than a megalomaniac suspect they'd be famous at some later date unless they were a military or public figurehead or a mass murderer?

I do think the early travellers had a sense that what they were doing was significant. Many of them left written records of their journeys (some of them now important historical and literary works) which in itself speaks to us down the years of calculated purpose.

My thinking is that the advent of the motorcar marks the end of high, historical adventure, although the first car to reach the Heerenlogement would almost certainly have arrived there with a sense of high adventure. Which puts the historical high-water mark at around 1910 or so.

There is an argument for breaking this rule in the case of Henry Pearson (1911), who was in the grand tradition of the explorers and collectors such as Thunberg, Mason and Zeyher in whose dusty steps he was following. Six years after his layover at the shelter, Pearson founded the Kirstenbosch National Botanical Gardens.

Someone who might well have stopped there but left no trace was JPH Acocks, one of South Africa's greatest ever travellers. John Phillip Harrison Acocks logged more than 1 000 000 miles between the years 1935 and 1952, mapping the natural plant communities of the country for the Department of Agriculture.

The harvest of his labours is an unexceptional-looking A4-format soft-back volume titled *The Veld Types of South Africa: Memoirs of the Botanical Survey of South Africa No. 57*. It is to this day, along with its accompanying wall map, a standard work for all students of biology, ecology and veld management in South Africa. I suspect even if Acocks had at some time on his long journeys laid his head on the Heerenlogement floor, he was just too modest a man to carve a selfie on the rock wall.

Many of the most notable names, Slotsbo, Le Vaillant, Bain and Zeyher among them, are clustered in an area of the shelter wall that measures about one and a half metres square. When I first visited and photographed it around three decades ago, you could see the names all clearly, as well as a sapling of a rock fig growing in a crack around which the names are clustered. That sapling is now a small tree, which has begun to obscure the central panel.

It is hard to resist the urge to remove it, but that would be vandalism.

Karoo Petroglyphs

Bushman Songs, Broken Strings and Stories That Sing on the Wind: Searching for Sacred Rocks in the Karoo

San rock painting sites in the mountain areas of South Africa are fairly well known. Much less so are the rock engravings, or petroglyphs, that lie scattered across the dry regions of the Karoo and Bushmanland. The two are as alike as they are different.

THIS JOURNEY INTO THE landscape of storytelling started as a photograph of a large, dark, spherical, solitary boulder lying on the flat arid veld. There must be tens, hundreds of thousands of rocks just like it lying all across the Karoo, many looking like marbles lying on some giant's playground.

They are bluish-black and polished to a high gloss by wind that carries the fine dust particles which work like a rubbing compound, nature's Brasso. Seen from a distance they shine and glitter like gemstones, maybe black pearls, lying scattered across the bleak scrub plains.

Some are the size of soccer balls, some Pilates balls and some as big as those balls they use to play car soccer on TV motoring shows. All of them are the remains of the hard dolerite, those ironstone layers that form the iconic flat-topped Karoo koppies and dark ridges that snake across the dry interior.

The horizontal layers are known as sills and the upright ones that create ridges are dykes, volcanic lava that was extruded into the softer sedimentary Karoo rocks before Africa existed. When those hard volcanic layers erode, the bits fall down the hills and eventually erode into litho-spheres. They are just about the hardest rocks on our planet; hit them with something hard and they ring like church bells.

But some are different, like the one in that photograph in the book *My Heart Stands in the Hill* that was so spellbinding. The natural colour of dolerite is a rusty red and the darker hue we see is really a patina (oxidisation) of aging. This one had been scraped and pecked to reveal the true colour, in the shape of an antelope standing on a line of ground and bending to drink.

This was no child's scribble or graffiti; it was far too precise. But what was it then, and who did it, and when, and what did it mean? If we dig and delve we find these "Bushman marbles" are connected to the surrounding landscape by invisible strands of cosmic energy. Let's go on a long and winding journey into the past and then far beyond...

The narrow *poort* through Nelspoort, flush with spring water and lined with tall reeds, used to be a stop-over on the generally barren national road between Beaufort West and the Three Sisters. Nowadays, what with the new N1 blacktop veering a ways to the west of the little settlement, only the rumble of the Trans-Karoo train marks the passing of time here.

Clambering around a low koppie nearby, local headmaster Lawrence Ratherham stopped a while to allow the train to pass. He pointed to the outline of a tortoise on one of the many dolerite boulders that dot the hill, then to the sky: "This used to be a sacred gathering place for the Bushmen," he noted. "But Nelspoort was the scene of one of the last big commando raids against them so now we don't know very much about them."

Nelspoort, with its ample water supply, was one of the last strongholds of the Bushmen in the Western Cape. Throughout the 18th century, the Dutch East India Company authorities in Cape Town sanctioned the killing of hunter-gatherers, not only by white settlers, but also the various "coloured" groups including Khoi, Griquas and Basters, some on horseback and with guns against poisoned arrows. No Bushman – man, woman or child – was spared the ferocious land-grab of these pastoralists.

Until recently, hardly anyone noticed these rock engravings, one of the richest collections known, as they sped this way and that along the N1. Even the residents of Nelspoort. Lawrence found them only by chance. As part of a holiday programme to give some sense of grounding to the rootless street kids from Beaufort West, Lawrence took them for walks in the veld that their ancestors would have known. It was here that one of them alerted him – "*Meneer, meneer, wat is dié?*" (Sir, sir, what are these?)

The schoolmaster was not sure, so he sought out people who might know and in time found himself under the mentorship of archaeological luminary Janette Deacon. On subsequent walks over the reptilian ridges and rounded dinosaur hills, Lawrence offered to pay the Beaufort street kids R2 for any scraped image they found and R5 for a fine-line engraving, or petroglyph as these rock depictions are called technically.

"They found thousands in the koppies around here," he says. But his most treasured image is one he found himself on a rock several kilometres west of the *poort*: the very faded image of a long-horned buffalo, a species that went extinct some 13 000 years ago. "My buffalo," he calls it. This find later proved important in dating all the petroglyphs in South Africa.

The images were created by one of three techniques, scraping, pecking or engraving with some kind of fine tool. Removal of the patina – the dark outer layer of oxidised rock – by the artist revealed the lighter reddish colour. By comparing one of known date (such as ships, horses or wagons for instance, as well as the youngest possible age of the long-horned buffalo) a repatination scale began to be developed and refined.

Although there are obvious links between the rock engravings discussed in this chapter and rock paintings in the Kamberg chapter, as well as the people who created them, there are also some marked differences. The first is that the engravings have a high percentage of abstract, mostly geometric patterns, whereas the paintings show mostly animals and human-like figures. Another noticeable difference is that most of the engravings appear to be relatively crudely rendered when compared with the exquisite artistry of the paintings.

The reason for these differences can be reduced at its most elemental to two words – water and media. Although the hunter-gatherers who lived on the arid plains of the southern African interior were closely related to those who roamed the eastern mountain ranges, they had little or no contact with one another and developed quite different languages and customs.

In terms of the art, the first difference is rather obvious: the plains Bushmen did not have soft sandstone cave walls to paint on, while the mountain dwellers did not have ironstone boulders to carve. This in itself led to a different approach to their respective arts, much like an oil painter and a scrap-metal sculptor, even though the purpose that underpins the images is a singular spiritual vision.

Then there was the fact that there is virtually no surface water on the plains. The entire existence of hunter-gatherers here would have revolved around finding water. Places with perennial water would have developed special significance, places of plenty where humans and animals congregated. Dolerite hills near the few known permanent water sources, such as Nelspoort and Wildebeeskuil near Kimberley, have dense concentrations of petroglyphs.

Isolated engraved rocks are found mostly where no permanent water exists. Rather than identifying a place of exceptional power, these isolated petroglyphs themselves imbued a place with power, most probably some kind of territorial marker denoting "home".

For hunter-gatherers in mountains rudely dissected with cascading mountain streams and an abundance of game and food plants year round, there would have been much more time to develop secondary skills. It is believed by some that this relative affluence greatly influenced the sophistication of the painted art of the mountain regions, as well as a more complex spiritual philosophy.

It is hard to have a deep and meaningful discussion with /Kaggan, God, when your every day is a grinding routine of dealing with drought and food scarcity. Also, in the mountains you would have had more time to spend on your art. And then, on a very practical level, it would have been easier to paint on a rock wall than to chip into one of the hardest kinds of rocks on the planet.

In rock paintings therianthropes, half-human, half-animal figures with antelope-type heads, are very common, while being very rare in rock engravings. With rain animals, what superficially appear to be badly executed hippos or other fat amorphous animals, the opposite is true. Therianthropes reference the deep hallucinogenic trance state and multifaceted experiences in the spirit world, while clearly rain animals represent an obsession with life-sustaining liquid. Both, however, depict a cosmology in which the supernatural state is populated by various animal spirits.

Also very more widely represented in the rock engravings on the arid plains than in painted images on the fertile mountains are usually symmetrical and often geometric patterns. Archaeologists have deduced that one category of them, those we can call star-burst patterns, refer to the visions a shaman or healer has when he (it is thought they were all men) descended into a trance state. These patterns were then often superimposed on familiar things, like tortoises or beehives.

Purely geometric shapes seem to proliferate from around 2 000 years ago, but here a new category of pattern, larger and more regular, appears on the scene. Most of these are to be found on the smooth glacial pavements along the Vaal and Orange rivers and their tributaries in the area between Kimberley and Prieska.

They are thought to coincide with the arrival of the first pastoralists in the region. We call these people Khoi, who brought with them cattle and sheep. In time they became immersed in the Bushman spiritual culture, but transferred the entoptic phenomena, the flashing geometric patterns that are perceived when someone first enters a trance state, onto things with which they were more familiar: bags, nets, stock kraals and the like, which in turn denotes possession.

The Khoi have been described as "Bushmen with sheep, or cattle", and their world view must have been a significantly more material one, with a stronger sense of ownership, or "mine-ness". The word "San", sometimes used to describe Bushmen, is in fact a Khoi word meaning "those without" or poor people.

Some researchers have linked the Khoi geometric patterns to rites of passage rather than broad spiritual conversations prevalent in the Bushman images. And mostly those relating to female sexual maturity, menstruation or a boy's first-kill dance. Fertility symbols are central to other forms of primitive art around the world, where procreation (of both people and livestock) was an overriding concern. Along with the mysteries of sex, pregnancy and childbirth.

Which is not to say the art of pre-Khoi times does not contain such fertility symbolism, just that it is not prevalent. At Driekops Island in the Riet riverbed near Kimberley, one of the outstanding engraved glacial pavements, there are no images of animals at all, only abstract patterns. This clearly shows a break in world views and the artefacts of people with livestock (Khoi) and those without (San).

Rock gongs are also common where we find concentrations of petroglyphs. These are boulders or slabs of rock which emit precise harmonics when struck with rock hammers. Rock gongs can be found throughout sub-Saharan Africa and were used by prehistoric people in ritual communications with the spirit world.

In areas once populated by Bushman clans, where you find rock gongs you invariably find rock art. There is one on the crest of the koppie at Nelspoort which shows well-worn strike spots. You can play it like a natural xylophone – a lithophone with direct dialling to the Bushman hereafter.

The total number of prehistoric rock art sites in South Africa is somewhere in the region of 30 000, so we can presume they must have been extremely important in the lives and customs of those people. But why?

There are a lot of theories about this but the only verbatim record is to be found in the Bleek-Lloyd manuscripts: the German linguist and his sister-in-law in Cape Town we first met at Kamberg. From them we learn that there were distinct grassland (Kimberley area), flatland (Kenhardt area) and mountain Bushman groups.

They shared a common core language (/Xam) and cosmology where /Kaggan was the supreme being attended by all manner of animal gods and spirits. In fact, all animals, including reptiles and insects, were god spirits, not all of them good. The symbols and metaphors between the Bushmen groups show a common underlying understanding of the natural and spirit world, although often separated by vast gaps in space, time and culture.

To begin to understand the meaning behind the rock engravings one needs first to gather the data. Apart from the abstract patterns, the imagery is dominated by big animals, including elephants, rhinos, ostriches, zebras (or quaggas), though eland are overwhelmingly represented. There are very few small, mainly food animals, such as springbok, steenbok and the like, which are – or were – more common in nature. It is inferred, therefore, that this art is not about food but some kind of primordial animism.

Comparing the Bleek-Lloyd stories to those collected in more modern times from Bushmen in the Kalahari, shows they all revolved around the healing trance dance. The ritual dance is invoked when a clan has cause to consult a higher power, in the case of disease, tragedy, drought, or perhaps to seek blessings from the ancestors in a time of plenty, or a birth, or a young person passing into sexual maturity.

During the course of the dance the clan's healer passes into an hallucinogenic state where he communicates with the spirit world, then returns to relate those experiences. Verbally almost certainly, although most likely in the form of ritualised storytelling, but also in art so that messages could be shared across space and time.

As the Trekboers pushed into the South African interior during the 18th century, the first thing they did was to occupy all the water points, thus depriving the indigenous people of both their physical and their spiritual sustenance.

His thinking strings had been broken, //Kabbo told Wilhelm Bleek, meaning that he had lost his link with both his land and his landscape. These strings were the stories that floated across his ancestral lands, stories "like the wind" that bound together small groups of people spread thinly across the implacable land.

The advent of radio-carbon dating has allowed scientists to begin to assemble a picture of prehistoric life. You cannot easily date a painted image or engraving, so you start with the things around them – stone tools, ostrich eggshell beads, bone fragments and charcoal. From this you begin to calibrate a rough time scale of the people who lived in the areas where the images occur.

Each new site studied reveals new information and so, piece by piece, a prehistoric art timeline for South Africa begins to emerge. For example, there seems to be a correlation between the oldest (most heavily repatinated) dated stone tools from some petroglyph sites and the finest incised hairline images.

The central piece of the puzzle is Wonderwerk Cave near Danielskuil, where what is believed to be the oldest known examples of human abstract expression (call it art if you will) have been found. Scientific dating of the layers of the cave floor gives us a time when the sand begins to flow in the cosmic timer of human artistic awakening, and that time is about 180 000 years ago, give or take a few thousand. Use of the cave by pre-humans could date as far back as 1.7-million years ago.

According to authors John Parkington, David Morris and Neil Rusch, the excavated record (stone tools, bones and beads) tells about the stomachs of the people, while the images at these sites reveal much about their states of mind. They believe the world of rock engravings is not tied as tightly to the shamanistic experience, as is the case of painted, mountain Bushman culture.

Rather, they argue, it is a reflection of the world of the hunter-gatherer life experience in the dry lands: the land, the animals, the weather, the over-arching sky that would have been a big-part player in life's drama, as well as the intersection of their lives with those of the animals and animal spirits. To them it was all part of the same natural and supernatural experience.

"We may never know [all the answers to all the questions raised when observing and studying the Karoo petroglyphs], but our habits as archaeologists encourage us to keep on wondering," they conclude.

Having confronted the questions of who, when and even why, and come up with some acceptable answers, it is strange that nowhere in the literature is the "how" meaningfully discussed. This is because scientists will not offer a view where no hard data exists (bless 'em), and there is none when it comes to this question.

Unlike in the case of ancient Egypt, where some people like to imagine fantastical forgotten engines and three-legged workers in space helmets, the truth is rather obvious to anyone who has actually travelled to the granite quarries outside Aswan where the obelisks were chiselled out of the bedrock. All it took were lots of stone masons and lots and lots of time.

The stone masons of ancient Egypt have long since passed on but they left their rounded dolerite hand hammers lying all around the quarry; dolerite being nominally harder than granite (Mohs scale 7–8 and 6–7 respectively, with diamonds topping the scale at a stellar 10). Not so in the case of Nelspoort, Wildebeeskuil, or Driekops Island where no kind of Bushman stone hammer or any kind of engraving tool has yet been discovered. It would be very hard to chip away at dolerite boulders with dolerite tools, but what else would a Stone Age artist have had at hand to work such hard surfaces?

The boffs don't like to go there, but surely the answer is glinting on the ground like a well-honed razor, not a shaving razorblade but a blade of reason like Ockham's. Ockham's Razor is the problem-solving principle devised by Franciscan friar William Ockham we met at Adam's Calendar. To recap, his principle states that whenever there are numerous complex and competing hypotheses, the simplest one is likely to be the most correct.

And so, by simple observation, what might we expect to find scattered (if ever so sparsely) across the great dry emptiness, glittering like tiny glass, or maybe dolerite balls in the harsh African sun? What else but diamonds?

Wilhelm Bleek's informants (having learned Dutch-Afrikaans) referred to specific places as a *brinkkop*. Some have been identified as significant ridges in their home territories from where they would observe the movements of game, and from where they would attempt to invoke rain upon the parched landscape. These ridges, invariably comprised of dolerite boulders, would take on great significance in the otherwise flat landscape as well as in the mental landscapes of the people who lived there.

And it is also there we tend to find their engravings. It is thought that *brinkkop* really means *blinkkop*, or shining hill. Looking out across the desolate Karoo surrounding Nelspoort, hill after hill shimmering with dolerite rocks, Lawrence Ratherham sweeps his hand and says "our diamonds".

The rock engravings of the Karoo are a dim echo of those strings; we see them and we hear them ever so faintly on the wind.

Sutherland

High Plains, Clear Skies and Starry, Starry Nights: Searching for Bright Objects and Dark Matter

The story of modern astronomy begins with maritime navigation and fixing the locations of stars in order to calculate very accurate time. Nowadays it's more about looking beyond the stars into deep space to try to see where time began. A very large telescope near Sutherland in the Northern Cape is part of that quest.

IT'S A BINARY WORLD OUT THERE – on-off, up-down, half full-half empty. And there are two kinds of people in it: those who look up at the sky and wonder what it's all about, and those who look up and measure it. But you'll need to travel to Sutherland to be able to tell one from the other.

Sutherland is not the kind of place that otherwise, normally, you would visit. There always seems to be a wind there, kicking dust down the Wild-West main street. Sometimes it's a hot wind that sucks the moisture right out of your lungs; at other times it forms an icicle at the tip your nose.

However, the place is much valued by sheep farmers, stock thieves (as the road signs attest) and astronomers, the kind of people who look up at the night sky and think: I wonder when it all began? The difference between them and the rest of us is that they have some astonishingly powerful tools to play with. But why *Sutherland*? Without even a moon shadow of a doubt there are more attractive places.

Like just about every other *dorp* in this country, the town formed around monthly *nagmaal* (communion), the resulting marketplace and the inevitable church. The current handsome church was built in 1899, a time when there were not many more than 200 permanent residents living in the 20-odd houses. The houses are not noticeably large.

In those days no one counted the *karretjiesmense* – the itinerant Khoi-San families who wandered the high plains in their donkey carts. These days nearly 80 per cent of the 2 800 permanent inhabitants are classified as coloured, mostly those who have traded in their old carts for RDP houses.

In fits of slow-country romanticism, a number of city folk have bought weekend homes in the village and most have lived to regret it. It snows almost every winter, which is when you realise we are, largely, a warmth-loving nation. If ever you plan to have a winter weekend there, best you have a bakkie and fill it to overflowing with firewood.

The place saw some hot action during the Anglo-Boer War, after the "khakis" had commandeered the kirk and the locals took great exception. For 10 hours a force of around 250 Boers on Rebelskop bombarded the British garrison, taking some care not to damage their church. The war graveyard today lies in the church grounds.

It is high, it is barren, it is stark and it is dry – other than when it is washed by flash floods. For the record (and this is official) Sutherland is the coldest town in South Africa, with an annual average of 11°C and an average annual low of 2°C. The coldest temperature recorded there is -16.4°C, although the farm Buffelsfontein in the Eastern Cape has given us the coldest temperature ever recorded in this country – a nose shattering -20.1°C.

The west Roggeveld, where you'll find Sutherland, is classified as having a semi-arid steppe climate. So does Moscow, the coldest capital city in the world where winter temperatures can drop to -40°C and snow often lies metres thick for several months of the year. The Russian astronomers who work at Sutherland must find the place positively sub-tropical in winter.

All that cold must have some positive effect on the creative juices, thinking of all the Russian literary greats, and the fact that those two giants of Afrikaans poetry, NP and his younger brother WEG van Wyk Louw, were born in Sutherland. One imagines long cold winter days and even longer and colder winter nights as being contributing factors.

Other than the well-woolled sheep, you can tell what else inhabits this barren steppe by checking the road kill: mainly bat-eared foxes and mongooses (meerkats mostly), a few jackals, sometimes a springbok and very occasionally a grey rhebok.

It is not the kind of place you would expect to find more than a dozen guest houses and guest farms, with a similar number of little eating nooks and bars. It's not the kind of place you would have visited in years past, and not many people did. But they do now, by all appearances.

In the early 1970s the South African Astronomical Observatory moved some telescopes from Cape Town to a hill nearby and suddenly the place was all abuzz with space fever. Places with names like the Jupiter Restaurant, Sterreland and Skitterland proliferated. Still, back then it was really only a small group of boffins bearing circular slide rules and pockets full of pens. (If you know what a circular slide rule is, you win a free weekend; if you've ever worked one, you get two.)

It all ramped up astronomically, so to say, around 20 years ago when the largest telescope in the southern hemisphere was placed on the highest hill outside the town. Nowadays you'll struggle to find a free bed over weekends. It's all about altitude and remoteness.

Sutherland is located on a scrub plain in the Northern Cape at an altitude of 1 450 metres. The hill upon which the telescopes are located (the silvered domes in the distance appear otherworldly and thought provoking) stands at 1 750 metres. It is famous for having very clear skies, not much rain, virtually no air pollution or that scourge of astronomers, light pollution. There are numerous similar locations, but none so close to Cape Town, "first light" for celestial observation in South Africa.

The Royal Navy established astronomical observatories at strategic harbours around the world in order to be able to fix midday at these points.

It was a time when maritime navigation was still a bit of a crapshoot. Being one second of the arc out in his calculations, a captain could run a ship of the Crown onto a reef instead of into safe harbour.

Calculating latitude was easy enough, with a bit of training: you just needed to work out the angle of a known celestial object above the horizon and reference it to a table. Longitude was the problem because for that you had to take a reading on the sun at precisely midday each day. Until accurate marine chronometers were developed in the mid-1700s, a ship's captain would typically have several clocks on board and have to estimate the degree of their inaccuracies, which, of course, would multiply during the course of a voyage. Reef ahoy!

King Charles II commissioned the Royal Observatory in London, designed by Sir Christopher Wren and opened for "first light" – the first image received by a telescope after its installation – in 1676. Now the Astronomer Royal could "apply himself with the most exact care and diligence to the rectifying of the tables of the motions of the heavens, and the places of the fixed stars, so as to find out the so much desired longitude of places for the perfecting of the art of navigation".

The Royal Observatory in Cape Town was established in 1820 on a low hill where the Liesbeeck and Black rivers meet. It was chosen as a place that could easily be seen by ships in Table Bay before the estuary, and then the Foreshore, were filled in and developed.

At Cape Town each day at exactly midday, as calculated by the observers on the hill that eventually became the suburb of Observatory, a flare pistol would be fired. These days it is a canon on Signal Hill. The other job of astronomers was to map, in this case, the southern skies. Knowing the names and exact locations of stars also aids navigation. Once the issue of time had been adequately resolved, astronomers set their sights on more and more distant stars.

In the late 1800s, the advent of long-exposure photography suddenly opened up a new vision of the heavens, which revealed the sky was much more full of light than anyone could have imagined.

While cataloguing stars had been good work for 18th- and 19th-century astronomers, come the age of precision scientific instruments, particularly photographic spectrometry, new frontiers opened. Once they knew where most of the visible celestial objects were, they wanted to know *what* they were.

A major breakthrough at the Cape Town observatory was the observation that the luminosity of a star is most often related to its mass. The installation of the 24-inch McClean Telescope in 1896 (housed in a domed building that was designed by Sir Herbert Baker) greatly extended this work.

But as astrophysics eclipsed star charting, the Cape observatory fell behind the times and its equipment became increasingly outdated. By the 1960s a few events collided which, at the time, would have seemed earth shattering, but in time would converge to take the observatory to new heights, literally.

The first was the slow creep of urban air and light pollution that had begun increasingly to obscure city-based astronomical observations the world over. The second was the bad political air emanating from South Africa. When the British Scientific Council (which had taken over cosmic matters from the Royal Navy) made the decision to close the Royal Observatory in Cape Town, darkness seemed to descend.

However, it was just the darkness before the new dawn in which was born the South African Astronomical Observatory (SAAO). For some years the local stargazers had been looking for a new site that would give them maximum observational advantage, and they had zoned in on a hill above Sutherland for that.

With this came the motivation for new equipment. First the 40-inch Elizabeth Telescope was moved upcountry in 1972. There followed other instruments from the Cape Town site, as well as a number of scientific installations by various other nations and also several private academic institutions from the USA to Japan.

But the star performer of the High Karoo stage was to be SALT, the

South African Large Telescope. It would be funded by a consortium of nations, including the United Kingdom, Germany, the USA, New Zealand and Poland, and more recently Japan, Russia and India. Each party would gain observing time in proportion to the size of their investment, and anyone else wishing to use the facility would have to shell out big bucks.

Two lines of stunted, weather-beaten pine trees stand alongside a narrow road, behind a high automated entrance gate to the SAAO facility on the Fraserburg road, exactly 15 kilometres outside Sutherland. They look more like two lines of war-torn soldiers returning from a battle than those marching off to one.

The road winds up a hill, the highest point. On moonless nights it is so dark up there you can barely see your hand in front of your eyes, or a 38-metre-high ice-white and silver domed building you know is right in front of you. Inside that building are people looking out. Some are looking for signs of light at the very edge of the observable universe, others for no light at all.

They are the light wizards of SALT, and they can see things one billion times fainter than you or I could on the darkest, clearest night of our lives. The wizards talk in billions: billions of stars, billions of galaxies, billions of supergalactic clusters, billions of years, billions of light years.

They are the billionaires of the universe and they cluster around computer monitors in the ops room looking for supernovas, black holes, dark matter and quasars near the edge of the imagined universe. There is a small handwritten sign taped to the window in the ops room: "Do not feed the astronomers."

In the old days, at places like Palomar Mountain in southern California, home of one of the greatest telescopes ever made, observers on the manual Hale Telescope had to survive through freezing winter nights on cookies and hot drinks, and by pacing around the catwalk inside the dome. Inside fully automated SALT no one is allowed inside the dome at night; telescopes these days are that sensitive.

Hale was the last of the great handmade telescopes. A single Pyrex glass slab was cast and then ground down and polished by hand. It took a team of polishers 15 years to get a perfect parabolic curve. But glass is a liquid and when it weighs 20 tonnes and slews around to track stars, it deforms ... ever so slightly, but more than enough to throw a distant object out of focus.

To compensate for this, a spider's web of mechanical arms and bearings and pistons and springs was built to support the mirror and give a tiny prod here, a little give there. We are talking about very, very small tolerances. The figure often quoted in the literature is just one thousandth the thickness of the page you happen to be reading.

For most of the 20th century the 200-inch, or 5.1-metre Hale was the most powerful telescope in the world. But its manufacture began in 1928 and it continually needed to be fixed with "kluges" by the boffins of Caltech who ran it. Although it is still in use, by the 1980s the gears and bearings and pumps and pistons had become worn, and there was no one left alive who had any idea how it all worked.

Not so at SALT. Everything about this space monster speaks of the automatic, electronic, digital age. For starters it is not one large, but 91 small individual hexagonal mirrors, each one-metre across, that are combined to work like a single 9.2-metre spherical mirror (its actual measurement is 11 metres across). It is the largest telescope in the southern hemisphere, modelled on the 10-metre Hobby-Eberly Telescope (HET) at the McDonald Observatory in Texas, but with some modifications.

HET and SALT are the second and fifth largest telescopes in the world respectively, after the effective 10.4-metre Gran Telescopio on La Palma Island and KEKs One and Two in Hawaii, both with effective 10-metre mirrors. There are currently two 30-metre optical telescopes (TMTs) under construction, one in Hawaii and the other in Chile. Then there are the radio telescopes like Meerkat up the road from Sutherland near Carnarvon, and the SKA (square-kilometre array) that could, theoretically, eventually have a working diameter about the same as the Earth.

Back at SALT things did not start off very well, and instead of looking back in time to the Big Bang, what they got was a big blur. In truth things did start off well, but soon after receiving first light in 2000, the images began to blur. For five extremely frustrating years no one could figure out why.

Those 91 individual mirrors each have to be perfectly aligned in order to render a single sharp image. To achieve this, 91 lasers are projected down from something called the Centre of Curvature Alignment Sensor that sits at the top of a calibration tower next to the dome. The focus of the constituent mirrors is then synchronised by software.

Adjustment of the individual mirrors is made by a spider's web of arms and bearings and pistons and pumps, much like Hale, but here it is all automated. You can imagine trying to find one tiny error among that hardware and software was like trying to find a black hole inside a distant galaxy. The telescope is controlled by professional operators in a process known as stacking: astronomers get their hands severely slapped if they try to touch any of the control keys.

The spanner in the works at SALT turned out to be the mounting material of the calibration sensor inside the 38-metre calibration tower. The designers had not taken into account the effect of gravity on the device. That is why today its date given for "first light" is 1 September 2005.

What the crowd of astronomers saw on their computer screens that day was an image showing globular cluster 47 Tucanae, open cluster NGC, spiral galaxy NGC 6744 and the Lagoon Nebula. Parabolic mirrors like Hale are great for looking at single objects, but spherical mirrors like SALT can scan much larger areas of the sky (up to one arc second – approximately the area of sky that would be masked by holding a grain of sand at arms length in front of you) at even higher resolution.

It can be a lonely life working up on that hill outside Sutherland. For starters it's a night-time gig and it's a very individualistic one. "There is a dark side to this work," one night owl confided. "By night four of five of a viewing cycle my psyche feels like it's regressed back to high school," admits a post-PhD stargazer.

Astronomy these days is mostly about spectronomy: looking at the colour bands coming from a distant object, and the emission and absorption lines that tell what elements it is made of. Also, what its red-shift value is, which tells how far away it is and how fast it is travelling away from us.

Later there is the inevitable talk about black holes, which is the hot topic of the day in the wake of the first one having been photographed just that week. Colliding black holes are even hotter. Some people who visit the observatory admit being terrified at the prospect of the Earth falling into one. They should be far more afraid of being hit by a Titan, or a Greek, says my guide.

Titans and Greeks are objects that orbit Jupiter and can range in size from a motorcar to one of the Great Pyramids. Apparently there are some 2 000 of them that could at any time be catapulted by gravity out of Jupiter's orbit towards us. "They are the drunk drivers careening around our Solar System, and every now and again one does hit us."

Like the one that hit Siberia back in 1908, causing an explosion equal to that of several nuclear bombs. It was one of the smaller ones. A big one would cause a global extinction. Every year around two billion tonnes of space debris lands on Earth, most of it in the oceans and mostly very small bits, the size of marbles. Sometimes they hit a car, or a house, and very occasionally an animal or person. Catch a falling star and put it in your pocket ...

One thing that makes SALT extra special is its low cost, relative to other big telescopes. Then there is the no small matter of the ease with which the 91 small mirrors can be cleaned. And you do have to clean the mirrors of all large astronomical telescopes. Since they point skywards hot grease from the various bearings of the cradle in which it hangs drip into it, as do droppings of birds and bats that fly around inside the dome when it is opened for night viewing.

The individual SALT mirrors can be taken out – extremely carefully – and cleaned, usually two at a time. It takes about a week to do two, and a full clean takes about a year. During this time no viewing time is lost and the large spherical mirror does not lose any clarity: it was designed that way, which why its effective diameter is a little smaller than its actual physical one. With the cost of one night's viewing set at around R400 000, there's a lot to lose if you get things wrong.

Beholding the wonder of SALT inside the dome (my visit was on a cloudy night, so no viewing was possible), my astronomer escort said: "This is about the best bang you can get for your bucks." It is certainly about the best Big Bang you can get too.

And then there's the issue of dark matter, which is a very hazy subject. All the billions of stars in billions of galaxies in billions of galactic clusters in an equally staggering number of super-galactic clusters, all the bright objects we can see in the sky, whether with our own eyes or through very large telescopes, might not be the main stuff that makes up our universe.

Dark matter is thought to comprise a staggering 99 per cent of the mass of the universe, but no one is sure. So dark matter really does matter, just the boffins have little idea what it is. It could be clouds of iron dust left over from the formation of stars and galaxies. Or it could be comets, or cosmic strings – what the boffs call tears in the fabric of space-time.

Inevitably this leads to ideas about measuring the size and shape of things, whether our universe is the only one, or just one of many in a super-universal cluster. Sometimes you feel compelled to find some dark place where you can look up at the night sky and wonder what it's all about.

There's a good place on a hill just up the road, or down, depending on which hemisphere you're in.

Companion Reading List

The Cradle of Humankind
Almost Human: The Astonishing Tale of Homo naledi *and the Discovery That Changed Our Human Story,* by Lee Berger and John Hawks (National Geographic, Washington DC, Jonathan Ball, Johannesburg, 2017)

The Johannesburg Museum of Military History
Black Sacrifice: The Sinking of the SS Mendi, 1917 by Dr Sandi Baai (National Heritage Council of South Africa, Johannesburg, 2017)

Mapungubwe
Mapungubwe: Place of Ancestors by Kgomotso PJ Masalesa (self-published, 2014)

Kruger National Park
Historical Sites of the Kruger National Park by Ron Hopkins (Ron Hopkins, Hoedspruit, 2013, 2014)
Jock of the Bushveld by Sir Percy Fitzpatrick (Penguin Books, Johannes-

burg, 1975. First published by Longmans, Green & Co, London, 1907)

South African Eden: Kruger National Park 1902-1946 by James Stevenson-Hamilton (Struik, Cape Town, 1993)

The Conservationists and the Killers: The Story of Game Protection and the Wildlife Society of Southern Africa by John Pringle (TV Bulpin/Books of Africa, Cape Town, 1982)

The Kruger National Park: A Social and Political History by Jane Carruthers (University of Natal Press, Pietermaritzburg, 1995)

Adam's Calendar

Adam's Calendar, Slave Temples of the Anunakki and Temples of the African Gods (Johan Heine and Michael Tellinger); *Slave Species of the Gods and Ubuntu Contributionalism* (Michael Tellinger) (various, mainly self-published under different imprints)

The Lying Stones of Marrakech by Stephen Jay Gould (Vintage-Random House, London, 2001)

Kosi Bay

Between the Tides: In Search of Sea Turtles by George Hughes (Jacana Media, 2012)

Isandlwana and Rorke's Drift

There have been too many books written about this day and the Anglo-Zulu War in general to mention. One considered to be a classic is *Zulu Rising* (various editions) by Ian Knight. A handy booklet is *Battles of KwaZulu-Natal* (Art Publishers), if you can find a copy. Better yet is the three-part audio book *Day of the Dead Moon* narrated by the now deceased Anglo-Zulu War expert David Rattray. The library at his old home, Fugitive's Drift, now a guesthouse, has a fine collection of historic books.

Mont-aux-Sources and the Amphitheatre

Barrier of Spears: Drama of the Drakensberg by Reg Pearse (Howard Timmins, Cape Town, first edition 1973)

A Camera in Quathlamba: Photographing the Drakensberg by Malcolm Pearse (Howard Timmins, Cape Town, 1980)

Drakensberg Walks and Best Walks of the Drakensberg by David Bristow (Struik, Cape Town, first edition 1988)

Kamberg, Game Pass Shelter

Images of Power: Understanding Bushman Rock Art by David Lewis-Williams and Thomas Dowson (Southern Book Publishers, Johannesburg, 1989)

Barrier of Spears by Reg Pearse (Howard Timmins, Cape Town, 1982). My thanks to Prof. David Pearce of the Wits Rock Art Research Institute for information about the Lewis-Williams, Bleek-Lloyd connection.

Lambazi Bay, Port Grosvenor

The Sunburnt Queen by Hazel Crampton (Jacana Media, Johannesburg, 2004)

The Caliban Shore by Stephen Taylor (Faber and Faber, London, 2004)

Hogsback

Frontiers: The Epic of South Africa's Creation and the Tragedy of the Xhosa People by Noel Mostert (Jonathan Cape, London, 1992)

The Garden Route

A Colossus of Roads by Patricia Storrar (Murray & Roberts/Concor, Cape Town, 1984)

Nieu Bethesda

This is My World: The life of Helen Martins, creator of the Owl House by Sue Imrie Ross (OUP, Cape Town, 1997)

Fossil Reptiles of the South African Karoo by MA Cluver (South African Museum, Cape Town, 1978)

Swartberg Pass and Die Hel

So High the Road by Jose Burman (Human & Rousseau, Cape Town, 1963)

A Colossus of Roads by Patricia Storrar (Murray & Roberts/Concor, Cape Town, 1984)

Die Hel: Diepkloofin by Aletta Hanekom (Gruisklippies Uitgewers/ Mosprint, Mossel Bay, 2015)

Herbal and Witblits Remedies from Die Hel by Dr J van Elfen and Hendrik "Hoed" Mostert (JJ van Heerden, Prince Albert, 2002)

Cape Point

Common Wildflowers of Table Mountain and Silvermine by Hugh Clarke, Bruce Mackenzie and Corinne Merry (Struik Publishers, Cape Town, 2013)

Currents of Contrast: Life in Southern Africa's Two Oceans by Thomas Peschak and Claudio Velasquez Rojas (Struik Publishers, Cape Town, 2005)

Heaven's Breath by Lyall Watson (Coronet Books/Hodder & Stoughton, London, 1984)

Hoerikwaggo: Images of Table Mountain by Nicolaas Vergunst (South African National Gallery, Cape Town, 2000)

Poacher: Confessions from the Abalone Underworld by Kimon de Greef and Shuhood Abader (Kwela Books/NB Publishers, Cape Town, 2019)

Sea Change: Primal Joy and the Art of Underwater Tracking by Craig Foster and Ross Frylinck (Quivertree Publications, Cape Town, 2019)

Table Mountain: A Natural History by Anton Pauw and Steven Johnson (Fernwood Press, Cape Town, 1999)

The Living Shores of Southern Africa by George and Margo Branch and Anthony Bannister (Struik Publishers, Cape Town, 1981)

West Coast Fossil Park

Langebaanweg: A Record of Past Life by QB Hendey (South African Museum, Cape Town, 1982)

Karoo Petroglyphs

Karoo Rock Engravings: Marking Places in the Landscape by John Parkington, David Morris and Neil Rusch (Krakadouw Trust, Cape Town, 2008)

Threads of Knowing: Tracing the Meaning of Southern Africa Rock Art by Helene Smuts (Rock Art Research Institute, Wits University, undated)

My Heart Stands in the Hill by Janette Deacon and Craig Foster (Struik, 2005)

My thanks to David Morris of the McGregor Museum in Kimberley for introducing me to Nelspoort headmaster and rock-art custodian Lawrence Ratherham.

Sutherland

First Light: Searching for the Edge of the Universe by Richard Preston (Abacus, London, 1987)

The Royal Observatory at the Cape of Good Hope: History and Heritage by IS Glass (Mons Mensa, Cape Town, 2015)

The Outer Layers of a Star by R van der Riet Woolley and W Stibbs (OUP, Oxford, 1953)

Longitude: The True Story of a Lone Genius Who Solved the Greatest Scientific Problem of His Time by Dava Sobel (Walker & Company, New York, 1995)

Searching African Skies: The Square Kilometre Array and South Africa's Search to Hear the Songs of the Stars by Sarah Wild (Jacana Media, Johannesburg, 2012)

About the author

David Bristow has been travelling the highways, byways, tracks and trails of South Africa since he was a teenager, both as a free-ranger and a professional travel photojournalist. Not many people know the place better than he. He is also an environmental scientist, storyteller and specialist tour guide.

David has a BJourn (hons) from Rhodes University in Grahamstown, and an MA in environmental sciences from the University of Cape Town. He has covered Africa and other parts of the world for the past 30-odd years as a travel and nature writer and a photographer, authoring more than 20 books along the way.

More recently he has turned to non-fiction narratives about the region. *Of Hominins* is the second in his series of "veld stories", the other being *The Game Ranger, the Knife, the Lion and the Sheep: 20 Tales about Curious Characters from South Africa* (2018).